THE FRUGAL MIND

1,479 Money $aving Tips
for $urviving the 1990s

CHARLOTTE GORMAN, Ed.D.

Nottingham Books
Denton, Texas

First Printing, Dec. 1990
Second Printing, Apr. 1991

The tips suggested in this book have worked for the author or are supported by research. All tips may not be applicable to everyone. Readers should use their own common sense and good judgement when choosing and implementing the tips. The author and publisher assume no responsibility for any errors, inaccuracies, and inconsistencies in the book. If a reader has a question about a specific tip, he or she should contact an expert in the field in which the tip falls.

See page 321 for ordering information.

Library of Congress Catalog Card Number: 90-61108

Nottingham Books Cataloging Data

Gorman, Charlotte
  The Frugal Mind: 1,479 Money Saving Tips for Surviving the 1990s

  1. Money Management. 2. Personal Financial Management. 3. Family
    Resource Management. 4. Money, Saving.

Includes Bibliography and Index

ISBN 0-9625856-0-2

THIS BOOK IS AFFECTIONATELY DEDICATED TO

My mother and father, Rosie and Buster Gorman, who began very early in my life to instruct me in the wise management of money and other resources. I thank them for teaching me not to be wasteful and for laying a good foundation upon which I could build over the years. I thank them, too, for instilling in me the virtues of hard work and determination.

My husband, Dr. C. Curtis Trent, who first suggested that I write this book and gave me the encouragement needed to complete it.

C. G.

CONTENTS

Preface   **xiii**

**1 HOW TO SAVE ON YOUR AUTOMOBILE
    EXPENSES**   **1**

    Introduction   1
    Ways to Save on the Purchase
       of an Automobile   2
    Ways to Save on Automobile Main-
       tenance and Protection   9
    Ways to Save on Gasoline   17
    Ways to Save on Parking   22
    Alternatives to Owning/Driving Your
       Own Automobile   23
    Ways to Save on Automobile Rental   26
    Sources for Additional Information   26

**2 HOW TO SAVE MONEY ON YOUR
    CLOTHING, SHOES, AND ACCESSORIES**   **29**

    Introduction   29
    Ways to Save on Clothing Purchases   29
    Ways to Save through Clothing Construction   40
    Ways to Save on Clothing Care and Repair   42
    Ways to Save by Recycling Clothing   48
    Ways to Save through Use of Discarded Clothing   51
    Ways to Save on the Purchase, Care, and
       Repair of Shoes   53
    Ways to Save on the Purchase, Upkeep, and
       Repair of Accessories   57
    Miscellaneous Ways to Save on Clothing, Shoes,
       and Accessories   58

**3   HOW TO SAVE ON YOUR
      COMMUNICATIONS EXPENSES**   60

    Introduction   60
    Ways to Save on Telephone Expenses   61
    Ways to Save on Personal Home Office
      Supplies   65
    Ways to Save on Postage   67
    Miscellaneous Ways to Save on
      Communications Expenses   68

**4   HOW TO SAVE MONEY THROUGH
      COUPONING AND REFUNDING**   70

    Introduction   70
    Ways to Save through Couponing   71
    Ways to Save through Refunding   74
    Couponing and Refunding Magazines   81
    Couponing and Refunding Clubs, Swap
      Sessions, and Conventions   81
    Miscellany   82

**5   HOW TO SAVE ON YOUR
      EDUCATIONAL EXPENSES**   85

    Introduction   85
    Ways to Save on School, College, and
      University Expenses   86
    Ways to Save on Informal Education   92
    Where to Obtain Free or Low-Cost Educational
      Information   94
    Miscellaneous Ways to Save on Educational
      Expenses   96

**6   HOW TO SAVE ON YOUR ENERGY
      COSTS**   100

    Introduction   100

Ways to Save on Heating Costs 100
Ways to Save on Cooling Costs 104
Ways to Save through Weatherizing Your
   Home 108
Ways to Save through the Use of
   Draperies, Awnings, Reflective Film,
   and Carpeting 110
Ways to Save on the Operation of Your
   Water Heater 111
Ways to Save in the Kitchen 113
Ways to Save on Lighting 120
Ways to Save in the Laundry 124
Ways to Save in the Bathroom 128
Ways to Save on the Operation of
   Entertainment Equipment 129
Ways to Save on Yard Care and
   through Proper Landscaping 129
Ways to Save by Taking Advantage of
   Special Utility Company Rates and Programs 130
Ways to Save through the Use of Alternative
   Sources of Energy 131
Miscellaneous Ways to Save on Energy Costs 132

**7   HOW TO SAVE ON YOUR
ENTERTAINMENT EXPENSES** 136

Introduction 136
Ways to Save through At-Home Activities 137
Ways to Save through Participating in
   "Public" Activities 140
Ways to Save through Hobbies 144
Miscellaneous Ways to Save on Entertainment
   Expenses 145

8   HOW TO SAVE ON YOUR FOOD COSTS 148

Introduction 148
Ways to Save on Food Purchases 148
Ways to Save through Couponing 162

Ways to Save through Food Preparation   163
Ways to Save through Proper Food Storage   165
Ways to Save on Eating Out   166
Ways to Save on Entertaining Others   169
Ways to Save through Growing Your Own
    Vegetables   171
Ways to Save through Preserving Your
    Own Foods   172
Ways to Save by Taking Advantage of
    Government and Other Food Programs   173
Miscellaneous Ways to Save on Food Costs   174

9   **HOW TO SAVE ON FUNERAL AND
BURIAL EXPENSES AND HOW TO
DEAL WITH RELATED ITEMS**   176

Introduction   176
What to do Before A Death Occurs   177
What to do After A Death Occurs   183
Source for Additional Information   188

10   **HOW TO SAVE MONEY ON GIFTS, GIFT
WRAPPING, GREETING CARDS, AND
DECORATIONS**   189

Introduction   189
Ways to Save on Gifts   190
Ways to Save on Gift Wrapping   193
Ways to Save on Greeting Cards   193
Ways to Save on Holiday Decorations   194

11   **HOW TO SAVE ON YOUR HEALTH
CARE COSTS**   196

Introduction   196
Ways to Save on Medicines   196
Ways to Save on Physicians' Charges   199
Ways to Save on Hospital and Outpatient
    Care Costs   201

Ways to Save on Dental Bills 204
Ways to Save on Eyeglasses and Eye Care
Costs 204
Ways to Save on Hearing Aids Costs 205
Ways to Save through Free and Low-Cost
Medical/Health Services 206
Ways to Save through Practicing
Preventive Medicine/Dentistry 208
Miscellaneous Ways to Save on
Health Care Costs 209

**12   HOW TO SAVE MONEY ON YOUR HOME
FURNISHINGS AND RELATED ITEMS** 213

Introduction 213
Ways to Save on the Purchase, Repair,
and Care of Furniture 213
Ways to Save on the Purchase of Window
Coverings 218
Ways to Save on the Purchase and Care
of Floor Covering 219
Ways to Save on the Purchase of Sheets,
Towels, and Tablecloths 220
Ways to Save on Interior Decorating and
Accessories 221
Ways to Save on Cooking Utensils, Dishes,
and Paper, Plastic, and Aluminum Products 223
Miscellaneous Ways to Save on Home
Furnishings and Related Items 224

**13   HOW TO SAVE MONEY ON YOUR
HOUSEHOLD APPLIANCES** 227

Introduction 227
Ways to Save on Purchasing Household
Appliances 228
Ways to Save on Appliance Repairs 233
Ways to Save on Purchasing Televisions 235
Ways to Save on Television Repairs 236

Miscellany   237

**14   HOW TO SAVE ON YOUR
      HOUSING COSTS**   239

Introduction   239
Ways to Save on Buying a Home   239
Ways to Save on Selling Your Home   246
Ways to Save on Renting   247
Ways to Save on Home Maintenance   248
Ways to Save on Moving Expenses   250
Ways to Protect Your Home from Burglars   252
Ways to Protect Your Home from Fire   257
Miscellaneous Ways to Save on Housing Costs   258

**15   HOW TO SAVE ON YOUR
      INSURANCE COSTS**   260

Introduction   260
Ways to Save on Automobile Insurance   261
Ways to Save on Disability Income Insurance   263
Ways to Save on Health/Medical Insurance   264
Ways to Save on Homeowners Insurance   267
Ways to Save on Life Insurance   270
Miscellaneous Ways to Save on Insurance   273
Sources for Additional Information   275

**16   HOW TO SAVE ON YOUR PERSONAL
      GROOMING EXPENSES**   276

Introduction   276
Ways to Save on Makeup Costs   276
Ways to Save on Hair Care Costs   277
Miscellaneous Ways to Save on Grooming
   Expenses   279

17 HOW TO SAVE ON YOUR VACATION
    EXPENSES   284

    Introduction   284
    Ways to Save on Vacation Travel Expenses   284
    Ways to Save on Vacation Lodging Expenses   287
    Ways to Save on Vacation Food Costs   291
    Ways to Save on Tourist Attractions   292
    Ways to Save on Vacations Abroad   293
    Miscellaneous Ways to Save on Vacation
      Expenses   295

18 HOW TO SAVE ON YOUR WATER BILLS   300

    Introduction   300
    Ways to Save in the Bathroom   301
    Ways to Save in the Laundry   303
    Ways to Save in the Kitchen   304
    Ways to Save on Household Cleaning   306
    Ways to Save in the Yard and Vegetable
      Garden   307
    Ways to Save on Car Washing   308
    Miscellaneous Ways to Save Water   308

BIBLIOGRAPHY   311

INDEX   313

NOTE TO READERS   320

ORDERING INFORMATION   321

THE AUTHOR   322

PREFACE

The Frugal Mind will help you save hundreds to thousands of dollars. One simple tip, if followed, could more than repay you for the price of this book. **If you follow the tips in this book, there is absolutely no way you can keep from saving money.**

Whether you are 18 or 80; are single or married; have an elementary school, a high school, or a college education; or are at the lower, middle, or upper income level, you will find helpful suggestions in this book.

This book is a practical guide for every day of your life. Many of the tips are based on my own experiences as a wife and homemaker in managing personal resources, and as a resource management educator and consultant--these tips have worked for me. The other tips are based on reliable research findings.

This book can change your outlook on managing your money and your life. Stretching your dollars will become a personal challenge. When you start getting more for your money and start accumulating more money, you will be pleased and motivated to continue getting more. Learn to think "frugality." Frugality is an attitude which must be developed. The more you save, the more you will want to save. Seeing how frugally you can live will become a pleasant daily goal. It will become a way of life--a happy and rewarding way of life.

My book does not include every possible tip for managing money. All of the tips may not be applicable to you. Use your own common sense and good judgement when choosing and carrying out the tips.

You may feel that some of the tips in this book are elementary or obvious. You are right; some are. You may think that surely people already do these things. Some do, but most do not. Even those people who are aware of some of these money saving tips may forget them; therefore, they don't practice them. I have tried to pull hundreds of tips together in one book to serve as an immediate reference for people who want to cut expenses, to have more money, and to get the most they possibly can from their dollars.

When you get home with your book, read it through as soon as you can from cover to cover. Then, start doing what it suggests. Keep the book handy at all times. Don't put it on a book shelf or in a drawer. Keep it right at your fingertips.

Make these money saving tips work for you as they have for me.

The Author

CHAPTER 1

HOW TO SAVE ON YOUR AUTOMOBILE EXPENSES

Frugality is a handsome income
Erasmus

INTRODUCTION

Next to housing and food, transportation costs (owning and operating a private automobile plus the cost of public transportation) represent the third largest expense for many people. Most people want to own one or more automobiles for social status, indication of success, recreation, a good feeling, or simply as a means for getting from one place to another.

But, the cost of owning and operating an automobile is probably more than you think. Even if we use the 1989 standard mileage rate of 25.5 cents per mile (for business use) allowed by the Internal Revenue Service, it would cost you $25.50 to drive 100 miles, $255 to drive 1,000 miles, and $2,550 to drive 10,000 miles.

Many people fail to take into consideration that the cost of owning and operating an automobile includes such items as insurance premiums, fees for registration, any personal property taxes you must pay on your automobile, parking costs at work or where you go shopping, cost of renting garage space at your apartment, depreciation costs, washing and waxing your car, gasoline, oil, maintenance, highway and bridge tolls, driver's license, repairs, annual safety inspections required by some states, new tires, and interest on the automobile loan. Furthermore, consider the interest you could receive on the money you are paying for owning and operating your automobile.

If you will follow the suggestions in this chapter, you should save hundreds to thousands of dollars each year on your transportation costs.

WAYS TO SAVE ON THE PURCHASE OF AN AUTOMOBILE

1. Ask yourself, "Do I really need an automobile?" "Is it absolutely essential that I have one?" "Could I take the bus?" "Could I carpool?" "Could I walk?" "Could I take a taxi in an emergency?" Do some real thinking before you rush out and buy an automobile. If you don't own one, you won't have the many expenses listed in the introduction to this chapter.

2. Ask yourself, "Do I really need to trade my present automobile for a different one?" "Is my present one still performing satisfactorily?" "Are the repair bills still quite low?" Even if your present vehicle needs some major repairs, would it be cheaper in the long run to have it repaired rather than trade it in for another one? Check with an auto mechanic whom you know and trust and get his or her opinion.

3. Ask yourself, "Do we really need a second or third automobile?" "Could the family get along without this additional car?" An additional automobile means another insurance premium, more personal property taxes, more maintenance costs, another registration fee, etc. Could the family plan and coordinate the use of the present vehicle or vehicles?

Sit down with your family and write down the alternatives to owning another vehicle. Could public transportation be used? Could one or more family members carpool? Could one family member walk? Could grocery shopping be done in the evening? Could you make arrangements with other parents to share the tasks of picking up and delivering school children? Owning more automobiles than is really necessary is spending money that perhaps could be used better elsewhere.

4. In general, try to keep your automobile for as many years as you can rather than trade it in for another one every year. Generally, the longer you keep your car, the lower will be the cost per mile to own and operate it. Of course, there will be eventually a point in the life of your car when it is just worn out and must be replaced. Proper care and maintenance will lengthen its life.

5. When shopping around for an automobile, consider how well the particular makes and models hold their values. Some makes and models have lower annual depreciation rates than others. The depreciation rate will make a big difference (money-wise) when you get ready to sell or trade in your car. Check at your library for the depreciation rates of various makes and models.

6. Check on buying this year's model "Demonstrator" automobile with very low mileage. You should be able to buy it much cheaper than a comparable new model. In addition to initial savings on the purchase price, the "Demonstrator" should require fewer trips to the dealership for minor repairs and adjustments, since, hopefully, it has received regular professional care and maintenance. Generally, you can expect that the "Demonstrator" will carry the full new automobile warranty--insist on it.

7. When a model of an automobile is being discontinued, haggle to get a much reduced purchase price on it. Dealers normally like to clear their stocks of these models before new models come in. Discontinued models should be much cheaper than models not being discontinued. Dealers might even be willing to take a loss on discontinued models just to get them off the lot. Their loss is your gain.

8. Consider buying a new automobile during the year-end closeout sale. You should realize significant savings.

9. Consider that it might not be wise to buy a new model of an automobile during its first year on the market. The bugs can be worked out usually during the first year, but it should not be at your expense.

10. When shopping around for an automobile, consider the cost of upkeep. For example, generally, the more accessories, the more expensive the upkeep; automatics normally are more expensive to keep up than manuals; and large tires are more expensive than small ones.

11. When shopping around for an automobile, a major consideration probably will be fuel economy. For instance, a small car generally gets better gas mileage than a large car, and a four-cylinder generally gets better gas mileage than an eight-cylinder.

Check the "fuel economy label" attached to the window of a new automobile for the average estimated miles per gallon for city and highway driving. Also, check the pertinent publications listed under "Sources for Additional Information" at the end of this chapter.

12. When you are shopping for a car, truck, or van, buy one with only the features, optional equipment, and accessories you really need and want. For example, if you never drive outside of the city, you probably shouldn't pay the added cost for a cruise control. If you don't really need an air-conditioner, then don't buy it. Not only does an air-conditioner cost hundreds of dollars, but it adds to the weight of the vehicle, thus reducing fuel economy.

If you never listen to the radio while driving, try to purchase a vehicle without one. Limiting the extras to only what you really need or want could save you hundreds to thousands of dollars on the purchase price, maintenance, and fuel costs. You may have to order the vehicle to get exactly what you want, which might take up to several months; but you will have and be paying for only what you really need and want.

13. Know what the warranties cover when comparing various automobiles. Warranties do vary with different makes and models. The extent of the coverage of a warranty could make a difference between your having to be out none, a little, or a lot of money should your automobile have problems.

14. Ask your friends, relatives, co-workers, and others about experiences they have had with particular dealers in buying a car and receiving service after the purchase, and whether they would buy another car from these dealers. Steer clear of those with "bad" reputations. For example, poor service or the lack of prompt service could result in your missing work or an important appointment.

15. Be careful about buying on impulse. Impulse buying could result in your paying more than what is necessary for an automobile. Get the information as suggested in this chapter before purchasing your vehicle. If you have your facts and figures, you should come out better, dollar-wise.

16. In general, the "smaller" the automobile, the less expensive it is to purchase, own, and maintain.

17. Never pay the "sticker" price for a new automobile. Instead, follow these steps:

a. Determine for yourself the dealer's cost (the price that the dealer must pay to the automobile manufacturer) for the particular new automobile in which you are interested. Refer to the pertinent publications listed under

"Sources for Additional Information" at the end of this chapter.

b. Determine the trade-in allowance you should receive for your used vehicle. (Use the wholesale price, because this usually is what the dealer would be willing to allow you.) Again, refer to the relevant publications listed at the end of this chapter.

c. Determine how much profit you are willing for the dealer to make. Remember, however, the dealer might have expenses such as rent, utilities, advertising, taxes, the salesperson's commission, etc. Start out low in your offer--you can always increase the offer. Because the profit margins do vary (perhaps as low as $100 or as high as $800 or more), you should shop around to locate a dealer who is willing to sell at the lowest profit.

18. If there is a glut on the "car lot" of the particular make or model of the automobile you want to buy, you should be able to get a better deal on that vehicle than on one that is such a "hot" seller that the dealership does not even have a single one on the lot and would have to order one for you. Make your offer accordingly.

19. Consider purchasing your automobile with a friend or relative with each paying one-half of the down payment, monthly payments, and upkeep. Ask a lawyer about the legal aspects of such an arrangement before finalizing the agreement. In general, co-ownership could cut your costs for purchasing and maintaining the vehicle in half.

20. Consider buying a good used automobile rather than a new one. Refer to the *Official Used Car Guide* listed under "Sources for Additional Information" at the end of this chapter for the retail prices of used vehicles. Then, you will have the money facts when dealing for the used automobile. Because profit margins on used cars do vary from dealer to dealer, you

should shop around to find a reliable dealer who is willing to sell at the lowest profit.

21. If you decide to purchase a used automobile, check with places which replace their "fleet" vehicles on a regular basis, such as: businesses, various organizations, universities, state governments, and companies with outside sales people to inquire about purchasing one of their vehicles when they are replaced with new ones. Also, check with private owners whom you know and trust. Of course, you can also check with new and used automobile dealers.

22. If you are looking for a used vehicle to buy, visit car rental agencies. Normally, their automobiles have been regularly serviced and properly maintained for customer use.

23. Before you purchase a used automobile, it would be wise to have a reputable mechanic whom you know and trust (one not connected with the dealer or other agency or individual who has the automobile for sale) to evaluate the vehicle for you. The charge for this service usually is low, but ask before-hand what the charge will be. The examination could save you from buying an automobile with serious problems or potential problems. It also may point out several minor problems which can be corrected easily but which you can point out to the seller and request a reduction in the asking price.

24. You might want to consider selling your used vehicle yourself through an advertisement in the newspaper if you feel you might get more for it than the dealer is offering you as a trade-in. You may be able to get several hundred dollars more by selling it yourself. Try this approach before you finalize arrangements with the dealer. If you can't get more by selling the vehicle yourself, then trade it in on the vehicle you are purchasing.

25. When trying to sell your used automobile, place a "For Sale" sign on the window of the vehicle, use word-of-mouth, put up notices on bulletin boards at your workplace and in your community, and place ads in organizational newsletters. The more outlets you use for advertising, the larger your audience of potential buyers and the greater your chances for getting more money for your vehicle.

26. Before you try to trade in or sell your used automobile, wash the outside, and follow your owner's manual relative to waxing the outside; clean well the entire interior, the trunk, and glove compartment; check the oil, water in the radiator, fluid in the windshield washer reservoir, and transmission and brake fluids; put enough gasoline in the tank so potential buyers won't run out of fuel while testing the vehicle on the road; check the tires and tire pressure; replace burned-out bulbs and headlights; and try to make the interior smell as pleasant as possible. All of these things will cost very little, and the returns should far outweigh the small investment.

27. If you must borrow money to purchase your automobile, find out the annual percentage rate (APR) the dealer charges on a loan. Then, check with your credit union and bank on their rates. In 1986, three automobile manufacturers were offering (through dealers) rates on new cars as low as 2.9 percent to just a bit over 3 percent. In March, 1987, at least one manufacturer was offering (through dealers) 3.7 percent on selected models of new cars. In the past couple of years, similar, low-interest rates occasionally have been offered by some automobile manufacturers. If you are offered a low interest rate by a dealer, make sure you are not paying a higher purchase price for the vehicle which might offset the advantage of the low interest rate.

28. When you are thinking about buying an automobile, consider how much your insurance on it will cost. Some vehicles are very expensive to insure, such as "high powered" ones. Also, because of such factors as age and/or driving record of the operator, insurance rates could be extremely high for some people. Make sure you will be able to afford the insurance before you purchase the vehicle. If you purchase the vehicle and later realize that you can't keep up the insurance payments, ownership will become a great financial risk.

WAYS TO SAVE ON AUTOMOBILE
MAINTENANCE AND PROTECTION

In general, follow the instructions in the owner's manual which came with your automobile. Proper maintenance, care, and operation of your vehicle should reduce total operating costs, improve fuel efficiency, and extend its life. (If your new automobile is still under warranty, the warranty may be voided if certain maintenance and repairs are not done by an authorized dealer.)

29. Change the oil as recommended. This will extend the life of the engine. Use the type and grade of oil recommended for your particular automobile. Mixing oils of different viscosities could be damaging to your engine and make starting difficult.

30. If you change your own oil, take your used oil to a local service station which serves as a collecting point for oil to be recycled--if there is such a station in your area. Recycling oil has obvious long-term financial advantages for all of us.

31. Have your vehicle tuned-up as recommended in your owner's guide or as otherwise needed. Properly tuned, it will perform more efficiently and use less fuel.

32. When you need to buy new tires, compare the warranties on various brands. All other things being equal or very close to equal, choose the tires with the warranty which provides the best financial advantage for you.

33. Shop around for new tires. The prices can vary from place to place on identical tires. Check such places as general discount-type stores, department stores, tire shops, automotive supply stores, auto repair shops, garages, mail-order catalogs, and service stations. Buy them where you can get the best overall deal.

34.   Watch for legitimate tire sales.   Primarily, watch the newspapers in your area for advertised specials.   The savings can be substantial.

35.   When you are shopping for new tires, ask if mounting and initial balancing are included in the purchase price.   A charge for mounting and balancing could wipe out the savings you are getting on the price of the tires.

36.   When buying new tires, figure the tire cost per mile to determine the best buy.   For example, with all other things being equal, a $40 tire with a 20,000 mile warranty would not be as good a buy as a $70 tire with a 70,000 mile warranty. Figure the tire cost per mile by dividing the purchase price by the number of miles.

37.   Consider buying "blemished" (blems) tires. The "blemish" will not decrease the wearability, performance, or safety of the tire; and it normally will carry the same warranty as an unblemished tire.   The cosmetic imperfection may be so minor that it is almost undetectable.   The difference in cost compared to an unblemished tire could be as much as 30 percent.

38.   Consider buying "black wall" instead of "white wall" tires. Black walls are usually cheaper.

39.   Check your tire pressure regularly.   Ask the service station attendant to check the pressure, or you can buy an inexpensive tire gauge and check the pressure yourself.   Tire pressure that is too low causes increased treadwear, so keep tires inflated at the recommended pressure.   The sooner your tires wear out, the sooner you will have to replace them.

40.   Balance your tires at the recommended mileage, or sooner if needed, to extend their lives and to give a smoother ride.   When you need new tires, buy them where periodical balancing is included in the purchase price, if the price is comparable to prices at other places which do not provide free balancing. The cost of balancing four tires over their lifetime could easily run $175 or more.

41. Have your tires rotated at the recommended mileage. When you need new tires, buy them where periodical rotation is included in the purchase price, if the price of the tires is comparable to the price at other places which do not give free rotations. The cost of rotating four tires over their lifetime could easily be $35 to $50.

42. You can rotate your tires yourself and save money. If the purchase price of your tires does not include periodical free rotation, save yourself up to $50 over the lifetime of four tires by rotating them yourself.

43. Keep the front end of your automobile in proper alignment to prevent abnormal wear to the tires. Alignment should be checked at the first sign of wear or as otherwise needed.

44. Take advantage of sales on tune-ups, oil changes, and other routine automobile maintenance. Be sure you know what is included and not included in the particular special. For example, must you pay extra for the oil filter on the oil change "special"? Generally, "specials" can save you up to 30 percent or more on maintenance costs.

45. Buy automobile air filters on sale and install them yourself. They are simple to install. You could save up to 50 percent compared to what the service station would charge for a filter. When you find filters on sale at a very good price, buy several at one time and reap the savings.

46. Buy automobile parts, oil, oil filters, air filters, headlights, antifreeze, and other items for your vehicle where they are the cheapest. They are often, but not always, cheaper at discount chain stores and are usually more expensive at garages, service stations, and service departments of automobile dealers. Call around to find the cheapest price. Remember to check auto parts stores and other places which sell auto maintenance items. Prices can vary a great deal from place to place.

47.   Check the antifreeze level in your automobile radiator before freezing temperatures occur. You can ask your service station attendant to check the level, or you can buy an inexpensive tester, and test the level yourself. If the level is low, buy some antifreeze (where you can get the best price) and add it yourself. After you have added the antifreeze, be sure to have it checked or check it again yourself with your tester to make sure your radiator and block are adequately protected from freezing. It is much cheaper to add antifreeze than replace your radiator or engine block.

48.   Before freezing weather, fill your windshield washer reservoir with a nonfreezing cleaner solution. Otherwise, your ordinary solution will freeze and will not be usable when needed--for example, mud or slush could be splashed onto your windshield obstructing vision and causing a serious accident. Accidents are expensive.

49.   Make as many automobile repairs as you can yourself, rather than hire them done. A large part of the cost of automobile repairs is for labor. By doing the repairs yourself, the labor part of the cost could be saved. For example, a part may cost $7; but the labor for installing it might be $30. Save that $23.

50.   Check in your area to see if there are do-it-yourself auto repair centers. You pay a certain amount per hour to rent a space and tools. You do your own work. Utilizing one of these centers could save you a great deal of money, particularly if expensive equipment is needed to make the necessary repairs to your vehicle.

51.   Do as much of your automobile maintenance yourself as you can, rather than pay others to do it for you. Some examples of relatively simple tasks you can perform yourself are: checking the engine oil level, adding oil, and changing the oil and filter; checking the transmission fluid level and adding fluid; checking the antifreeze level and adding antifreeze; checking the brake fluid level and adding fluid; checking the air filter and replacing it; checking the water level in the radiator and adding water; checking the windshield washer reservoir and adding windshield washer solution; replacing fuses; replacing light bulbs and headlights; installing a new battery; checking the air pressure in the tires and adding air; and replacing a flat tire with the spare.

52.   Spend a small fee to take a course on simple, basic auto repair and maintenance. Call your local vocational-technical school or institute, local high school, local junior college, or County Extension Service to see whether the personnel there offer such a course or if they know where such a course is available. You should be able to save on repairs and maintenance many times over what you may pay for the course.

53.   When you use self-service gasoline pumps, don't forget to check such things as your automobile's oil level, brake fluid level, transmission fluid level, radiator water level, windshield washer reservoir level, and tire pressure. Neglecting these things could result in expensive problems for you and your vehicle.

54.   Use the gasoline octane recommended for your automobile. Your vehicle will run better, and you will get the most efficiency from your fuel.

55.   Consider having your car undercoated (rust-proofed) to help prevent rust, especially if you live near salt water, in areas where salt is put on roads in icy weather, or in other areas where rusting is a major problem. Rusting can require replacing your car long before its time. (Compare the cost of having the job done with that of buying the rust-proofing materials and doing the job yourself.)

56.   Ask that guarantees related to repairs or services for your vehicle be put in writing. If you have repairs or services done at national chain stores or shops, keep copies of all bills and guarantees in your vehicle, should you have trouble with these same problems while you are away from home. The unfulfillment of verbal guarantees could take money out of your own pocket when trouble arises with the same problem.

57.   When having your automobile repaired, ask for a written estimate of the costs. Otherwise, you might receive a bill for twice the amount you expected to pay.

58.   Check with friends, relatives, acquaintances, and co-workers for suggestions of qualified, honest, and reliable auto mechanics. In both the short and long run, you could save yourself some frustration and money.

59.   When you need repairs on your automobile, shop around and compare prices. Check at auto repair shops at new car dealers; with mechanics at local service stations; with independent general auto mechanics; and at specialty shops, such as muffler shops and transmission repair shops. With all other things being equal, choose the place with the lowest estimate for the cost of your needed repairs. Prices do vary from place to place.

60.   Prepare a written, dated, and signed list (keep a copy for yourself) of repairs or services you want done on your automobile and leave it with the mechanic. If you don't leave such a list, you could return and find some of the things you wanted done left undone; or you might find charges on your bill for things you did not authorize.

61.   Park in parallel parking slots rather than angled slots so that other people can't open and bang their automobile doors on the sides of your vehicle. After several years of door-banging, your automobile could have hundreds of dents and places where the paint has chipped away. If the condition is bad enough, your automobile might need a new paint job; or the condition could lower the sale price or trade-in value of your vehicle.

62. Don't hit the curb when parking and turning corners. Also, slow down when driving on rough roads. These precautions will help keep the front end in alignment and also minimize damage to your tires, thus extending their lives.

63. Park your automobile under your carport or in your garage to protect it from the weather. Bad weather--such as hail and windstorms--can damage your car and could necessitate expensive repairs or lower your vehicle's trade-in value.

64. Park your automobile under your carport or in your garage to protect it from the sun. The sun can fade the outside paint and the inside upholstery. It can, also, over an extended period of time, weaken the upholstery and cause it to deteriorate. Lack of protection from the sun could create a need for a premature paint job and premature replacement of upholstery--each of which represents money out of your pocket.

65. If you don't have access to a carport or garage, consider buying a flexible automobile cover for your vehicle to help protect it from such things as the sun and inclement weather.

66. Do not park your car under trees which drip sap or in which birds roost. The paint on your car could be ruined, and a new paint job is costly.

67. Use floor mats in your automobile to help keep your carpet from getting soiled. Well-kept carpets will add to your vehicle's appearance and may help you get a better price when you trade or sell. Floor mats also will help prevent the carpet from wearing out and having to be replaced.

68. Keep your automobile clean inside. A vehicle whose interior has been well-kept should bring a higher price when it is traded or sold.

69. Keep the outside of your automobile clean to help preserve the finish. Follow the automobile manufacturer's instructions on washing and waxing. A vehicle whose finish has been well preserved should bring more money when it is traded or sold.

70. Wash the outside and keep the inside of your car clean yourself rather than hire it done. At $7 (and upward) for a car wash, you could spend $84 or more a year if you have it washed just once a month. That's $840 or more over a ten-year period.

71. Drive defensively to reduce the possibility of having an accident. Be on alert and pay attention to your driving at all times when you are behind the wheel. An accident may cost you some money even if you have automobile insurance and health insurance and even if it isn't your fault. Also, many people are reluctant to buy a vehicle that has been in an accident.

72. Before you leave on a trip, be sure that your automobile is in good running condition. Have your mechanic check it out if you are not certain everything is in good shape. While you are on the trip, always stay with your vehicle when you stop for gasoline or other services at a service station, especially along the interstate highways. Unscrupulous service station owners or attendants could slash a tire, water hose, or fan belt, for example, and charge you an exorbitant price for replacement.

73. If you are away from home and want to use a public restroom, park your automobile in a place that is visible to passersby, lock the doors, and spend as little time as possible away from your vehicle. The less time you are away from it, the less likely it will be bothered.

74. When you stop for a meal at a restaurant, try to park your car where you can see it while sitting in the restaurant. Keeping it in sight could prevent someone from breaking into or damaging your car.

75. Park your automobile in a well-lighted area at night. Thieves operate best in the dark.

76. To help deter thieves, keep your vehicle doors locked at all times. Do so while your vehicle is parked in the shopping mall parking lot as well as in the front of your church. I personally know a woman who left her keys in her unlocked car which was parked in front of the church on Sunday morning. When she came out of the church after services, the car was gone.

77. If you have a garage, keep your automobile in it when it is at home. Keep your vehicle doors locked and the garage door closed at all times when the car is inside. Don't tempt a thief or make it easy for him or her to break into or steal your automobile.

78. Consider installing an alarm system in your automobile to deter thieves.

WAYS TO SAVE ON GASOLINE

79. Ask yourself every time you plan to use your car, truck, or van, "Is this trip really necessary?" Every mile you drive your vehicle will cost you an average of 25.5 cents. (See the "Introduction" at the beginning of this chapter.) If the trip is not necessary, think twice before using your vehicle.

80. Drive at a conservative speed on the highway. According to the U.S. Department of Energy, most automobiles get about 20 percent more miles per gallon on the highway at 55 miles per hour than they do at 70 miles per hour.[1]

81. Consider purchasing an automobile which gets the best gas mileage. For example, generally, the following get better gas mileage: lighter weight vehicles, vehicles with smaller engines, vehicles with manual transmissions, those with four cylinders, and those with fewer accessories. Check the "fuel economy" labels attached to the windows of new automobiles to find the average estimated miles per gallon for given makes and models. Also see the section, "Sources for Additional Information," at the end of this chapter for references on gas mileage.

82. Decrease the number of short trips you make. Short trips drastically reduce gas mileage. If an automobile gets 20 miles per gallon in general, it may get only 4 miles per gallon on a short trip of 5 miles or less. The U. S. Department of Energy says that trips of 5 miles or less make up 15 percent of all miles driven each year, but these trips burn 30 percent of the gasoline.[2]

83. Cut down on the number of shopping trips. Try to plan your shopping so that you can run all of your errands in fewer trips. Combine trips. Driving to run errands many times a week can become very expensive.

84. Run necessary errands on your way to and from work. You can also run errands during your lunch break by walking to nearby stores, the library, and other places.

85. Make a list of all errands in order of their location before you leave home. Move from one to the other without back-tracking. Backtracking requires additional gasoline.

86. Run errands when the traffic is least congested. You will minimize stopping-and-going and, thus, save on gasoline.

87. Don't drive all the way across town to save five cents on an item. As pointed out in the "Introduction" to this chapter, it costs 25.5 cents a mile to own and operate an automobile. If you drive 10 miles, it will cost you $2.55.

88. When shopping several grocery stores, consider how far they are from each other and whether you could still save money over the cost of automobile ownership and operation if you drove to all of them to purchase, for example, advertised specials.

89. Minimize stopping-and-starting. It wastes gasoline.

90. Try to drive at a steady pace. Try to avoid unnecessary and repetitious speeding up and slowing down. Jerky driving uses more gasoline.

91. Try to avoid, as much as possible, stop-and-go traffic. It increases fuel consumption.

92. Accelerate smoothly and moderately. Accelerating very rapidly uses more gasoline. Jumpy starts and fast getaways can burn over 50 percent more gasoline than normal acceleration.[3] Once you have reached your desired speed, keep a steady pressure on the accelerator, just enough to maintain the speed.

93. Warm-ups should not exceed one minute. The gasoline consumed in long warm-ups is not offset by any great improvement in engine performance.[4]

94. Turn off your engine if you stop for more than one minute. Restarting the automobile will use less gasoline than idling for more than one minute.[5] Don't wait until you unbuckle your seat belt, turn off the lights, turn off the air-conditioner, gather items from the seat to take with you, etc. before you turn off the engine. When you turn off the ignition, your gasoline costs stop.

95. Run your automobile air-conditioner only when really necessary. Alternatively, use the economy vent. Running the air-conditioner results in more fuel consumption and fewer miles per gallon of gasoline.

96. If your automobile is equipped with a cruise control, use it when possible. It helps you get better gas mileage. Most automobile manufacturers recommend, however, that the cruise control not be used in heavy traffic for safety reasons.

97. Change the air filter when needed. A clogged filter wastes gasoline.

98. Change the fuel filter at regular intervals. A dirty filter reduces fuel economy.

99. Have your automobile tuned-up as recommended in your owner's manual or as needed. A poorly tuned engine could consume three to nine percent more gasoline than a well-tuned one. The tune-up will pay for itself in gasoline savings and performance.[6]

100. Check your tire pressure regularly. Keep your tires inflated at the recommended pressure. Tire pressure that is too low will increase rolling resistance and reduce gas mileage. You can lose about two percent in fuel economy for every pound of air pressure under the recommended pounds per square inch.[7]

101. Consider radial tires. The use of radial tires can mean from three to five percent improvement in gas mileage in the city, seven percent on the highway, and 10 percent at 55 miles per hour after the tires have warmed up for 20 minutes. Radials also last longer. (Remember: Never mix radials with conventional tires on the same axle.)[8]

102. Keep the front wheels of your vehicle in proper alignment. If the wheels are out of alignment, the vehicle will use more fuel.[9]

103. Remove unnecessary weight from your automobile. Generally, the lighter the vehicle, the less gasoline it will use. An extra 100 pounds decreases fuel economy about 1 percent for the average car, and 1.25 percent for a small car.[10]

104. Vacation near home this year. Most of us fail to see and enjoy the attractions in our own city or state. Instead, we tend to drive long distances for a vacation. People hundreds or thousands of miles away from us drive to see our attractions, and we drive to see their attractions even though we haven't seen our own nor have they seen their own. Discover some exciting things close to home this year and save hundreds of dollars in transportation costs.

105. Shopping by mail can save gasoline. However, make sure you aren't spending more on the items you order than you would pay for them in a local store plus the cost of operating your car at 25.5 cents per mile. (See the "Introduction" to this chapter.)

106. Instead of driving around, telephone around to compare prices, to find out about the availability of an item, or to get other particular information. Telephoning will save on your transportation costs (and help reduce impulse buying.)

107. Order needed items over the telephone and have the items delivered to you if the overall delivered cost of the items is less than the price of the items on the shelf in the store plus the cost of driving your automobile to the store and back. Some drug stores, small neighborhood grocery stores, cleaners, department stores, and other types of stores and businesses provide "free" delivery service.

108. Shop around for the best price on gasoline. There could be as much as 30 cents or more per gallon difference in price at different places that sell gasoline.

109. Some service stations advertise "Save 4 cents per gallon when you pay cash." For example, by paying cash rather than using your credit card, you could save 60 cents on a 15-gallon purchase. Such savings could accumulate to a relatively large amount over time. If a service station does not advertise savings for paying cash, you may wish to ask the manager or owner if he or she would be willing to offer such a saving to you if you pay cash rather than use your credit card.

110. Pump your own gasoline. Save as much as 10 cents to 30 cents per gallon.

111.   Don't overfill your gas tank.   The gasoline draining down the side of your automobile is lost and may also damage the finish on your car.

112.   Figure your gas mileage each time you purchase gasoline.   If the miles per gallon begin to drop, you can check for possible causes and make the necessary adjustments or repairs.

WAYS TO SAVE ON PARKING

113.   Park in a public parking garage or lot some distance from the main downtown area, and your parking charges should be less.   Normally, the farther away from downtown, the cheaper the parking fee.   A distance of 8 to 10 blocks might just provide the daily exercise you need.

114.   If there are houses with garages, driveways, front yards, or accessible back yards within the vicinity of your job, ask the residents if they would be willing to rent a parking space to you.   If you can negotiate a price lower than the cost of parking in a public parking lot or garage, then consider renting a space.

115.   When you drive downtown to shop, find out which stores have their own free or reduced-price parking lots or garages or provide free or reduced-price parking in agreement with a nearby garage or lot.   Take advantage of this type of parking when appropriate, and save money.

116.   If free, unassigned parking is provided for employees where you work, be sure you arrive early enough to get a parking space.

117.   Check on monthly parking rates as opposed to daily rates.   If you need parking space every day, you may find that monthly rates are to your advantage.

118. If free street parking is available in the vicinity where you work, then arrive early enough each day to take advantage of the free parking.

ALTERNATIVES TO OWNING/DRIVING YOUR OWN AUTOMOBILE

119. Carpool. Drive your automobile only part of the time to and from work and to various other activities. For example, if you could carpool with just one other person, you could save 50 percent on the cost of gasoline for getting to and from work. Carpool with three others and save 75 percent. Try to locate others interested in carpooling by:

a. placing an advertisement in the newspaper. The ad could read: "Would like to carpool Monday through Friday from Avalon to Greenwood and back. Call-------."

b. contacting nearby friends, relatives, and others who drive daily to the vicinity where you work and ask if they would like to carpool.

c. putting a note on the bulletin board at work saying that you would like to carpool from Avalon to Greenwood and back Monday through Friday. Put your name, department, and telephone number on the note.

d. checking the telephone directory under "Carpool" to see if there might be a listing which you could contact. That office may have a list of people from your area who would like to carpool.

120. Some employee associations and employers buy vans or small busses for use in transporting employees to and from work at a reasonable daily, weekly, or monthly fee. Usually, one of the employees drives the vehicle. Riding in the van should be less expensive than driving your own automobile. Check it out.

121. Ride to work with someone and pay him or her so much per day or week. If you know of no one going by or near where you work, place an advertisement in the newspaper stating something like this: "Need a ride daily to work, from West Collier Street to the Gibson Building in downtown Witberg and return. Will pay. Call-------." Paying someone else for a ride should be cheaper than driving your own automobile.

122. Consider riding a bicycle. Use a bicycle path, if possible (if it is safe). If you have to ride on the street, be extra careful. Some people in cars often have little sympathy for bicyclists. When you reach your destination, lock your bicycle with a strong chain to a stationary structure. Consider moving close enough to your job to ride a bicycle to work. It can be a very cheap means of transportation and will require little upkeep.

123. Think about a motorcycle. Although this is a relatively cheap alternative to driving your car, it can also be very dangerous. Be extra careful.

124. Consider a moped. Mopeds get outstanding gas mileage, but they can be dangerous.

125. Limit your use of the taxi since this method of getting around can be very expensive. However, it is an alternative to owning and driving your own automobile; and, for some, it may be the best alternative.

126. Rent an automobile. (See the section on "Ways to Save on Automobile Rental" in this chapter.)

127. Lease an automobile. Since a wide variety of different leasing arrangements is available, check with several different companies on the actual overall cost to you for leasing to determine whether it would be cheaper for you to lease or to buy an automobile.

128. Use public mass transportation, such as the bus, subway, and train, to get to and from work, to do shopping, to get from the airport to downtown, to run errands, etc. Public transportation should be much cheaper than the overall cost of owning and operating your own automobile.

129. Take advantage of senior citizens', disabled persons', students', and children's discount fares on public transportation.

130. Send your children to school by public mass transportation (if safe and cheaper to do so) rather than drive them to school. Using public transportation should be less expensive than driving your own automobile. Have your children ride the school bus if one is available where you live--there should be no cost.

131. Arrange with other parents to share the responsibility of taking children to and from school and other activities. Sharing will decrease your transportation costs.

132. Walk to work (if close enough) and to nearby shops, grocery stores, and other places instead of driving. Consider moving close enough to your job to walk to work. Walking is free (and it is also healthy).

133. If you have time, take a bus or train instead of a plane for long-distance travel, if the bus or train would be cheaper than the plane, which is usually the case.

134. Mail payments for bills and send letters when possible. This will be much cheaper than driving your car to pay a bill or deliver a message.

135. Call and have grocery orders and medical prescriptions delivered to you, have dry cleaning and laundry picked up and delivered, and take advantage of various other delivery services, if there is no charge for delivery or if the cost of delivery is less than it would cost you to use your own automobile.

136.   Use your telephone to comparison shop, visit with friends, and give and obtain information. Telephoning should be cheaper than driving your automobile.

WAYS TO SAVE ON AUTOMOBILE RENTAL

137.   Shop around for the best price on automobile rental. In addition to calling the major car rental agencies, check with smaller agencies, some of which rent older used cars (three to five years old). Rates are much cheaper for the older cars.

138.   If you qualify, inquire about a senior citizens' rate or percentage discount on rental vehicles.

139.   Ask professional organizations and other organizations to which you belong if they have discount agreements with various car rental agencies. If so, request a special discount card, if your membership card is not sufficient. Such discounts can be 10 percent or more.

SOURCES FOR ADDITIONAL INFORMATION

140.   To find out a dealer's cost (the price that the dealer must pay to the automobile manufacturer) for new vehicles, read the following publications at your public library:

> *Edmund's (current year) New Car Prices*
> *Carputer's (current year) New Car Yearbook*
> *Consumer Guide Auto Series (current year)*
> *Foreign Car Prices*

141.   To find out current wholesale prices, retail prices, and loan values of used automobiles, consult the following publication at your public library, bank, or credit union:

Official Used Car Guide

142. For information on automobile owners' experiences with various makes and models of automobiles, ask for the following at your public library:

> *Consumer Reports*
> *Popular Mechanics*
> *Road and Track*

143. For information on gas mileage, review the mileage test results published by Consumers Union. (Check at your local public library.) Also, ask your automobile dealer for free copies of the following or check at your public library:

> *EPA/DOE Gas Mileage Guide*
> *Gas Mileage Guide for New Car Buyers*

144. Ask your public librarian for other publications not listed in this section with information on various makes and models of automobiles.

ENDNOTES

1. U.S. Department of Energy, *Tips for Energy Savers* (Washington, D.C., 1986), p. 26.

2. U.S. Office of Consumer Affairs and U.S. Department of Energy, *Your Keys to Energy Efficiency* (Washington, D.C., July, 1985), p. 6.

3. *Ibid.*

4. *Ibid.*

5. *Ibid.*

6. U.S. Department of Energy, *Tips for Energy Savers* (Washington, D.C., 1986), p. 28.

7. *Ibid.*

8. *Ibid.*

9. U.S. Department of Energy, *1987 Gas Mileage Guide* (Washington, D.C., October, 1986).

10. U.S. Department of Energy, *Tips for Energy Savers* (Washington, D.C., 1986), p. 28.

CHAPTER 2

HOW TO SAVE MONEY ON YOUR CLOTHING, SHOES, AND ACCESSORIES

Mend your clothes and you
may hold out this year
George Herbert

INTRODUCTION

Clothing represents a large outlay of money for many individuals and families. However, if you follow the suggestions in this chapter, you should be able to decrease your expenditures for clothing, shoes, and accessories by up to 75 percent or more per year.

WAYS TO SAVE ON CLOTHING PURCHASES

1.   When you are considering the purchase of some item of clothing, ask yourself: "Do I really need that garment?" "Do I really need a new white shirt, or will the ten white ones I already own be sufficient?" "Should I buy another business suit with five good business suits hanging in my closet?" An answer

of "no" to these and similar questions can save you money--
money you can put into your savings account or use for other
purposes.

2. Make a list of clothes you need to buy. Be careful about
buying on impulse. Even if certain items are on sale, resist the
temptation to purchase them if they are not on your "needs"
list. For example, as a business executive, you have on your list
the following items: A solid navy suit and a solid medium gray
suit. Don't buy a white suit and a red jacket, instead, just
because you think they would look good on you.

Stay with your list and don't spend more than you have
budgeted for clothing. If you buy on impulse, you may have to
use the money which was intended for the items on your list.
If so, you will have to come up with additional money for those
needed items.

3. Before you shop at any other place for clothing, shop the
garage sales first. Clothes will, almost always, be much cheaper
there than anywhere else. However, don't expect to find the
quality and quantity of what you need by going to one or two
garage sales per year. You probably will have to spend from
several hours each month to several hours each week and go to
half a dozen or so garage sales each time to find what you
need.

When you do go to a garage sale, always take a tape measure
with you. The size may no longer be inside the garment, or the
garment may have shrunk due to laundering. A pair of men's
slacks labeled "34 inches in length" may really be only 32 inches
or less, due to shrinkage. A size 10 in one dress may not have
the same measurements as a size 10 in another dress. You
may find that a size 8 or 12 fits okay.

In addition, you may not have the opportunity to "try on" the
clothes before you buy them unless you slip them on over the
clothes you are wearing, so don't wear heavy, bulky clothes on
your shopping trips. If you forget to take a tape measure and

you can't try them on, you could always hold them up to you and get some idea of the fit.

Some of my favorite and most stylish clothes came from garage sales and at very low prices. For example: I have purchased blouses for 25 to 50 cents, skirts for 25 cents to $1.00, dresses for 10 cents to $1.50, a new jogging suit with long sleeves and long pants for $1.50, and almost new full slips for 25 cents. I have found women's suits for $1.00 to $2.00. I have purchased suits, sportcoats, shirts, and slacks for my husband at enormous savings!

Garage sales usually are excellent places to find baby and children's clothes which often show very little wear and cost only a fraction of the price charged in stores for comparable new clothes.

4.   Check stores which sell clothes which have been previously worn. Clothes are almost always much cheaper at these stores than they can be purchased new at "new" stores. Such clothing stores might be called thrift shops, secondhand shops, used clothing stores, resale shops, clothing exchanges, or second-time-around shops. Try these stores for men's, women's, children's, and baby clothes. Some shops even specialize in designer clothes. These clothing stores may be run by churches or charitable organizations, or they may be privately owned. Check your telephone directory and the classified section of your newspaper for help in locating the stores.

Buying secondhand clothing is rapidly becoming an accepted practice in all segments of society. The stigma once attached to wearing secondhand clothing has all but disappeared. Today, people are admired for finding a used bargain. Andie MacDowell, who played the role of Jane in the motion picture "Greystoke," purchases many of her clothes secondhand from thrift shops.[1]

5. Check out used stores operated by organizations such as the Salvation Army and Goodwill Industries. In addition to other items, they will have used clothing at low prices.

6. Go to factory outlets. New clothing usually is offered at good discounts. Don't always assume that there is a major flaw in a garment sold at a factory outlet. Even if there is a flaw, it may be so minor that it really doesn't matter. The clothes may not even be seconds or imperfect garments. The clothing may be first-quality surplus items, samples, or discontinued lines.

I purchased a garment once at a factory outlet at a considerable saving, simply because it was slightly soiled. After one washing, it looked beautifully white. Caution--Even though you normally will find clothing at a large discount at factory outlets, don't always assume that you are getting the best deal possible. You may be able to find the same or a comparable item "on sale" at a cheaper price at a department store. Shop around.

7. Check out the "bargain basements" at various department stores. Some offer expensive clothes at discounts, while others specialize in less expensive lines of clothes.

8. Shop the discount stores. Prices are almost always cheaper there. Such stores may feature manufacturers' closeouts, slightly "irregular" items, and first quality clothing at discount prices.

9. When you need to buy clothes, consider placing an advertisement in the newspaper. (Hopefully, the newspapers in your area provide free ads of a noncommercial nature.) For example, your ad might read: "Want to buy good, used boy's clothes, size 6. Call-------." "Want to buy long, formal dress, misses size 10 or 12. Call-------." "Want to buy good, used maternity clothes, size 14 or 16. Call-------." "Want to buy good, used tuxedo, size 42 long. Call-------." "Want to buy good, used man's solid navy blue suit, size 40 regular, 34 inch waist, and 32 inch inseam. Call-------." "Want to buy used baby clothes for girl. Size 12 months. Call-------." You should be able to get clothes at great savings through an ad.

10. Purchase "seconds" or "irregulars" if the flaws are so minor that they are not noticeable to others and do not decrease the comfort or durability of the garments. Even if a belt is missing, you always can buy a belt to match or use one of those hanging in your closet. A puckered seam usually can be taken out and resewn. "Seconds" and "irregulars" normally are much cheaper than comparable "first quality" garments.

11. Shop around for the best price. In general, don't buy the first thing you see at the first store you enter. You may find the identical item next door or down the street for less money.

12. Buy most of your clothes only when they are on sale, preferably 50 to 75 percent or more off. It usually is only a matter of time until most clothes will be on sale. It should be a very rare occasion when you will need to pay the full price for a garment. For example, end-of-the-season sales can save you quite a lot of money on your clothing expenditures.

13. Buy most of your clothes in simple, classic, basic, traditional, and conservative styles which will not look outdated in a year, but rather will stay in style for many years. Thus, your overall clothing expenses over the years should be much less.

14. Limit your purchases of "fad" clothing. "Fads" usually go out-of-style in a year or less. Having to buy a new wardrobe each year could get relatively expensive. If you do purchase a "fad" garment, spend as little as possible on it.

15. Buy multipurpose, versatile garments, such as a tweed sport coat, a dress with a jacket, a skirt and blouse, slacks which can be worn with several shirts or blouses, a two-piece dress, a reversible jacket, a shirt which would look good with or without a tie, a jacket which can be worn with several different skirts or pairs of slacks, a garment which can be "dressed up" or "dressed down" for different occasions, a shirt or blouse which can be worn as a lightweight jacket, a shirt and blouse which can be worn outside as well as inside of slacks and skirts, a reversible vest, and a suit with an extra pair of coordinated slacks. You should need fewer clothes if the ones you buy are multipurpose; and, as a result, you probably will spend less money.

16. When you buy a raincoat, consider a fabric one with a detachable, warm lining. The coat with the lining in can be worn in cold weather. The lining can be removed when the weather is warm. If you live in an area with a relatively mild climate, such a dual-purpose coat could eliminate the need for an additional overcoat and save you money on your clothing costs.

17. Limit your purchases of seasonal clothes. Rather, select most of your clothes in year-round fabrics and styles. Seasonal clothes could spend six months out of the year occupying space in your closet. This could be compared to your savings account drawing interest only six months out of the year. If you can wear most of your clothes year-round, you should need fewer clothes and be able to reduce your clothing costs. (Of course, in extremely cold climates, a few heavy, "winter" clothes may be necessary.)

18. Build your wardrobe around a few basic colors. Concentrate on "separates," so you can mix and match the different color-coordinated garments for a different look, thus expanding your wardrobe. If none of the garments in your wardrobe can be coordinated, you are limited to wearing a garment in only one way rather than in several combinations. You should need fewer garments if you can coordinate most of them. Fewer clothes should mean that you have less of your money tied up in clothes.

19. Simply limit the number of garments in your wardrobe. In general, fewer clothes should mean less money invested in clothes. For example, a few years ago a female acquaintance of mine had few other clothes than the following in her business wardrobe: A two-piece, woven, wool and polyester blend navy suit; a two-piece, woven, wool and polyester blend beige suit; a matching silk skirt and long-sleeved blouse of a multicolor design, but with the predominant color being mauve; a long-sleeved mauve blouse; and a pair of navy pumps with one-inch heels. She mixed and matched these items, always looked well dressed, and didn't have to spend hours worrying about what to wear each day.

If you are a businessman, you could limit your business wardrobe in a similar manner. For example, you might limit your business suit wardrobe to only four suits.

Consult current books on business dressing for essentials for your business wardrobe.

20. Limit your purchases of clothing decorated with frilly lace or other trimmings which may wear out before the rest of the garment. Especially limit such ornamentation on children's clothes. Since children are "rough" on clothes, the lace, etc. will be even more susceptible to wear and tear. If you do buy clothes with ornamentation, make sure it is sturdy enough to last as long as the garment itself. Otherwise, you could find yourself having to replace clothing prematurely. Replacing clothing costs money.

21. Buy garments which are well constructed (especially children's clothes). Inspect each garment carefully and completely before you buy it. If garments are poorly constructed, you may find that they have to be discarded after minimum wear. Replacing them costs money.

22. In general, buy clothes with no more than an absolute minimum of ornamentation. Highly ornamented clothes could go out-of-style more quickly than plain ones. Being able to wear your clothes for several years will save greatly on your clothing bill.

23.   Buy clothes that feel good on you. If you have doubts about a garment, don't buy it. If it doesn't feel good on you, you will never be completely happy with it; and you probably will wear it very rarely. You will have wasted your money, since the garment will only be taking up space in your closet.

24.   Don't buy a garment that is skintight. If you gain several pounds, you may be unable to wear it; and you will have wasted your money. You should allow, also, for possible shrinkage if the garment is to be washed.

25.   If possible, try on clothes before you purchase them to make sure they fit. For example, a junior size 7 dress in one brand may not have the same dimensions as a junior size 7 in another brand. Also before you buy, be sure that the store will honor a refund or an exchange if you decide later that the garment does not fit or does not suit your needs. If the store has a no-exchange or a no-return policy, make absolutely sure the garment fits you and your needs exactly before you buy it. Following the above suggestions could prevent you from having to bear the expense of a garment you can't or won't wear.

26.   Save the sales slip, labels, hangtags, important "papers," extra buttons and thread, and special packaging for a garment you buy. Take them with you if you return to the store for a refund or an exchange. Having proof of purchase when you return a garment may mean the difference between getting the adjustment you desire and having to keep the garment.

27.   When purchasing clothes for adults, look for wide seams to let out should you gain weight. Narrow seams will not permit you to increase the size, thus you may have to put garments aside until you lose weight. If you don't lose weight, you will have wasted your investment in the garments. In addition, you may have to purchase more clothes.

28.   When purchasing women's skirts or dresses, look for deep hems to let out if styles change to longer lengths. Letting the hems down saves you the cost of replacing the clothes.

29. Buy slightly soiled new garments at significant savings. Wash or dry-clean them, and they should be as good as "first-quality" garments. Don't buy them if you don't think the spot, etc. will come out.

30. Don't assume that expensive "designer" clothes are always better quality than other clothes. My husband has a "designer" shirt which is twice as difficult to iron and doesn't look as good as his other shirts. The "designer" shirt cost four times as much as some of his best-looking shirts. Don't buy clothes just because they have a "designer" label. You could be just wasting your money.

31. Don't have older clothes altered if you can buy comparable used items for less than the cost of the alterations. For example, don't pay $6.00 to have a blouse taken up if you can buy a comparable one at a garage sale for 25 cents.

32. Convince yourself that buying only certain expensive "labels" of clothes is not essential and that you will judge a garment first by its quality and ability to serve your purposes before you look at the "label." You could save a sizable amount of money by not being a "label" person.

33. In general, don't buy at expensive, prestige clothing stores. The prices of garments at such stores usually are significantly higher than identical or comparable items at other stores.

34. If you are purchasing a piece of clothing such as a shirt, blouse, jacket, or sweater which will be worn with other items, think about what you have in your present wardrobe. Buy the color and style that will go with the largest number of your garments. The greater the number of items with which you can wear your new purchase, the more wear you can get from it and the fewer clothes you should have to buy.

35. Buy baby and children's clothes in sizes somewhat larger than needed, since they outgrow their clothes so quickly. Of course, you don't want the garments to be so large that they look unattractive; but neither should you buy a "perfect fit." Replacing quickly outgrown clothes can put a strain on your clothing budget.

36.   In general, buy some of your baby and children's clothes as cheaply as possible since they are outgrown so fast. Shop carefully, and you won't have to sacrifice quality or style.

37.   Buy children's clothes with built-in growth features, such as elastic in the waist (which expands), cuffs on the slacks (which can be let down), knitted clothes (which "give"), deep hems (which can be let down), and generous seam allowances (which can be let out). These features will enable children to wear the clothing for a longer period of time as they grow, thus decreasing the need for additional clothing.

38.   Before purchasing an item of clothing, consider its care cost, particularly dry cleaning. For example, the care of a nonwashable blouse or shirt which might need to be dry-cleaned after each wearing could become very expensive if worn frequently. The cost of dry cleaning a nonwashable, light-colored suit which may need cleaning after one or two wearings could, over time, amount to more than the original cost of the suit. Even a dark-colored, nonwashable suit will need to be cleaned eventually.

Dry cleaning is becoming more and more expensive, and it adds to the overall cost of a garment. So, limit your purchases of clothes which must be dry-cleaned. Of course, some clothes, including most good-looking men's and women's business suits, must be dry-cleaned; and this will have to be built into your clothing budget. Be sure to read the care label attached to a garment before making a final decision on whether or not to purchase it.

39.   Limit your purchases of clothes which must be washed separately. They will require washing by hand (which wastes your valuable time), or they will require separate washing in the clothes washer. Washing one piece of clothing at a time in

a clothes washer seems to me to be an unwise use of water and electricity.

40. Buy wash-and-wear, permanent press, and wrinkle-resistant clothing whenever possible. Washing is cheaper than dry cleaning. Permanent press clothing will require little or no ironing (ironing uses electricity). Wrinkle-resistant clothing will need little or no pressing between wearings. Save your money and your valuable time for other pursuits.

41. When buying knee highs, thigh highs, and regular hose, buy several pairs of the same color. When one "stocking" gets a run (visible to others), you can wear its mate with a "good" mate from another pair. This process can reduce your hosiery bill by a sizable amount.

42. Buy several pairs of socks in the same color and style. When one sock wears out, don't throw the pair away. Save the good sock and wear it with a mate from your sock drawer. Cut your sock expenses by a considerable amount.

43. When you buy panty hose, buy several pairs of the same color and style. When one leg in each of two separate pairs gets a run which is visible to others, cut off the leg portions (which have the runs in them) just below the reinforced part of the panties. Put aside the leg portions which have the runs. Wear the remaining leg and panty of each pair at the same time. This will give you a great deal more wear from your panty hose.

44. Launder washable ready-to-wear garments before you make any alterations to them. They could shrink. If you wait until after they are altered to launder them, they then may be too tight or too short and unwearable. If they are unwearable, you will have wasted your money and will be out the cost of replacement.

WAYS TO SAVE THROUGH
CLOTHING CONSTRUCTION

45. If you don't know how to sew, check the newspaper advertisements, the telephone directory, and various other sources (such as fabric stores and friends) for information on locating a seamster in your area. Or, you might want to take a simple, introductory sewing course to help you get started sewing. Call your County Extension Service for information on such a course. Being able to sew could save you money on making, altering, and repairing your and your family's clothing.

46. Make a garment at home if it would be cheaper than purchasing it ready-made. Add up the costs of the fabric, lining, pattern, trimmings, buttons, zippers, snaps, hooks and eyes, hem tape, seam binding, interfacing, thread, etc. Next, check to see how much a similar, new garment would cost on sale.

Don't just assume that you can always make a particular garment cheaper than you can buy it new. Also, I have said nothing about the hours of your time which will be needed to make the garment. Do you have extra time? Do you enjoy sewing as a hobby? Is sewing relaxing for you? You will, of course, take these and other things into consideration when deciding whether to make or buy a new garment.

47. Crochet or knit sweaters and other clothing if this is cheaper than buying them ready-made. Total the costs of the pattern, crochet thread or knitting yarn, needles, and any other supplies. Compare this cost with the price of a new sweater or other garment of comparable quality available on sale at various stores and other outlets. For example, most stores will reduce the price of sweaters by up to 75 percent or more at the end of winter. Your purchase can be worn for a while and then stored away until next fall.

Don't just assume that you can knit a sweater, for example, for less than you will have to pay for a new one. It is important that you consider the time involved in crocheting or knitting. Unless you crochet or knit as a hobby or just have extra time on your hands, figure in the cost of your time before you invest it in making your own garments.

48. Save appropriate nonwoven, used fabric softener sheets (similar to some nonwoven interfacing) and use them when possible as interfacing in sewing. Why buy all of your interfacing if these sheets will serve some of your purposes?

49. Save and reuse clothes patterns if possible. Even if you have had them for a number of years and they are slightly out-of-style, minor changes could make them stylish again. With patterns ranging in price from $3.00 to $6.00 and more each, it would make good common sense to reuse your old patterns. A friend of mine recently made a dress from a pattern which her grandmother had used to make a dress for her own daughter over 25 years ago. No changes had to be made in the pattern to make it stylish.

50. Buy individual envelopes of clothes patterns with each envelope containing several different garments or versions of garments which you can use, such as two different pairs of slacks and two different jackets, three different shirts, two different pairs of slacks and shorts, or a long and a short skirt and a blouse with and without sleeves. Buying these types of patterns should cut down on the number of patterns you need to buy.

51. Trade clothes patterns with relatives, co-workers, neighbors, club members, and friends. Trading can cut your outlay of money for patterns.

52. If you have clothes patterns you know you will never use again and you cannot trade them, sell them. You can recover part of your cost.

53. Make children's clothes with built-in growth features such as elastic in the waist, cuffs on the slacks, knitted fabrics, deep hems, and generous seam allowances. These features will enable children to continue to wear their clothes for an extended period of time and reduce the overall clothing budget. (See number 37 in this chapter.)

54. Launder washable fabric before you cut out and make a garment. If you make the garment before pre-shrinking the fabric, you may find that the completed garment is too short or too tight to wear after you wash it; and you will have wasted your time and money. Also, be sure to launder zippers, woven interfacings, lining fabric, lace, and other items if they are not pre-shrunk.

55. Use your leftover scraps of fabrics to make "patchwork" skirts, jackets, vests, and other items of clothing. Such garments can be quite stylish, and the cost will be minimal.

WAYS TO SAVE ON CLOTHING
CARE AND REPAIR

56. Take care of minor repairs to clothes before the repairs become major ones. For example, resew a small section of lace before the entire piece of lace needs to be resewn or replaced; restitch a small section of hem before the whole hem rips out; resew a loose button before it comes off and is lost; repair small rips before they become large rips; and resew seams when only a small break has occurred. Minor repairs are less expensive than major ones.

57. Don't discard garments with broken zippers. Repair or replace the zippers. Repairing or replacing zippers is cheaper than buying new garments. I have repaired zippers in several pairs of my husband's slacks and in my own clothes.

58. Put decorative patches on torn, heavily soiled, and overly worn areas of clothes. By using patches, you can extend the useful lives of garments. Some clothes, however, may have to be removed from the "dress" category to the "yard-work" or "lounge-around-the-house" category; but they may still be worn.

59. Repair or replace torn lace and other trimming rather than discard a garment. Trimming is cheaper than a new garment. In some cases, the trimming can be completely removed and not replaced; and the garment will still look good. Regardless of whether you repair, replace, or remove the trimming, continuing to wear the garment will save you the cost of buying another one.

60. Replace worn-out or badly stretched elastic rather than discard the clothing. Use your good judgement, however. For example, replacing the elastic in a pair of underwear which is nearly worn out may not be worth the cost of the elastic.

61. When a button comes off and is lost, replace the button rather than discard the garment. If you can't find a button like the one lost, replace all the buttons with a different set. A set of buttons will cost less than a new garment.

62. When you are working in the kitchen, wear an apron or a smock over your "good" clothes to protect them. Make sure it covers your clothes adequately. Grease spots and stains could make your "good" clothes unsuitable for wearing in public and necessitate the purchasing of another outfit.

63. Wear old, less desirable clothes for jobs such as cooking, cleaning, and yard work and save your "good" clothes.

64. Use underarm dress shields to absorb perspiration and protect certain garments from becoming stained. If a garment becomes badly stained and if the stain cannot be removed, it will be unsuitable for wearing in public and will have to be relegated to the "old clothes" category. A replacement will cost money.

65. When going out in the rain, wear a raincoat to help protect your clothing. Also, carry an umbrella to help protect your briefcase, handbag, or other things you are carrying.

Water could cause damage to your clothing and other items; if they must be replaced, dry-cleaned, or restored, this means money out of your pocket.

66. Protect the clothes you are wearing when you brush your teeth, shave, apply makeup, and fix or spray your hair. I wear an old, lightweight nylon duster to protect my clothing. A man could wear a robe or an old shirt. If clothes are not protected, they may be damaged or need to be laundered or dry-cleaned as a result.

67. Cover garments hanging in your closet if they are worn only occasionally. They can collect dust and may have to be laundered or dry-cleaned before they can be worn again.

68. Store your clothes away from sunlight to prevent fading. Badly faded clothes may have to be discarded or relegated to "around-the-house wear."

69. Protect your woolen clothes from moths by storing them in moth-proof bags or a cedar chest or closet, or by using moth repellents in your regular closet and other storage areas. Moth holes can ruin a garment completely. Check the labels on your clothes to find out their fiber contents.

70. If you discover mildew on clothes in your closet, remove the mildew as soon as possible. One or more of the following may prevent any further mildew: Leave the closet doors open to allow air to circulate and to admit light. Leave an electric light burning in the closet to provide light; it might also provide enough heat to keep moisture down. Place a chemical moisture absorber in the closet. If neglected, mildew can damage your clothes.

71. Store your knitted clothes in such a way as to prevent them from stretching out of shape. For example, you may want to fold knitted sweaters rather than hang them on hangers. Most knitted skirts and dresses probably could be folded lengthwise and then folded in half over slack hangers. A garment stretched out of shape may have to be washed or dry-cleaned to restore its shape. It may not even be possible to restore the shape to some badly stretched garments.

72. Hang your jackets, suits, blazers, and coats on special contoured wood or plastic "suit" hangers to help retain the shape of the neck, collar, shoulders, and sleeves. Using such hangers should prevent your having to "press" them before you wear them.

73. See that children change from "school" or "dress" clothes when they come home. Adults should make similar changes. This procedure will save "good" clothes.

74. Don't remove the care-instruction labels which are sewn into garments. You will need to refer to them for caring for the clothes. Also, if you eventually sell the garments, the new owner will need the information. Proper care is an important factor in extending the useful lives of clothes.

75. When an item of ready-to-wear clothing becomes soiled, follow the instructions on the care label of that particular garment. Also read all the other labels and hang tags which came with the garment. For example, should it be washed in cold, warm, or hot water? Should it be dried on a flat surface, or can it be dried in a clothes dryer? Must it be dry-cleaned? Proper care will extend the lives of your clothes.

If you follow the care instructions, but a garment fades more than it should, colors "run," it shrinks an abnormal amount, or it is damaged in some other way, return it along with the sales slip and hang tags to the store where it was purchased. Explain the situation and ask for an appropriate adjustment. Most stores will honor your request.

76. When you buy fabric, ask the salesclerk for a care label for that particular fabric. If a care label isn't available, write down the fiber content and the care instructions on a piece of paper. By following the care instructions, you can extend the life of the fabric. (See item 75 above on what to do if damage results when you have properly followed all the care instructions.)

77.   Remove stains from clothing as soon as possible, before the stains "set." Stains not removed can ruin the look of a garment. Call your County Extension Service and ask for a stain removal chart or booklet.

78.   Wash your swimsuit after each wearing to remove dirt, suntan lotion, perspiration, and chlorine to prolong the life of the garment.

79.   Use coin-operated, self-service dry cleaning machines at the laundromat when possible to dry-clean some of your nonwashable clothes.   By using these machines, your dry cleaning expenses will be much less than the cost of sending all of your nonwashable clothes to a full-service dry cleaners.

80.   Send only those clothes which *require* dry cleaning to the cleaners. Launder those which are washable at home and save the expense of dry cleaning. Even some clothes on which the label states "Dry-clean only" can be washed safely. However, make sure that you know absolutely that the particular garment can be washed safely before you wash it and perhaps ruin it forever.

81.   Launder or dry-clean clothes only when they need it. Some clothes can be worn a second or third time or more before laundering or dry cleaning. On the other hand, if you leave dirt, stains, and perspiration in clothes too long, the garments could be damaged. Use your good judgment on when garments should be washed or dry-cleaned.

82.   Hand wash delicate garments instead of tossing them into the washing machine, and they should last longer.

83.   Wash clothes in cold water to minimize fading and shrinking.

84. Don't dry clothes in the dryer if they are susceptible to abnormal shrinkage. They could shrink so much that you would be unable to wear them.

85. Dry garments containing elastic on low heat. High heat can damage elastic and may result in your having to repair or replace such garments.

86. Remove clothes from the dryer as soon as they are dry. This could eliminate or minimize the need for ironing. Ironing consumes electricity and your valuable time. Overdrying clothes also could shorten their lives.

87. Be careful where you sit. Make sure that where you are going to sit is not dirty or greasy. Keep a couple of paper towels in your briefcase or purse to wipe off a seat when there is a need. Sitting in a soiled seat may cost you $5.00 or more at the dry cleaners.

88. Don't put heavy or bulky objects in your pockets if there is a chance they might damage the pockets or cause them to lose their shape. Damaged or sagging pockets can ruin the looks of a garment.

89. Be careful not to snag your clothes. (Knits are particularly susceptible.) Bracelets, rings, purses, briefcases, luggage, and rough seats are some of the things which could cause snags. Snags in a garment could minimize its good appearance.

If you do get a snag, don't cut it off. Rather, use a "knit puller" to pull the snag to the inside of the garment. If you cut off the snag, a noticeable hole could eventually develop in your garment.

90. When you remove your clothes, check them to see if there are any loose buttons, tears, seams which have broken threads, loose hems, spots, or other problems. Taking care of such problems when they are minor ones will be easier and cheaper than treating them after they have become major problems.

91. When you take off a garment that is damp from rain or perspiration, let it dry before hanging it in the closet, putting it in the clothes hamper, or putting it aside to take to the cleaners. Damp garments are susceptible to mildew attack.

92. Stop runs in unseen areas of hose and panty hose by dabbing the ends of the runs with fingernail polish so that you can get additional wear from them.

WAYS TO SAVE BY RECYCLING CLOTHING

93. By recycling your clothes, you can continue to wear them and not have to discard them because they are out-of-style, are stained, have shrunk, have stretched, are torn, are too big or too tight because you have lost or gained weight, or are overly worn in some places. Make the needed changes, repairs, etc. By wearing your clothes longer, you can postpone the expense of purchasing other clothing.

94. Go shopping in some of the "high-class" stores and check out the new styles. Then, go home and see what you can do with the clothes you already own to achieve a similar look. For example, if large, lace collars are "in," you could buy or make a detachable one to wear with some of your dresses and blouses. If wide belts are "the rage," you could update some of your garments by adding belts.

If scarves and large chunky jewelry are popular, you could buy a scarf and a piece of costume jewelry to perk up your wardrobe. If textured hose are being worn this season, could a pair or two give a lift to your last season's clothes? Would a new tie and handkerchief bring new life to one of your old business suits? Would new fashion buttons improve the look of a garment? Update and perk up your wardrobe with the latest "trendy" inexpensive accessories and cut the costs of being "in style."

95. Update your clothes by adding a new shirt, blouse, jacket, vest, or other item of clothing.

96. If the lapels on a coat or jacket are too wide to be "in style," cut them or have them cut down to an acceptable size. The cost will be much less than that for a new coat or jacket.

97. Detach the skirt portion of a dress at the waist and make the dress into a skirt. Use part of the bodice to make a waistband for the "new" skirt.

98. Remove and reverse overly-worn or frayed collars. If you don't sew, consult a seamster and compare the cost of reversing such collars with the cost of new garments. The difference could be substantial. By reversing the collars, you could get additional wear from the garments.

99. When the cuffs of shirts and blouses have become overly worn or a hole has been worn in the elbow area, cut off the sleeves and make short-sleeved or sleeveless garments.

100. When sweaters have stretched at the bottom of the sleeves, put elastic in these areas to restore a proper fit. This is cheaper than buying new sweaters.

101. When the elbow or other sleeve areas of long-sleeved sweaters have become overly worn or have developed holes, cut off the sleeves and make short-sleeved sweaters.

102. Use decorative patches and appliques to cover rips, stains, and worn places in garments to extend their lives.

103. Use appliques, decals, and decorative stitching to modernize garments.

104. If you lose or gain weight, adjust the size of as many of your clothes as possible by taking them up or letting them out, rather than buy new clothes. A complete new wardrobe can be quite expensive.

105. When children outgrow their clothes, make them wearable again by letting down hems, adding ruffles to the hems, and letting out seams.

106. If slacks or jeans have shrunk too much in the length, shorten them to a stylish length.

107. When holes wear in the knees of trousers, cut off the legs and make them into shorts or put "patches" over the holes.

108. If skirts are too "full" for the present styles, take out some of the fullness or take the skirt fabric and cut out a new skirt from a pattern.

109. If there is too much fullness in the sleeves of shirts, blouses, dresses, or jackets to be stylish, take out some of the fullness.

110. If the legs of slacks are too wide, cut them down to fit the current style.

111. If collars are too wide, cut them down or remove them and go "collarless."

112. If ties are too wide, alter them or have them altered to the proper width. A few years ago when the styles changed from wide to narrow ties, my husband had about a dozen of his favorite ties altered. The cost was $3.00 per tie, or about one fifth of the cost of a comparable new tie.

113. Hand clothes down from the largest child to the next largest child and so on, if the clothes are still in suitable condition. Of course, don't neglect buying some new clothes for the smaller children who always get the hand-me-downs.

Also, you might want to change the handed-down clothes in some ways to make them look a little different and "new," such as making knee pants or shorts from slacks, cutting the bodice off the dress and making a skirt, making short sleeves from long sleeves, adding a different belt, adding a lace collar to a blouse or dress, adding decorative appliques, or embroidering a design on a garment. Handing down clothing could save a tremendous amount of money on clothing the children.

114. If you have a two or three-piece outfit, and one or two pieces can no longer be worn, try to salvage the remaining one or two pieces and save money on your clothing expenditures. For example, you may have gained weight in the hips, and the slacks are too tight and cannot be let out; but the matching jacket fits fine and will go with several pairs of other slacks you have. You ripped the blouse beyond repair, but the matching skirt can be worn with several other blouses you have. Your denim jeans are worn out, but the matching denim jacket has several years of wear left in it.

115. Before you discard any item of clothing, ask yourself, "Is there anything I can do to this garment so that I (or family members) can continue to wear it?" An answer of "yes" will help you save money on your clothing expenses.

WAYS TO SAVE THROUGH USE OF DISCARDED CLOTHING

116. Use the fabric from good, out-of-style and outgrown clothes for making other clothes. For example, you could make small children's clothes from some of the fabric. A woman's dress could be made from a very full skirt. An apron could be made from the fabric of most any item of clothing. Scarves, ties, purses, belts, and handkerchiefs could be made from small pieces of used fabric. Patchwork clothing and quilt tops could be made from scraps. Some bodices could be converted to blouses. By utilizing previously-used fabric, you save yourself the expense of buying the fabric.

117.   Cut up badly worn garments and use them as cleaning and dusting rags. For example, a 100 percent cotton, knitted man's undershirt makes an excellent dusting rag. Utilizing the worn garments saves you the cost of buying cleaning and dusting cloths.

118.   Salvage all usable parts of worn-out garments such as buttons, zippers, elastic, hem tape, seam binding, trimming, decals, belts, hooks and eyes, snaps, appliques, and shoulder pads. Having these on hand decreases the need for buying such items.

119.   Donate discarded clothes to charity. (You could let this replace some of your cash charitable contributions, thus decreasing the amount of cash paid out of your pocket.)

120.   Have a garage sale and sell discarded clothes. Garage sales are growing in popularity and have become regular weekend outings and forms of recreation for many people. You could make extra money from the sale.

121.   Swap good discarded children's and adults' clothing, maternity clothes, and other items of clothing with friends. By swapping for items you need, you can save the money you would have spent to purchase these items.

122.   Sell good, discarded clothing to privately-owned thrift shops. Not only do you get the clothes out of your way, but you make money by doing so.

123.   Put an advertisement in the newspaper to sell good, discarded clothing. What you have to sell may be just what others want. Your advertisement might be worded similar to this: "Four good, used men's suits for sale. Size 40 regular with slacks 34 inches in waist, 33 inches long. Call -------."

124.   Put your nicest and most stylish discarded clothes in a consignment shop. The clothes should be clean and in good shape. (You get a percentage of the money from the sales, if and when the clothes sell. Items unsold after a specified length of time are returned to the owner.)

125. If your clothes qualify, sell them to a "Vintage" clothing store. These stores sell "antique" clothes which are 20, 30, and 40 years old. (These clothes usually demand a higher price than newer, used clothes.)

WAYS TO SAVE ON THE PURCHASE, CARE, AND REPAIR OF SHOES

126. When considering buying a pair of shoes, ask yourself, "Do I really need another pair of shoes?" For example, "Do I really need a new pair of black shoes, since I already have four pairs of good, black shoes in the closet?" Answering "no" to such questions could save you a sizable amount of money.

127. If possible, wait until needed shoes are on sale--preferably at 50 to 75 percent or more off. My favorite pair of high-heel shoes was regularly priced at $56. I bought them on a closeout table for $3.00. Nearly all shoes (men's, women's, and children's) will eventually be put on sale. Rare should be the case when you would need to pay full price for a pair of shoes.

128. If you really do need a pair of new shoes and you cannot find them on sale, shop around for the best full price. For example, the price of an identical style and brand of shoe can vary from store to store.

129. Check out the garage sales. Shoes, especially ones still in very good condition, are usually rare, but not impossible to find, at garage sales. I have purchased some in like-new condition, so be on the lookout. Spray the insides of all secondhand shoes with a commercial fungicide to avoid the chance of getting athlete's foot.

130. Check factory outlets. (See number 6 in this chapter for information on factory outlets.)

131. Consider "seconds" and "irregulars" if the flaws are so minor that it really doesn't matter, and if they don't affect the comfort or fit. "Seconds" and "irregulars" will be cheaper than the same "first-quality" shoes.

132. Consider "samples." Watch the newspaper for advertisements of sales on shoe "samples." You can usually get them at considerable savings.

133. Buy shoes which will stay in style beyond one season. Choose simple, basic, classic, conservative, and traditional styles. Such shoes should be stylish for many years and, thus, should decrease the need to buy additional shoes as soon.

134. Avoid (or drastically limit) the purchase of "fad" shoes, which are in style for very short periods. If you do buy fad shoes, pay as little as possible for them. If you do pay more than a small amount for them, you will have more to lose when the shoes are no longer stylish.

135. Buy a pair of shoes in a color and style which can be worn with many of your clothes, not just one particular garment. The more clothes with which you can wear a pair of shoes, the fewer pairs of shoes you should need.

136. Buy children's shoes slightly larger than needed so that the children can wear the shoes longer. Of course, you don't want to buy shoes which are uncomfortably large or damaging to your children's feet. Use your good judgement. The children could wear thick socks and switch to thinner socks as their feet grow.

137. Be careful about buying shoes on impulse. Make a list of the styles and colors of shoes you need and try to stick to it. Otherwise, you could end up with a closet full of shoes which match very few of your clothes. In addition, the more shoes you buy, of course, the less money you have left to use else-where or put in your savings account.

138. When you are buying shoes, buy ones which can be worn for several occasions, if possible. For example, a pair of office shoes may be comfortable enough for a day of shopping and dressy enough for dinner out. The more occasions on which you can wear a pair of shoes, the fewer pairs you should need.

139. Buy shoes in which you feel "good." If you don't like the shoes a great deal in the store, you probably won't like them any better when you get them home; and your money invest-ment will spend most of its time on the shoe rack in your closet.

140. Buy shoes that are comfortable. If they are not comfort-able during the five minutes you wear them in the store, they probably won't be comfortable after you have worn them for hours in the office or on shopping trips. Thus, you will probably end up not wearing them; and you will have wasted your money.

141. If possible, try on shoes before you buy them. A size 6AA in one brand or style may not fit the same as a size 6AA in another brand or style. Once you have scuffed the soles, you usually can't return or exchange them for another size. Also, if you bought them on sale, you may not be able to return them or exchange them anyway. Your money will be lost.

142. Limit your purchase of light-colored shoes which might not look as good for as long a time as darker-colored ones. Lighter colors have more tendency to show scratches, stains, and evidence of having been repaired.

143. Have shoes repaired rather than buy new ones. For example, have the shoe shop replace worn heels and soles, resew straps, and make various other repairs. However, use your good judgement. For example, it probably would be a poor investment to put new heels and soles on a pair of men's shoes which are practically worn out in all other places.

144.   Replace broken or badly worn shoe laces to extend the lives of the shoes instead of discarding the shoes. New laces could also perk up the look of older shoes. New laces certainly will cost less than a new pair of shoes.

145.   Insert pads inside of shoes, wear socks, or wear thicker socks than you've been wearing for a better fit, instead of discarding shoes which have stretched. Continuing to wear the shoes will decrease the need for buying additional ones.

146.   Launder washable shoes by hand in the bathroom lavatory, bathtub, laundry room sink, or a bucket or other container of water rather than run them through the cycles in the washing machine. Washing them in the washing machine could shorten their lives, and you will have to buy new ones sooner.

147.   Keep your shoes clean and polished to extend their lives.

148.   Wear rubber or plastic overshoes or galoshes in rainy and snowy weather to protect your shoes.

149.   Protect your leather shoes from mildew. If you detect mildew on shoes in the closet, leave the shoes outside the closet after you have cleaned off the mildew so that they can get light and air, or lay a package of chemical moisture absorber in the shoes when they are in the closet--one or both of these suggestions could remedy the problem. Mildew could damage shoes and cause you to have to buy new ones.

150.   Have children to change from "good" shoes to "play" shoes if they are going to "play." Adults should do likewise. Changing shoes will help "good" shoes to stay in that category for a longer period of time.

WAYS TO SAVE ON THE PURCHASE, UPKEEP, AND REPAIR OF ACCESSORIES

151. Buy your accessories on sale instead of paying full price for them. It is usually just a matter of time before most accessories will be reduced by 25 to 75 percent or more in price. Rarely should you need to pay full price for accessories.

152. If you absolutely must pay full price for accessories, then shop around for the best price. Prices for similar accessories usually vary substantially among stores.

153. Shop at garage sales, thrift shops, discount stores, factory outlets, and bargain basements for your accessories. Accessories should be the least expensive at these places, unless you can find "super" sales at other types of stores. Andie Mac-Dowell, who played Jane in the film "Greystoke," purchases many of her accessories secondhand from thrift shops.[2]

154. If you lose the back off one of your pierced earrings, rather than throw the pair away, buy a new back; or, if you have another pair of pierced earrings, use the back from one of those earrings. Even buying a new back should be cheaper than buying a new pair of earrings.

155. If you lose the back off a tie tac, instead of throwing the tie tac away, buy a new back; or, use the back of one of your other tie tacs. Even buying a new back should be less expensive than purchasing another tie tac.

156. If your beads break, restring them instead of discarding them. "String" would be cheaper than a new strand of beads.

157. If your chain necklaces and bracelets break, have them repaired instead of discarding them, if you can have them repaired cheaper than you can buy new ones.

158. Make sure the clasps are secure on your jewelry, including watches, so that there will be less chance of your losing your jewelry. Occasionally, check their security. If you lose them, you will have to replace them (which costs money) or do without them.

159. Check out chain jewelry stores. These stores usually sell similar items at a lower price than "independent," "individual" jewelry stores. For example, the price of a pair of pearl pierced earrings with a 14 karat gold "back" was $75 at one independent jewelry store and $60 at another one. I bought a comparable pair at a discount chain jewelry store for $40.

160. If you buy "expensive" jewelry, choose basic, classic, simple, and traditional designs which will stay in style. Having to replace "expensive" jewelry which is no longer stylish can greatly upset your bank account.

161. If you are buying faddish accessories, pay as little as possible for them. Then, when their short lives are over, you will not have "lost" as much money.

162. Have your "good" jewelry checked occasionally by a jeweler to make sure stones are still secure and that settings have not worn to the point that stones could be lost.

163. Compare the warranties when shopping around for a watch. Put the warranty and sales slip for the one you do buy in a safe place at home for use should the watch need an adjustment or repair while it is still under warranty.

MISCELLANEOUS WAYS TO SAVE ON CLOTHING, SHOES, AND ACCESSORIES

164. If you haven't worn some clothes, shoes, and accessories for several years, consider selling them. You can use the money to purchase items you will wear.

165. When you find items (such as hosiery, underwear, socks, and handkerchiefs) you regularly wear or use on sale at considerable savings, stock up. Why pay full price?

166. The best deals (largest discounts) in stores are normally found on end-of-the-season leftovers. For example, I have purchased new $30 slacks for $1.00, new $12 belts for $1.00, new $1.83 underpants for 33 cents, and numerous other new items at "giveaway" prices.

167. When you are shopping for clothes, shoes, and accessories, go straight to the sales racks and tables. In many stores, the true bargain items will be in the back of the store. The savings could be drastic.

168. When you want to buy an article of clothing, a pair of shoes, a pair of hose, a piece of jewelry, or some other item to match items in your wardrobe, take the items with you to make sure you match them correctly. If you don't take the items with you, you may buy something which doesn't match; and there is always a possibility you can't return or exchange it, especially if you bought it on sale or at a garage sale.

169. When hose or panty hose get small "picks," wear them inside out; and the small "picks" will be less noticeable.

170. Wear knee highs rather than hose or panty hose with slacks. Knee highs should be sufficient and generally are cheaper than hose or panty hose.

ENDNOTES

1. Sydney Baker, "Lady Tarzan," *Fair Lady*, Cape Town, South Africa, August 22, 1984, p. 68.

2. *Ibid*.

CHAPTER 3

HOW TO SAVE ON YOUR COMMUNICATIONS EXPENSES

Ah, make the most of what we yet may spend
Edward Fitzgerald

INTRODUCTION

In today's world, the telephone is considered by many to be a necessity rather than a luxury. However, without careful thought and management, the costs can play havoc with your budget.

Unnecessary expenditures for personal home office supplies and postage, which may seem insignificant at the time, can add up to a substantial amount of money over the period of a year.

If you follow the suggestions in this chapter, you should be able to decrease your monthly telephone bill by up to 60 percent or more. You should be able, also, to decrease considerably the amount you spend on personal home office supplies and postage.

WAYS TO SAVE ON TELEPHONE EXPENSES

1. Consider whether having a telephone in your home is absolutely essential, especially if you have access to a phone at your place of work, if there is a pay phone near where you live, if there is a pay phone or other available phone in your apartment building, or if you have access to a neighbor's phone in case of an emergency. If you realize that a telephone is not absolutely essential, don't install one; or if you have one, have it disconnected immediately. Save yourself the monthly expense of a telephone.

2. Be on a party line, if possible, rather than a private line. The base rate for a party line is cheaper in most areas. Call your local telephone office and ask if a party line is available where you live.

3. Check to see if "local measured service" or other special services are offered by your local telephone company. Determine whether one of these services would be cheaper and meet your needs as well as the regular, monthly flat-rate service. If you make only a few calls per month, an alternative to the regular, flat-rate service could save you money. For example, the monthly base rate for local measured service is usually much cheaper than the base rate for regular, traditional service. Some telephone companies offer several different measured service options. Make sure you get all of the details of the various "services" before you make a switch, because there usually is a fee to switch from one type of service to another.

When we lived in Little Rock, Arkansas, my husband and I switched to local measured service, and our monthly base rate decreased by 75 percent. We paid a fraction of a cent up to several cents for each minute we talked depending on the distance and the time of day we made the call. Even with the number of calls we made each month, the complete monthly bill for the measured service was less than half of the monthly base rate for the regular, flat-rate service.

4.   If you are on "local measured service," on which you pay for telephone calls by the length of time you talk, make a list of the items you want to cover before you dial the number. Having a list should help you limit your call to the shortest period of time possible and keep your telephone costs within reason. Make your calls when the cheapest local rates are in effect.

5.   Check with your local telephone company to see whether it offers a decreased monthly rate for low-income persons who qualify.

6.   Have only one telephone in your home, if at all possible. Each additional telephone increases your monthly bill, if you rent the phones. If you purchase an additional phone, the purchase price must be added to your overall communications expenses.

7.   Consider installing an extra-long extension cord on your telephone instead of adding another telephone. The phone can be moved easily into another room for privacy.   A cord generally will be cheaper than another phone.

8.   Don't purchase the extra services (such as call waiting, multiple listings, speed calling, call forwarding, and unlisted numbers) offered by most telephone companies unless there is a valid reason for doing so. These extras add to your telephone costs.

9.   Check into buying your own telephone from the telephone company or other reliable source rather than renting one for a monthly fee from the telephone company. Buying could be cheaper in the long run. I purchased several new telephones on sale at $3.95 each plus tax at a discount department store. When they wear out, I'll just throw them away. It will be cheaper for me than paying $2.00 or more per month to lease the least expensive type of phone. Consider your own situation, however, before you rush out and buy a telephone.

10.   When buying telephones, compare the warranties before you buy. If quality and prices are comparable, buy the phone carrying the best warranty.

11.   Buy or rent the least expensive telephone that will meet your needs.

12.   Check with several companies offering long distance telephone service to determine which company offers the best deal (money-wise) for your particular long-distance needs. Get all of the details on what each company offers and does not offer.

13.   Limit the number of long distance calls you make. Write letters instead. A postage stamp generally is cheaper than a long distance call.

14.   Limit the length of your long distance calls. Use a one-minute egg timer for timing calls. The shorter the calls, the less they will cost.

15.   Before you place a long distance telephone call, jot down the items you want to cover during the call. Having such a list before you will prevent your using valuable time trying to remember what you want to say or discuss and should decrease the number of minutes you talk. Fewer minutes mean a smaller charge.

16.   Dial your own long distance calls from your home or business phone. This method is cheaper than going through an operator.

17.   Dial your long distance calls direct when the rates are the cheapest. Check your telephone directory for direct-dial rates for different times of the day and days of the week. For example, you can save around 40 percent when the night and weekend rates are in effect. Also, on some holidays, the evening rate applies all day. Never make long distance calls when the full rate is in effect, except when really essential.

18. Eliminate person-to-person long distance calls. This is the most expensive type of call.

19. Long distance calls may be more expensive if you call from your hotel or motel room. If possible, arrange before-hand for your party to direct dial a call to you at your hotel or motel at a designated time.

20. Make your long distance telephone calls from your home or office rather than from a pay phone. Using a pay phone will be more expensive than dialing direct from your home or office. Of course, if you are a considerable distance from your home or office and must make a long distance call, the pay phone may be your only alternative.

21. Use your telephone credit card or have your call charged to a third number only when it is absolutely necessary. Such calls are much more expensive than dialing direct from your home or office.

22. Rather than having family members or other parties calling collect (other than in emergencies), make prearrange-ments for a time when you may dial them direct. This way, you can eliminate costly collect calls from children who are away at boarding school or college, from family members who are away on vacation, or from your spouse who is away on a business trip. Collect calls are much more expensive than direct-dialed calls.

23. If you dial long distance and reach a wrong number, have a poor connection, or have other problems, hang up and dial the operator immediately and ask for credit on the call.

24. Keep a list of long distance calls you make so you can check your record against your monthly phone bill. Errors can be made, or an unauthorized person or persons might charge calls to your number. If calls appear on your bill which you did not make, call your telephone company and explain the situation. These calls should be deducted from your bill.

25. If you don't know a particular long distance telephone number within your area code, dial 1-555-1212. If the party for which you want the number is located outside your own area code, dial 1-area code-555-1212. After you get the desired number, dial it direct yourself. Asking the operator to place the call for you will be more expensive.

26. Dial free 1-800-555-1212 to obtain toll-free telephone numbers (numbers you can call without a charge to you) for particular people, companies, banks, businesses, organizations, and other establishments which have 800 numbers. There are thousands of toll-free numbers. It is quite possible that the persons and establishments you need to call have toll-free numbers. Why pay for long distance calls if you can call toll free?

27. Use your telephone directory to locate a local number rather than pay to have "Directory Assistance" look it up for you.

28. If you have reported to the telephone company that you are unable to make or receive calls because your telephone is "out of service," you generally are entitled to receive a proportionate credit on your telephone bill for loss of service lasting 24 hours or more. If you experience this loss of service, inquire at your local telephone office about such a credit.

29. If you happen to "lose" your money in a pay phone, use another phone to report the loss to the operator. The telephone company will send you a refund.

WAYS TO SAVE ON PERSONAL HOME OFFICE SUPPLIES

30. Use the front and back of nonbusiness letter writing paper when you write more than a one-page letter. Not using the back is really a waste of money. If you normally spend $50 a year for personal letter writing paper, you could cut this amount in half by writing on both sides of the paper if you usually write two-page letters.

31. When you receive mail, don't throw away any of the envelopes. Save them for holding such items as receipts, important papers, income tax records, coupons, refund forms, and postage stamps. Also, you can cut appropriate envelopes open at the top and both ends and fold them out flat. The insides of most envelopes provide a clean sheet of scratch paper. The flat sheets, also, can be cut into several small pieces for short notes and reminders to yourself.

32. Use the clean backs of previously used sheets of paper for things like writing grocery lists, writing menus, jotting down notes, making lists of things to do, and writing rough drafts of letters and speeches. With the exception of the final copy, I used the clean backs of used 8 1/2 x 11 inch sheets of paper for writing this book. If you start now saving paper with one clean side (junk mail, letters, etc.), I think you will be amazed at the stack of usable paper you will accumulate. Why would you throw away usable "scratch paper" and then go out and buy scratch pads?

33. If you need a few extra copies of something you are writing or typing, make carbon copies rather than photocopies, if carbon copies will serve your purpose. Making carbon copies usually will be much cheaper.

34. When a pencil becomes too short to use comfortably, unscrew the top from the bottom of a used-up ball-point pen, remove the insides, and insert the top of the pencil into the bottom part of the ball-point pen. Assuming that people discard pencils when they are only two-thirds used, a substantial sum of money could be saved, over time, by using pencil holders so that most of the remaining one-third of the pencils can be used.

35. Pick up free calendars from banks, businesses, and other places around town instead of buying them, especially if they

provide enough space on each date to jot down appointments, birthdays, and other important items.

36. You can make your own calendar by drawing vertical lines on 8 1/2 x 11 inch sheets of paper. Make boxes by drawing horizontal lines across the vertical lines. Write the dates in the upper right-hand corners of the boxes. Make one sheet for each month and staple the sheets together. You will have a calendar with room to write in appointments and other items, and the cost will be much less than purchasing a similar calendar.

37. Rewind and reuse the correction tapes on "self-correcting" typewriters. I have rewound and reused tapes as many as five times each and have had acceptable results. Correction tapes are expensive. The more times you can reuse them, the less your outlay of money for replacements.

38. When you find items which you use regularly (such as writing paper, typing paper, pencils, pens, carbon paper, file folders, and typewriter ribbons) on sale at considerable savings, stock up.

39. Pick up seashells and rocks with interesting shapes and colors and use them for paperweights instead of buying paperweights.

WAYS TO SAVE ON POSTAGE

40. Use post cards whenever possible instead of paper and envelopes. First-class postage for post cards measuring 3.5 by 5 inches to 4.25 by 6 inches is much cheaper than first-class postage for sealed envelopes. Unless there is a real need for sending your message in an envelope, use a post card.

41. Send Christmas and other holiday post cards rather than cards in envelopes. Post cards require less postage. (See number 40 above.)

42. Use aerogrammes when writing to someone in a foreign country. They are available at your post office. The postage is less for aerogrammes than for international airmail letters. For example, in 1990, an aerogramme sent from the United States cost 39 cents. The postage for an international airmail letter weighing up to 1/2 ounce was 45 cents. When you use aerogrammes, you also save your own writing paper and envelopes. For instance, if you write internationally 50 times a year, you could save $3 per year on postage plus the cost of 50 envelopes and at least 50 sheets of writing paper.

43. Use postage-paid envelopes when possible. Ask your bank for a supply for mailing in deposits. Check with other establishments with which you do business and ask if they provide postage-paid envelopes for paying bills.

44. When you send articles such as books, catalogs, gifts, or other items by mail, ask at your post office and find out the cheapest rate for such items. You may be surprised at the amount of postage you can save.

45. Buy an inexpensive set of postal scales (or diet scales which weigh in ounces) and weigh your outgoing mail. Don't guess how much it weighs and how much postage will be required. By weighing your mail, you can be sure you are not using too much postage. My husband and I bought a set of diet scales for weighing our letters and small packages for $2.97 plus tax. We estimated that we saved enough on postage the first few weeks to pay for the scales.

MISCELLANEOUS WAYS TO SAVE ON COMMUNICATIONS EXPENSES

46. Never send cash through the mail. There is always a possibility that your mail will pass through dishonest hands, or it could be lost.

47. Use free classified ads whenever possible. Some newspapers offer free ads if they are of a noncommercial nature.

CHAPTER 4

HOW TO SAVE MONEY THROUGH COUPONING AND REFUNDING

Industry, perseverance, and frugality,
make fortune yield

Franklin

INTRODUCTION

As a couponer and refunder, you should be able to save between $30 and $200 (or maybe more if you have a large family) per month on expenditures for food eaten at home and out, toiletry items, paper products, medical items, household cleaners, personal grooming aids, and dozens of other items. That's $360 to $2,400 or more a year. Just think what you could do with that much extra money!

Each year, manufacturers make thousands of different refund offers available to consumers. Hundreds of billions of manufacturers' cents-off store coupons are distributed annually. Also, thousands and thousands of restaurant and fast-food coupons and various miscellaneous coupons are issued. American consumers could save billions of dollars each year by redeeming coupons and responding to refund offers.

Read this chapter to see how you can get your part of those billions of dollars through couponing and refunding.

WAYS TO SAVE THROUGH COUPONING

1. Save every coupon (manufacturers' cents-off store coupons, restaurant and fast-food coupons, and others) you come across. Don't throw away a single one unless it has expired. If you can't use some of them, trade them to other people for ones you can use. Every coupon is potential money in your pocket.

2. Organize your manufacturers' cents-off store coupons. First, get out a dozen or so used business size envelopes (from the stack you have been saving). Label each envelope with the category of coupons you plan to place in it. For instance, you might label one envelope with the words "canned vegetables, fruits, and soups." Another might be labeled "meats and main dishes." Another could be "toiletry and personal grooming aids." Another might be "breakfast foods."

Use categories or groupings which are most convenient for you. Next, sort out your coupons and place them in the appropriate envelopes. By having your coupons organized, you will be more inclined to use as many as you can. The more coupons you use, the less money you will have to take out of your pocket for your purchases.

3. Label a used business size envelope and store all your restaurant and fast-food coupons in it. If you keep all these coupons in one place, you will be more apt to use them.

4. Label a used business size envelope "miscellaneous" and put in this envelope such coupons as, "Two suits cleaned for the price of one"; "As a newcomer to our community, bring this coupon in for a free box of assorted candies"; and "Bring this coupon to our portrait studio for a free 8 by 10 color portrait." Keeping your miscellaneous coupons together in one place should encourage you to take advantage of as many of them as possible.

5.   Purchase coupon books if the coupons can save you more money than you must pay for the books and if the coupons are for items you can use.   Various promotional businesses and nonprofit organizations sell such books from time to time. Generally, the coupons are for items provided by local businesses.   Buy several books if the potential savings are great enough.   These books might contain coupons for such things as: a free sandwich at a fast-food place; free tire rotation; a studio portrait for $1.95; a free dinner entree with the purchase of one; or a free houseplant.

6.   Always use coupons whenever and wherever possible and save money.   Make sure you never leave home to go shopping without taking all your coupons with you.   You might invest in a small file box or other suitable container (with a handle) for storing and carrying your envelopes of coupons.   If you take your car, put your coupons in the trunk of your car when you are not using them to decrease the chances of their being stolen while you are out on your shopping trip--they are the same as money!   If you have your coupons with you on your shopping trip, you can take advantage of outstanding, unadvertised specials when you find them and save even more money with your coupons.

7.   Use restaurant and fast-food coupons.   These coupons may be for such offers as: "Two dinners for the price of one," "Buy one sandwich and get one free," "Free hamburger with the purchase of a chicken sandwich," "One-half price buffet from 4 to 6 p.m.," "Get a free order of french fries with the purchase of a sandwich," "Two dollars off any entree," and "Pizza--1/2 price on Wednesdays."   There are usually dozens of such offers available at any one time.   With careful planning, rarely should you have to pay full price for eating out.

8.   Wait and shop on days when grocery stores double or triple manufacturers' cents-off store coupons.   (Some stores occasionally triple coupons and are willing to lose money on the coupon items just to try to attract new customers.) If you shop on days when the stores deduct only the face values of your coupons from your bill, you are losing money. If the grocery stores where you usually shop do not have double or triple coupon days, consider switching stores. However, make sure that the stores which offer these extra coupon savings aren't charging a lot more for their products than the stores at which you regularly shop.

9. Don't buy a particular brand of a product just because you have a manufacturer's cents-off store coupon for it if you can buy another equally acceptable brand or the generic item for less without a coupon.

10. Before you go shopping, pull and put all of the coupons you plan to use that day together in one envelope. By doing this, it will be much easier for you to use them. While you are out, you will not have to go back through your entire inventory of coupons to locate the ones you had planned to use. If it is easy for you to use the coupons, you will be more inclined to use them.

11. Go through each category of your inventory of coupons on the first day of each month and pull out all of the ones which will expire that month and clip the expiring coupons with a paper clip to the front of the envelope containing the rest of your coupons in that category. By doing this, you will be less likely to let the opportunity to use them pass. Throw away the coupons that expired at the end of the previous month.

12. Where do you find manufacturers' cents-off store coupons? Here are some suggestions: in the food section of the daily newspaper; in the Sunday newspaper; in certain magazines; inside and on the outsides of specially marked packages; in the mail, so always open your "junk" mail--it may contain valuable coupons; in a box at the front of some grocery stores; at swap sessions where you can swap coupons you don't want for ones you can use; at coupon and refund clubs where you can trade coupons; from friends and relatives who have saved them for you; from newspapers which friends and relatives who are not into couponing have saved for you; from representatives of companies in stores on particular days offering free samples of certain products and handing out coupons for these products; and from company representatives who are handing out coupons as you come into the store.

The larger the number and variety of coupons you can collect, the greater your potential to save money on your purchases.

13. If particular issues of newspapers and magazines have "good" coupons, buy several copies if you can save more than the cost of the newspapers or magazines. For example, a newspaper may have $10 worth of high-value manufacturers' cents-off store coupons for items you use routinely. You might profit by purchasing eight or ten copies of this issue.

WAYS TO SAVE THROUGH REFUNDING

<u>NOTE</u>: You might already have many of the qualifiers (requested on the refund forms) just lying around your house. Qualifiers are proofs-of-purchase, and they are required by companies in refund offers. Qualifiers are further discussed later in this chapter.

14. Save all refund forms you come across. If you can't use some of them, then trade them for forms which you can use. There probably is someone out there who would like to have your refund form for receiving $1.50 back on the purchase of a package of chewing tobacco. Refund forms are potential money in your pocket.

15. Keep your refund forms organized, and you will be better prepared to take advantage of refund offers. Here is one way you might organize your refund forms: First, get out twelve used business size envelopes (from the stack you have been saving). Second, write January on one of them, February on another, and so on through December. Third, sort out your refund forms by the expiration dates and put the forms in the appropriate envelopes. Being organized will help you to take advantage of as many refund offers as you can.

16. Never leave home to go shopping without your inventory of refund forms. You might need to refer to them while you are out shopping. For example, you find a shampoo on sale for $1.00 and you think you have a refund form for $1.00 back on the purchase price. If you have all of your refund forms with you, you can easily check to see if you have one for the shampoo.

17. Search actively for items for which you have refund forms if you can use the items or give them as gifts and if the amounts of the refunds are worth your efforts. The following are just a few examples of refund offers in which I have participated:

> a. I bought a bottle of Pert shampoo at a "Dollar" store for $1.00 plus five cents sales tax. I sent in the refund form plus the required qualifiers and received a $1.00 refund. So, I got a bottle of Pert for the price of a postage stamp, five cents for tax, and 1/2 cent for an envelope.

> b. I received a refund for the entire purchase price of $1.89 plus 9 cents tax for sending in the required refund form and qualifiers for a bottle of Secret roll-on deodor- ant. My cost was the price of a postage stamp plus 1/2 cent for an envelope.

> c. I received a refund for the entire purchase price of $3.50 plus the sales tax of 18 cents for a bottle of Viadent mouthwash. I was out the cost of a postage stamp and 1/2 cent for an envelope.

> d. A refund form offered a $1.59 refund on the purchase of a bottle of Ban roll-on deodorant. Responding to the

issuance of the refund offer by the manufacturer, Wal-mart advertised the Ban for $1.59. The bottle of deodorant actually cost me a postage stamp, 8 cents for sales tax, and 1/2 cent for an envelope.

e. I received a $2.00 refund in a Kiwi shoe polish refund offer. The price I paid for the polish was less than $1.00, so I made nearly a dollar profit on this offer--even after paying for a stamp and an envelope.

f. I have also received such refunds as these: $4.00 on a 4.5 pound can of Crisco shortening, $4.99 on a 168 ounce box of Clorox laundry detergent, $3.00 on six pairs of men's Hanes briefs, and $10.00 on 20 packs of Eveready batteries.

The list could go on and on. With very little effort, you can get refunds similar to these.

18. When you send in refund forms, be sure to fill in all the blanks correctly, completely, and legibly and enclose the required qualifiers. Use small envelopes if possible; they are cheaper than the business size. Try to keep the weight of your letter at one ounce or less--peel off thick cardboard backings and trim all qualifiers as closely as possible. Additional weight could require more postage and reduce the amount you will actually realize from the refund offer.

19. Write down and keep the following information about every refund offer to which you respond: Name of the refund offer; the mailing address where you sent the form; what qualifiers you sent; date sent; and what you are supposed to receive. Some refund forms will list an address to which you may write if you have not had a response within a certain length of time. Write this address down, also. Keeping the above information will help you in following up on a refund offer in which you are participating but from which you have not yet received your refund.

20.   If you have not received a response to a refund offer (check, coupon for a free product, or merchandize) within 12 weeks after submitting the form and qualifiers, write to the head office (corporate headquarters) of the company offering the refund.   Normally, this is not the same address to which you sent the refund form.   The head office address usually is found on the product package, and sometimes it is listed on the refund form itself.

I have written (I have called if they had toll-free numbers.) to the head offices about several refunds which I had not received and have gotten very nice, apologetic letters along with refund checks, coupons for free products, or whatever the refund offer was promising.   Since most refund offers are handled by clearinghouses which receive thousands of refund requests, it is always possible that one will be misplaced.

21.   When you write to the head office (corporate head-quarters) of the company offering a refund to inquire about your refund, use a post card, not a letter in an envelope.   The postage for a post card is much cheaper.   Every penny saved on postage is important in refunding, since postage is a relatively large part of your overhead.

22.   Where do you find refund forms?   The following are some suggestions:

> a. Search for pads of forms on the shelves throughout stores. You should take no more than one of each form. Taking more than one deprives others of the opportunity for a refund.

> b. Check bulletin boards at the front of the store. Take only one of each form.

> c. Look through special mailouts to your address, so be sure to open all of your "junk mail."

> d. Examine newspapers.

e. Swap with friends. Get a group together for a swapping session.

f. Explore boxes at the fronts of various stores. Shoppers put in refund forms when they have some they don't need. Others take out ones they can use.

g. Flip through magazines, especially "women's" magazines.

h. Ask the cashier whether he or she has refund forms under the counter. Take no more than one of each different form.

i. Investigate file cabinets or boxes in the store office or at the courtesy/information/exchange desk. Ask the manager or the person at the desk if you may look through such cabinets or boxes. Take only one of each different form.

j. Observe the outsides and insides of specially marked packages.

k. Ask relatives and friends to save refund forms for you.

l. Put a note on a store's bulletin board saying, "I will trade refund forms. Call -------." Be sure to clear with the manager before you place a note on the bulletin board.

m. Join a coupon/refund club where you can exchange refund forms. (Organize one if there is not one in your area.) Better still, join several clubs.

n. Trade forms through the mail. Some couponing and refunding magazines have classified sections with ads placed there by people who would like to trade refund forms. You send forms to these advertisers; and they, in turn, will send you an equal number of forms of similar quality. Often, the advertisers will be from other states, so you may receive some forms which are not available in your area.

o. Trade refund forms by mail with people you know.

p. Purchase refund forms through the mail. Some couponing and refunding magazines have ads placed there by people who sell refund forms.

q. Place an ad in the newspaper. Some newspapers offer free ads of a noncommercial nature. Your ad might read: "I want to exchange refund forms. Call-------."

r. Write to companies. When all of the refund forms have been taken from a pad on the shelf at a store or on the store's bulletin board, the cardboard backing will sometimes give an address to which you may write to request one of the forms.

Collecting as many refund forms as possible increases your potential savings.

23. A word about qualifiers: In general, save the entire product package. One manufacturer may require the proof-of-purchase (POP) seal for a particular refund. Another may request the net weight statement, another may ask for the hinge off the top of the plastic bottle, and one may want the plastic lid from a coffee can.

You can never be totally sure just what qualifier a manufacturer will request in a particular refund offer. You can no longer afford to save only box tops and universal product codes (UPCs)--the bar codes consisting of lines with numbers below them. Unless you save virtually everything, you could miss out on many refund offers and the opportunity to save money.

24. Organize your qualifiers. Separate qualifiers for storage. For example, all cereal boxes may be flattened and placed in one large box; soup, fruit, and vegetable can labels could be placed in a smaller box; toothpaste boxes and soap wrappers may be placed in yet another box; and flattened facial tissue boxes may be placed in another.   Small qualifiers may be stored in used envelopes.   Being organized should help and encourage you to respond to more refund offers.

25.   The following are some examples of qualifiers: box tops; fluid ounce statements; ingredient listings; proof-of-purchase (POP) seals; the names of the products; the ends of pouring spouts; the universal product codes (UPCs); instructions for preparation; the net weight statements; the side, front, or back panels; the product symbols or "logos"; box bottoms; the round circles where the prices are stamped; certain statements on the containers; warranty statements; instruction sheets; inner seals; tear strips; entire labels from cans, jars, and bottles; the cap liners; complete outer wrappers; neckbands; plastic lids; individual wrappers, such as wrappers from individual bandages; owners' manuals; and instruction manuals.

26.   The following are some sources of qualifiers:

a. Items you purchase.

b. Friends, relatives, and co-workers. Ask them to save qualifiers for you.   If they save quite a number of qualifiers for you, you may want to give them an occasional gift of an item you receive through your refunding activity or something else as a token of your appreciation.

c. Coupon/refund club meetings, swap sessions, and Refunder's Conventions. Trade your qualifiers here.

d. Newspapers. Place ads such as: "I would like to trade or buy qualifiers. Call--------." "I need five box tops from Kelloggs Cornflakes, two hinges from the top of Pert shampoo bottles, and six cardboard backs from Duracell size D batteries. Will pay or swap. Call--------." Hopefully, your local newspapers offer free ads of a noncommercial nature. If they do not, after paying for the ads, you may not realize enough profit to make it worth the effort of putting the ads in the papers.

e. Couponing and refunding magazines. Check the ads to see if the qualifiers you need are offered for sale or for swapping.

27.   Always save all cash register tapes. Many refund offers require that the dated cash register tape with the price circled be sent in with the refund form and the necessary qualifiers.

COUPONING AND REFUNDING MAGAZINES

28.   Couponing and refunding magazines are good sources of information on couponing and refunding. The following are some of the magazines which I have requested sample copies of, subscribed to, or otherwise had access to over the years: *Couponing, Moneytalk, The National Supermarket Shopper, No Form Needed Roundup, Refunder's Digest, Refunders Hotline,* and *Roadrunner Refunder.*   Inquire at your local library for names of current couponing and refunding magazines, subscription rates, and mailing addresses.

COUPONING AND REFUNDING CLUBS, SWAP SESSIONS, AND CONVENTIONS

29.   Consider joining a coupon/refund club in your area, nearby area, or even one farther away but still within a reasonable distance from you. By belonging to one or several clubs, you have a greater chance of getting good coupons and refund forms as well as qualifiers you want.

30   If there isn't a coupon/refund club in your area, get a group of friends (15 to 20 makes a good number) together and start one. You might want to place an ad in the newspaper, such as: "If you are interested in joining a coupon/refund club, call-------." Clubs usually meet once a month in the home of a different member each time or at a place such as a bank, church, library, or community center. Members bring to each meeting coupons, refund forms, and qualifiers which they wish to trade. The club decides how the exchanges will be made. For example, will refund forms be exchanged "one for one" of equal value? Will coupons just be put in a box from which anyone can freely choose? The club may or may not have officers, charge a membership fee, or serve refreshments.

31. An alternative to organizing a coupon/refund club is the informal swap session. You could call a few friends and invite them over to have a cup of coffee and to swap coupons, refund forms, and qualifiers.

32. From time to time, informally swap coupons, refund forms, and qualifiers with friends, relatives, neighbors, and people with whom you work.

33. Attend Refunders' Conventions. These usually are one- or two-day events (usually on weekends) where up to 100 or 200 couponers and refunders get together in a large meeting room with dozens of long tables to exchange coupons, refund forms, and qualifiers. Normally, there is a registration fee to cover convention expenses. Door prizes might be given. Perhaps there's a banquet. Sometimes free merchandise is given by manufacturers to each person attending. There might also be contests. (You may even want to organize a convention yourself.) You should come away from the convention with many dollars worth of useful coupons, refund forms, and qualifiers.

MISCELLANY

34. When you are writing out your weekly menus and weekly grocery list, include as many of the grocery store weekly specials as possible; and at the same time, plan to use as many

manufacturers' cents-off store coupons as you can. Also, keep in mind the refund forms you have. For example, you have planned to have frozen broccoli at one meal next week; but canned spinach is on sale, and you have a coupon for 25 cents off (and it's double coupon day). By doing a little adding and subtracting, you realize that you can serve spinach for less than one-third the cost of serving broccoli. Wait until broccoli is on special, which probably won't be very long. Then you can buy several packages of broccoli and put them in the freezer.

You, also, included canned whole kernel corn in one of your menus for next week because you have three coupons, each of which enables you to buy one can of corn and get one free. (Since the coupons will expire in four days, you can't wait another week to see if the store might put the corn on sale so you could save even more.) You also have a refund form and can receive a $1.00 refund for five corn can wrappers.

You have a coupon for a free quart of milk with the purchase of one pound of cheddar cheese. So you buy cheddar this week instead of Swiss cheese. You have a refund form for $1.00 back on the purchase of a particular brand of cookies which are also on sale this week for "two for the price of one." So, this week you buy these cookies instead of your usual brand.

Planning your menus so that they will be nutritious but at the same time using as many coupons and taking advantage of as many refund offers as you can will be well worth the hour or so it will take you for this planning. Simply stated, whenever possible, buy the item on sale, use a coupon with it, and then send in the qualifiers for a refund. With careful planning, you will be surprised at how often this combination is possible. You could save quite a lot of money each week on your grocery bill.

35.   Be on the lookout for "good," unadvertised specials on which you have coupons and/or refund forms. Take advantage of those specials which offer a financial advantage.   For example, even if you had not planned to buy xyz cookies, but you found them on sale at half-price for 85 cents and you have a 50 cent coupon (and it's double coupon day) plus a $1.00 refund form for them, you could purchase them, make a profit on the transaction, and have a free bag of cookies besides.

36.   Be on the lookout for "Specially Marked Packages." These will have coupons and/or refund forms on the outside or inside.   I recall purchasing a box of crackers on sale for 99 cents.   On the back of the box was a refund form offering a 99 cent refund.   My cost for the box of crackers was a postage stamp, five cents for sales tax, and 1/2 cent for the envelope.

CHAPTER 5

HOW TO SAVE ON YOUR EDUCATIONAL EXPENSES

Waste Nothing
Franklin

INTRODUCTION

Educational expenses for you and/or your family represent a sizable outlay of money. The average annual cost of attending a four-year public college in 1987 was $5,604 and an average of $10,199 for attending a four-year private college.[1] Attending graduate school adds thousands more to the cost of getting an education.

The rapid advances in technology over the past few years have forced many adults back into the "classroom" to upgrade their skills or learn new trades. The costs of these educational experiences can be quite substantial. There is hope, however. If you will follow the suggestions in this chapter, you should be able to keep your educational expenses much below average.

WAYS TO SAVE ON SCHOOL, COLLEGE, AND UNIVERSITY EXPENSES

1. Send your children to public, tax-supported schools rather than to private schools. Even at a very conservative estimate of $100 per month for nonboarding private school fees, you would spend $10,800 per child in twelve years for elementary and high school education in addition to the costs of transportation. At $200 a month, this figure would be $21,600. The fee at many nonboarding private schools could easily exceed $200 a month.

2. Attend a public college or university rather than a more expensive private one. You are paying taxes to support public institutions, so take advantage of your investment.

3. Attend a public two-year community college or junior college for the first two years. Expenses usually are less than those at a four-year public college or university and normally much less than those at a private institution.

4. Avoid out-of-state tuition by attending a public college or university in the state where you live, if the course of study you wish to pursue is available in your own state. Out-of-state tuition can be up to six times greater than in-state tuition.

5. Shop around for the least expensive college or university which will adequately meet your particular educational needs. Tuition, room and board, and other fees do vary from institution to institution. If the quality of education is comparable, then choose the least expensive college or university.

6. Take an overload of courses each semester if you are a good student. Also, attend summer sessions. By doing these two things, you could complete the requirements for an undergraduate degree in three years instead of the usual four. Cutting one year from your degree program should reduce the expenditures for your college education.

7. Live at home, if possible, rather than in the college or university dormitory. Room and board are large expense items at educational institutions.

8. If you are inclined to join a sorority or fraternity and live in the local chapter house, compare the costs of room and board there with the costs of living in a dormitory or a shared apartment. If the overall expense of living in the chapter house is greater, consider opting for the dormitory or apartment.

9. Enroll in credit courses conducted by colleges and universities through television, radio, or amplified telephone hookups. Contact the educational institutions in your area and inquire about such courses. By taking advantage of these methods of instruction, you can pursue your education and be employed full time. Also, you can eliminate the expense of driving to a campus to attend classes.

10. Attend night and weekend courses offered by most colleges and universities. You can take these courses and work at a full-time day job. If you are married, if both you and your spouse work at full-time day jobs, if there are small children in the home, and if both spouses wish to attend night or weekend classes, arrange the schedules in such a way that one parent can baby-sit while the other attends class.

11. Enroll in college courses offered off campus. Such courses may be held at a local public school, in a church, in a conference room at the local bank, in a room at the local community center, or in another appropriate place. Write nearby colleges and universities and ask for a schedule of off-campus courses. Depending upon the distance from your home to the college or university, you could save considerably on your travel expenses by taking the off-campus courses.

12. Take college courses offered during the summer if you work at a nine-month job (for example, as some school teachers do). Consider using your vacation time to continue your education if you work at a twelve-month job.

13. Take college courses by "correspondence." Check with various colleges and universities for information on taking courses by mail. I took one such course from a university hundreds of miles away and had to travel to a nearby college only once in connection with the course--to take the final comprehensive examination. By taking correspondence courses, you can save the expense of regular travel to a campus and work at a full-time job.

14. Enroll in college courses designated as "independent study." Such courses require only infrequent visits to the campus to confer with instructors. Costs for travel and time away from your job are reduced to a minimum.

15. Ask your high school counselor, college financial aid officer, and college placement officer about apprenticeship programs and cooperative educational programs. For example, you might go to college for one semester and work for one semester, and so on. One of these programs might enable you to get a college education which you otherwise would be unable to get. Some programs may even give college credit for certain work.

16. Enroll in an "external degree" program and complete your college education off campus. Check with your public library, colleges, and universities for information on external degree programs. These programs allow you to work at your own pace, and they save you the expense of traveling to the campus to take regular courses. Also, they allow you to work at a full-time job.

17. Take advantage of "testing-out" on certain college courses. Many institutions of higher learning make this option available to students. If you are well versed in a particular subject, ask about testing-out on specific courses. Study up and take the test. If you score high enough on the examination, you may receive college credit for the course and reduce the number of credit hours you will have to take for your degree.

18. With all other factors, such as costs and quality of education, being equal, enroll in the college or university which offers you the best financial aid package.

19. Check with the financial aids officers at various colleges and universities in which you have an interest and with your local high school guidance counselor; ask for information on student financial assistance. Ask about fellowships, scholarships, grants, loans, and other available assistance, including any aid available directly from the colleges and universities themselves from money they have received from alumni and various other sources. Also, ask about help available through federal and state programs.

Apply for all financial aid for which you are eligible. Financial aid can lower the costs of your college education.

20. If you are employed by a college or university, check with your immediate supervisor and determine whether you and/or members of your family are eligible for free or reduced tuition at the institution where you are employed. Some institutions of higher education pay tuition at other institutions (some even pay out-of-state tuition) for children of faculty members.

21. Ask your employer whether the organization or company for which you work offers college financial aid for employees and their families. Many do. Some provide time off from work for employees to take college courses. Others may pay the total cost of such courses.

22. Check with your labor union and determine what, if any, college financial aid is offered for members and their families.

23. Check with trade associations and professional organizations related to the college major you wish to pursue. Ask your librarian for help in locating names and addresses. Write and ask whether they provide financial assistance for study in a particular specialty in which they are involved. For example, if you plan to pursue a degree in home economics, contact the

American Home Economics Association and your state home economics association. Many trade associations and professional organizations do provide assistance.

24. Financial aid for college study often is available directly through fraternal organizations, civic clubs, and other groups, such as:

    a. American Legion
    b. Lions Clubs
    c. Rotary Clubs
    d. Kiwanas Clubs
    e. Masonic Lodges
    f. Elks
    g. 4-H Clubs
    h. Extension Homemakers Clubs
    i. Daughters of the American Revolution (DAR)
    j. Garden Clubs
    k. Parent Teachers Associations (PTAs)
    l. National Organization for Women (NOW)
    m. Chambers of Commerce and Jaycees
    n. Business and Professional Women's Clubs
    o. Boy Scouts and Girl Scouts
    p. Churches and other religious groups

Check with the above and others which may come to your mind.

Ask at your library for names of other groups and for the mailing addresses of the various ones you plan to write.

25. Go to your public library or college and university libraries and ask for "Foundation" directories. Most of the major foundations registered in the United States will be listed along with the types and amounts of grants or scholarships they provide. Apply for any aid for which you may be eligible.

26. Check directly with some of the major corporations, businesses, and manufacturers and ask about their college financial aid programs. You might try such organizations as Kelloggs, General Foods, General Mills, General Motors, Sears, IBM, Ford, Chrysler, and others. Ask your librarian for a reference which lists the names and addresses of major U.S companies, corporations, and manufacturers. Write them.

27. If you have earned outstanding grades in high school, ask your high school guidance counselor about the possibility of obtaining a National Merit Scholarship. These are available to a limited number of students each year. If you qualify, submit an application.

28. Ask your librarian for information on scholarships that may be available for certain groups such as women, Indians, African Americans, and disabled persons. If you qualify, submit an application.

29. Check with the R.O.T.C. office at the college or university you plan to attend and ask about a R.O.T.C. scholarship.

30. Check directly with banks, credit unions, and other lending institutions for information on low-interest educational loans.

31. If you are an unmarried child of a retired, disabled, or deceased worker, check with your nearest Social Security Office to see if you are eligible for benefits which could help with your educational expenses.

32. If you are a single or married veteran or the child, spouse, or surviving spouse of a veteran, check with your nearest Veteran's Affairs office to see if you are eligible for benefits to help with your educational expenses.

33. If you are planning to pursue graduate study, write directly to the head of the college or university department in which you hope to major and inquire about the availability of teaching or research assistantships and fellowships. Also, ask about any other possible financial assistance.

34. Buy used college textbooks. They are cheaper than new ones. Check the college bulletin boards, campus newspaper ads, and campus and local bookstores. You might place an ad in the campus newspaper and/or notes on campus bulletin boards reading: "I would like to buy a used copy of *Social Problems* by John Doe, second edition, 1990. Call-------."

WAYS TO SAVE ON INFORMAL EDUCATION

35. Attend free and low-cost educational workshops, programs, lectures, seminars, and other activities conducted or sponsored by accountants; stockbrokers; hospitals; government agencies; financial planners; lawyers; banks; churches; colleges; libraries; and various other individuals, clubs, groups, or organizations.

36. Some institutions of higher education offer relatively inexpensive noncredit courses. Check with your nearby colleges (including community or junior colleges) and universities and ask if such courses are offered in your geographical area. Ask for a schedule. One university with which I am familiar called its program "Dollar College" because many of its noncredit courses were offered at $1.00 each.

37. Participate in free and low-cost educational activities offered by your County Extension Service. Activities are offered in a wide range of topics in the broad areas of agriculture, home economics, community development, health, and youth work.

38. Observe your state legislature and the U. S. Congress in session and sit in on open meetings of your city and county governments. These activities will provide you with a free education in local, state, and federal government. If you have children, take them with you. You might also arrange for a group, such as the members of a club to which you belong, to visit the above.

39. Observe various courts in session. Such observations will provide you with a free education on the workings of your judicial system. Go on your own, take your children, or take an interested group with you.

40. Tour your state and national capitols. The capitols in most states and the U.S. capitol in Washington, D. C., maintain various permanent and temporary exhibits. These tours can provide you with a quick refresher course in history, government, and other subjects at no cost.

41. Enroll in the Elderhostel program. Elderhostel is a private, independent, nonprofit organization which cooperates with a network of hundreds of colleges, universities, and other educational institutions throughout the United States and around the world. It offers educational programs in an academic setting for adults who are 60 years of age and older. The "students" live on campus, eat in the college or university cafeteria, and attend daily classes. Normally these noncredit courses last for one week, and the costs are relatively low.

Contact institutions of higher education in your area for more details on the Elderhostel program. You can also write to: Elderhostel, 80 Boylston Street, Suite 400, Boston, MA 02116 for information.

42. If you are a senior citizen, take advantage of free and low-cost activities offered by senior citizen centers and organizations. Activities or topics may include genealogy, painting, quilting, writing, current events, crafts, woodworking, archeology, financial management, bridge, movies, bowling, fishing trips, nutrition programs, vegetable gardening, dance classes, flower growing and arranging, lawn care, exercising sessions, gourmet cooking classes, citizenship programs, tours to points of interest, "armchair" travel, and many others.

43. Take advantage of free and low-cost educational activities sponsored by various youth, women's, men's, mothers', and parents' groups, plus dozens of other groups.

44. Take free tours to such places as a radio station, television station, fire station, factory, and other interesting places. Call such places and ask when tours are scheduled or if one can be arranged for you, for you and your family, for your club, or for a group of friends. Agree on the time and date for the tour and tell the person in charge the number of people he/she can expect.

45. Participate in educational trips or tours offered by various groups, organizations, and colleges. Such trips or tours may vary in length from one-half day to several weeks. These "group" activities usually are cheaper than similar ones you arrange for yourself.

46. Visit museums, art galleries, and historical restorations which have free or low-cost admission.

47. Visit the zoo and become familiar with the world of animals. Some zoos may offer free admission. Others offer free admission on certain days and/or during certain times of the day. Go when admission is free.

48. Take your own nature walks, bird-watching outings, and educational hikes.

WHERE TO OBTAIN FREE OR LOW-COST EDUCATIONAL INFORMATION

49. Check with your County Extension Service for free or low-cost educational publications on agriculture, home economics, community development, health, and working with youth.

50. Order free informational booklets, pamphlets, and brochures by mail instead of buying publications with similar content. Ask your librarian where free information on particular topics may be ordered. Also, requesting free information on post cards will cost less in postage than sending the requests in envelopes.

51. Pick up free educational pamphlets, booklets, and leaflets at such places as banks, libraries, insurance companies, Red Cross offices, Cancer Society offices, physicians' offices, health departments, hospitals, dentists' offices, stores, shopping malls, hotels and motels, restaurants, colleges and universities, churches, businesses, government offices, utility companies, telephone offices, and dozens of other pertinent places. Whenever you go into any place, always keep your eyes open for free literature.

52. Buy used books of an educational nature at book fairs, garage sales, and thrift shops. Many can be purchased for as little as 25 cents or less.

53. If you must buy a set of encyclopedias, rather than use the sets at the library, buy a late edition used set. Place an ad in the newspaper which might read: "Wanted--a good used set of late-year World Book encyclopedias. Call-------."

54. When buying new books, buy paperbacks, if possible, rather than hardcovers. Normally, paperbacks are much cheaper.

55. Listen to educational programs on the radio.

56. Watch educational television. There are many excellent programs aired daily.

57. Watch educational programs on commercial television. Many worthwhile educational programs are aired almost daily. The programs may deal with nature, wildlife, peoples and cultures of other countries, medicine, health, nutrition, arts and crafts, business opportunities, exercise, economics, biology, history, outerspace, new technology, fashions, agriculture, politics, public events, consumer issues, and numerous other areas.

58. Check out books from the public or college library instead of buying them, particularly if you have no need to keep them after you have read them once. However, if you will need to refer to the book almost daily (such as the book you are now reading), buy it--preferably in paperback.

59.   Read magazines and other periodicals at the library. Set aside some time on a regular basis to spend reading there. I can scan most magazines in about 30 minutes. I would not pay $10 for three magazines that I could read at the library in less than two hours. I, personally, would not pay to subscribe to the _Congressional Record, Federal Register_, or other relatively expensive publications if they are available at the library. I would read them there.

60.   Spend some time occasionally at the library just reading encyclopedias. My husband recalls that one of his most valued learning experiences came from reading the encyclopedia as a child.

61.   Discontinue subscriptions to magazines which you do not find time to read. Better still, discontinue most subscriptions and read the periodicals at the library.

62.   Read the magazines you find in various places where you usually have to wait, such as barber shops, beauty shops, doctors' and dentists' offices, insurance offices, government offices, auto garages, car washes, and other places.

MISCELLANEOUS WAYS TO SAVE ON EDUCATIONAL EXPENSES

63.   Read the dictionary. Every home should have a dictionary. Just take some time to sit down and simply read it. Also, if you hear a word or see a word in something you are reading and don't know the meaning, look it up in the dictionary. This is an excellent way to increase your vocabulary.

64.   Increase your vocabulary by working crossword puzzles. Begin with very simple puzzles and work up to more difficult ones. A "book" of crossword puzzles can be purchased for around one dollar.

65. Join clubs and groups of an educational nature, if membership dues are relatively low. There are dozens of clubs that fall into this category, such as 4-H Clubs, Extension Homemakers Clubs, reading clubs, historical societies, and garden clubs.

66. Check with your State Employment Office to see what free training or retraining opportunities are available. Take advantage of those that will meet your needs.

67. When inquiring about particular educational activities and publications, ask about special rates or discounts for senior citizens, disabled persons, students, children, groups, organizations, government employees, military personnel, etc.

68. If you are employed, ask if the organization or company would be willing to pay, for example, all or part of your expenses for taking certain job-related college courses, attending job-related workshops or seminars, purchasing job-related educational materials (such as books and tapes), and subscribing to job-related educational magazines and newsletters.

69. Take advantage of the educational fringe benefits already established by your employer. For example, some employers provide employees with three weeks of educational leave each year. Others may provide part or all of the expenses for attending a national professional conference or workshop. Taking advantage of these and other educational fringe benefits saves you money on the cost of your education.

70. Take advantage of free adult education programs. Check with your local adult education office. Local programs may include learning to read and write, obtaining a high school equivalency certificate, learning job skills, and taking courses just for fun.

71. Go "window shopping." This is a free way to educate yourself on the latest clothing fashions, latest trends in home furnishings, newest features in household equipment, latest developments in automobiles, and dozens of other interesting topics.

72. Develop your own "learning experiences." If you really want or need to learn something, sit down and write out exactly what it is that you wish to learn--whether it is how to delegate tasks or how to grow roses. Next, make a list of sources where you can obtain the information or training you need. Select the most economical source which will meet your needs. Then proceed with your "learning project."

For example, assume that you have decided to purchase a home, and you have never purchased one before. What do you need to know? Certainly, you need to know about such things as the types of homes that are available and the price ranges; types and availability of home loans; interest rates; warranties; construction materials; taxes; insurance; advantages of paying to have the home inspected by a professional prior to making an offer on the home to determine the "condition" of the house and appliances; average maintenance costs; closing costs; the potential for continued appreciation in the prices of homes in the location where you are considering the purchase; and average utility costs.

What are some of the sources of the information you will need? Some examples are as follows:

a. Perhaps a nearby college is offering a two-week, noncredit night course on "Purchasing Your First Home" for a fee of $100.

b. A local real estate company has a two-day course for $25 on the same subject.

c. The library has shelves of free information.

d. You have a friend who is in real estate and home construction.

e. Your co-worker has just bought her first home.

f. Your real estate agent is very knowledgeable about all of the details of purchasing a home.

Choose the least expensive source(s) of information which will meet your needs.

ENDNOTES

1. "College Tuition Costs Outpace Inflation," *Kansas State Collegian* (Manhattan, Kansas: Kansas State University), February 25, 1987, p. 8.

CHAPTER 6

HOW TO SAVE ON YOUR ENERGY COSTS

*Economy is the science of avoiding unnecessary
expenditure, or the art of managing our
property with moderation*

Seneca

INTRODUCTION

Forty-eight percent of the energy used in the home is used for heating and cooling. An additional 16 percent goes for heating water. Refrigerators and freezers use 12 percent. The remaining 24 percent is used for lighting, cooking, and operating appliances.[1]

By saving energy, you can save money. If you follow the suggestions in this chapter, you should be able to decrease your utility bills by up to 50 percent or more.

WAYS TO SAVE ON HEATING COSTS

Caution: Older persons should be careful not to turn the heat too low, because they are more susceptible to hypothermia, which develops when body heat is lost to a cool or cold environment faster than it can be replaced. Infants and people with certain diseases are also especially at risk.[2] People with circulatory problems and those taking certain types of medications may also be vulnerable.[3]

If you or someone in your home is at risk, you should seek and follow a physician's advice on both winter and summer temperatures in your home.

1. If your home is equipped with a central heating system, try setting the thermostat between 65 and 70 degrees F in the winter during the day. Use a room thermometer to check the temperature in your home if your particular type of heating unit (for example, a baseboard, through-the-window, or portable unit) does not give the temperature in degrees. Experiment--you may be able to turn the setting down even a few more degrees and still be comfortable. Each degree makes a difference in the utility bill.

2. To save on your utility bill, turn down the heat considerably or turn it off at bedtime during the winter. (See number 3 below for exceptions.) Use extra cover or an electric blanket for added warmth.

3. If you are going to be away from home, turn the heat down to save on your utility bill. Maybe even turn the heating unit off if you will be away for an extended period of time (if your pipes are well insulated so your water will not freeze and burst the pipes, your houseplants or other items will not freeze, and you don't leave a pet in the house).

4. If you have a central heating system, consider if you really need to use it all the time when heating is needed. If you could comfortably use only one or more small areas of your house, you may want to buy some type of additional heating unit(s) with just enough capacity to heat those areas of your house, rather than operate the central system and heat the entire house all the time. For example, if you live alone and you have a large two-story house, you may want to close off the upstairs and live in the downstairs, or close off all but one bedroom, one bath, the den, and the kitchen.

Check with your County Extension Service about the economics of closing off part of your house and heating only certain areas and about what type of heating unit(s) to buy; you should be able to save a substantial amount on your heating bill. When you have guests and want to heat the entire house, then you can use the central heating system.

5. If you are building a new home or replacing your present heating unit, check to see if, in your area, a gas heating unit, an electric heating unit, or a fuel oil heating unit would be cheaper to operate. Consider building or buying accordingly.

6. If you plan to buy a new gas heating unit, ask your gas utility office and dealers in gas heating units about the potential savings of electronic ignition (rather than a pilot light which burns all the time). You should realize significant savings on your gas bill with electronic ignition.

7. If you plan to buy a new electric heating unit, consider installing a heat pump for heating and cooling your house. A heat pump can cut your use of electricity for heating by 30 to 40 percent and also might provide some savings in cooling costs.[4] Ask experts about the possible benefits of using a heat pump in your geographical area.

8. If you plan to buy a new furnace, check around for the most energy efficient models.

9. Turn off the gas furnace pilot light during the summer. The pilot light uses gas; thus, it increases your gas bill.

10. Close off unused rooms, and close the heating/cooling vents going into the rooms. It is a waste of money to heat these rooms. (This does not apply if you have a heat pump system. Closing vents could harm your heat pump.)[5] Caution: Before you close any vents, get the advice of an expert on

whether it is advisable to close vents in your home, and, if so, which vents.

11. Keep the doors of cabinets, pantries, closets, and storage rooms which are inside the house closed. It is a waste of money to heat them unless there is some vital reason for doing so.

12. During cold weather, when you are inside the house, wear several relatively loose, warm layers of dark-colored clothing. Wear warm socks and "closed" shoes. Wear long underwear and slacks. Wear long-sleeved blouses, shirts, and sweaters. Wearing such clothing should enable you to keep the heat at a lower setting.

13. During the winter months, when you are inside the house, wear a hat to help you stay warm. A large amount of body heat is lost through the head. Wearing a hat should enable you to reduce your home heat a little.

14. During the winter, while you are inside the house, wear a scarf around your neck to avoid significant heat loss through the neck. Wearing a scarf should enable you to lower the heat a bit.

15. Use the kitchen and bathroom ventilating fans sparingly during cold weather. In just one hour, these fans can blow away a houseful of heated air.[6] Turn them off just as soon as they have done their jobs.

16. During cool weather, after you have turned off the oven and after the food has finished cooking, open the oven door to allow the remaining heat to help warm the kitchen.

17. Make sure that draperies, furniture, and other items are not obstructing the heat coming from the heating vents. If heat is obstructed, then you are not getting the full benefit of the heat for which you are paying. For example, if a floor vent is positioned so that most of the heat from the vent is going behind the draperies, then you are definitely wasting money. Inexpensive plastic heat directors can be purchased that will direct the flow of heat out into the room.

18. Have your heating unit checked periodically by a professional service person to make sure it is operating at peak energy efficiency.

19. Clean or replace the filter regularly (every month or so depending on the frequency of use of the unit) in your heating/cooling unit. When the filter is dirty, the energy efficiency of the unit is reduced.

20. Dust or vacuum radiator surfaces frequently. Dust impedes the flow of heat.[7]

21. Insulate accessible heating ducts in unheated areas, such as the attic. Insulation minimizes heat loss during the winter.

WAYS TO SAVE ON COOLING COSTS

Caution: See the information under Caution at the beginning of the section on "Ways to Save on Heating Costs" in this chapter.

22. If you have a central cooling system, consider if you really need to use it all the time when cooling is needed. If you could comfortably use only one or more small areas of your house, you may want to buy some type of additional cooling unit(s) with just enough capacity to cool those areas, rather than operate the central system and cool the entire house all the time. For example, if you live alone and you have a large two-story house, you may want to close off the upstairs and live in the downstairs, or close off all but one bedroom, one bath, the den, and the kitchen.

Check with your County Extension Service about the economics of closing off part of your house and cooling only certain areas and about what type of cooling unit(s) to buy; you should be able to save a substantial amount on your cooling bill. When you have guests and want to cool the entire house, then you can use the central system.

23. If your home is equipped with a central cooling system, and it gets hot enough to turn on the system, try setting the thermostat during the summer between 78 and 80 degrees F during the day. (Use a room thermometer to check the temperature in your home if your particular cooling unit--such as a window air-conditioner--doesn't give the temperature in degrees.)

Experiment. You may be able to turn the thermostat up a few more degrees and still be comfortable during the day. You probably will be able to turn the temperature up even a little more when you go to bed at night. You may even be able to turn the unit off on some nights and still be comfortable. Perhaps you could run the fan and/or open the windows on other nights. Experiment to find the ways in which you can stay comfortable and use the least amount of energy.

24. Consider a heat pump for cooling and heating your home. A heat pump can cut your use of electricity for heating by 30 to 40 percent and also might provide some savings in cooling costs.[8] Check with experts about the possible benefits of using a heat pump in your geographical area.

25. Make sure that draperies, furniture, and other items are not obstructing the flow of cool air coming from the cooling vents. If the cool air is obstructed, then you are not getting the full benefit of the cool air for which you are paying. For example, if a floor vent is positioned so that most of the cool air is going behind the draperies, then you are definitely wasting money. Inexpensive plastic air directors can be purchased which will direct the flow of air out into the room.

26. Use the kitchen and bathroom ventilating fans sparingly if the air-conditioner is on. In just one hour, these fans can blow away a houseful of cooled air.[9] Turn off the fans just as soon as they have done their jobs.

27.   Close off unused rooms, and close the heating/cooling vents going into these rooms. It is a waste of money to cool unused rooms. (This does not apply if you have a heat pump system. Closing vents could harm your heat pump.)[10] Caution: Before you close any vents, get the advice of an <u>expert</u> on whether it is advisable to close vents in your home, and, if so, which vents.

28.   If you are going to be away from home, turn up the thermostat on your cooling unit. (If your particular type of unit, such as a window air-conditioner, doesn't display a degree reading, then merely turn the setting on the unit so that it will cool less.) Turn the cooling unit off if you will be away for an extended period of time and if there isn't a crucial need to keep the house "cool" while you are away. Unnecessary cooling is a waste of money.

29.   If you are using a window air-conditioner to cool a room, then turn off the air-conditioner if you are going to leave the room for several hours. Less energy will be required to recool the room than the unit will use if you leave it running.[11]

30.   Use ceiling or portable fans to enhance your air-conditioning unit. The fans help circulate the air and make the higher temperatures feel cooler. As a result, you should be able to raise your thermostat setting some and still feel as comfortable as you would at a lower setting without using fans. Each degree you raise the thermostat setting makes a difference in your cooling expenses.

31.   Use ceiling, portable, and/or window fans instead of your air-conditioner whenever possible. In general, fans use less electricity than air-conditioners.

32.   Turn off your air-conditioner and open the windows (if it is safe to do so) whenever the weather permits. Outside air is free. Therefore, make sure some of the windows in your home can be opened.

33. Install an attic fan to cool the house and use it whenever possible. Open the windows in the house, and the fan will pull air from the outside into the house and exhaust it through the attic. Using the attic fan when possible rather than the air-conditioner will help keep your cooling costs down. (Determine whether it is safe to leave the windows open where you live.)

34. When the air-conditioner is not on, use the exhaust fans in the kitchen, bathroom, and other areas to expel hot air from the house. In general, fans use less electricity than air-conditioners.

35. Don't use covering when sleeping at night in warm or hot weather. It is a waste of energy (money) to cover up with a sheet, a blanket, and maybe even a bedspread, and then lower the thermostat setting so you won't be too warm under all of that covering. The less covering you use, the less cooling you will need.

36. Close the doors of cabinets, pantries, closets, the laundry room, and storage rooms located inside the house (unless there is a valid reason for leaving them open) when the air-conditioner is on. It is a waste of money to cool such places without a good reason.

37. During warm and hot weather, wear lightweight shoes and lightweight and light-colored clothing in the home to minimize the need to use fans and the air-conditioner.

38. Have your air-conditioner checked periodically by a professional service person to make sure it is operating at peak energy efficiency.

39. Clean or replace the filters regularly (every month or so depending on how frequently you use the units) in your central heating/cooling unit and window air-conditioners. When the filters are dirty, the energy efficiency of the units is decreased.

40.   In warm and hot weather, keep the sunshine out of your home by using awnings on the outside of windows and/or by closing draperies, blinds, shades, or other inside window coverings in sunny windows. Keeping the sunshine out will decrease the need for mechanical cooling.

41.   In warm and hot weather, keep the incandescent lights off whenever possible and as low as possible when they must be on. Incandescent lights give off heat. (Fluorescent lights give off almost no heat.)

42.   Turn off the furnace pilot light during the summer. A pilot light gives off heat.

43.   Use vents and exhaust fans to expel heat from the attic to the outside. Otherwise, excessive heat in the attic could escape into your house.

44.   Insulate accessible cooling ducts in uncooled areas, particularly those ducts that pass through the attic. In warm or hot weather, the temperature of the cool air will rise while it is passing through uninsulated ducts. Insulation will minimize this unwanted heat gain inside the ducts.

45.   If you live in a warm climate, a light-colored roof can help keep your house cooler than a dark roof.

WAYS TO SAVE THROUGH WEATHERIZING YOUR HOME

Weatherize your home to minimize heat loss during the winter and heat gain during the summer--thus, save on your heating and cooling costs.

46.   Check the insulation in your home--such as in the attic floor; exterior walls; the floors above unheated crawl spaces; the floors of rooms above an unheated garage; and the floors above an unheated basement.   Talk with reputable insulation dealers, your local building inspector, your utility company, or your County Extension Service to find out the R-Values recommended for your geographical location (in other words, your climate) for specific areas of your house and for the correct instructions for installing insulation.

If you don't have enough insulation or none at all, add the appropriate amounts.   (If you don't feel confident in checking your present insulation and installing additional insulation, if needed, then hire a professional to do the job.)

The R-Value is the insulation efficiency rating; the R number stands for the resistance to winter heat loss and summer heat gain.[12]   The higher the R-Value (R number), the more effective the insulating capability--in other words, the greater the resistance.

47.   If installing insulation inside the outer walls of your existing home is not affordable or readily feasible or if you live in a rented house or apartment, an alternative is to hang thick draperies or draperies with a bonded lining or separate lining, quilts, or other "insulating" items over the full length and width of the inside of the outer walls.

48.   Install tight-fitting storm, double-pane, or triple-pane windows. A much less expensive alternative is to tape a sheet of thick, clear plastic to the inside window frames.

49.   Install storm doors. A much less expensive alternative for any doors which can be permanently closed during the winter months is to tape a sheet of thick, clear plastic to the inside door frames.

50.   Use caulking to seal cracks in and around nonmoving parts of your home, such as doors which are no longer used and the stationary parts of windows. A less expensive alternative is to stuff cracks with paper or rags.

Use weatherstripping to seal other cracks such as those around doors which are in use, around the moving parts of windows, around room air-conditioners, and around the access "door" to the attic.   You could save as much as 10 percent or more on your annual energy costs by caulking and/or weatherstripping the doors and windows in your home.[13]

51.   Cover window and through-the-wall air-conditioning units during the winter.

52.   Replace broken window panes.   If you can't afford replacements, tape up the breakage or put cardboard over the panes. If the pane is missing, cut a "pane" from heavy cardboard and put it in the opening.

53.   If electrical outlets are drafty, install specially made insulating pads to reduce the draftiness. Put special "plugs" into unused outlets.

**WAYS TO SAVE THROUGH THE USE OF
DRAPERIES, AWNINGS, REFLECTIVE FILM,
AND CARPETING**

54.   In general, keep the shades, blinds, draperies, and other window coverings closed during the summer, when possible, (if you don't have the windows open for ventilation) to help keep the heat out of your house.

55.   Use awnings over windows to help keep unwanted sunshine out of your home during the summer. Remove the awnings or roll them up during the winter to allow the sunlight in to help warm your home. (Remember, however, that the sun can fade your carpeting, upholstery, draperies, bedspreads, etc.)

56. Put reflective film on the windows which receive direct sunlight to help reflect the rays of the sun away from your house during the summer.

57. Use draperies and/or other window coverings to reduce heat loss from your house during the winter.

58. Open the draperies, shades, and blinds in the sunny windows during the day in cool and cold weather to allow the sun to help warm the house. (Don't forget, though, that the sunlight can fade items, such as upholstered furniture and carpeting, within your home.) Close the window coverings at night to reduce heat loss.

59. Use thick padding and carpet on as much floor space as possible to provide warmth and reduce heat loss in cold weather.

WAYS TO SAVE ON THE OPERATION OF YOUR WATER HEATER

60. Reduce the temperature setting on your water heater to the lowest effective and acceptable temperature. Most owners' manuals recommend a setting no higher than 120 degrees F for most household uses. However, if you have a dishwasher and if it doesn't have its own internal heating element, the manuals recommend that the water heater be set at 140 degrees F. Turning the water heater down from 140 to 120 degrees F could save 18 percent of the energy used at 140 degrees F; even reducing the setting by 10 degrees will save more than six percent in water heating energy.[14]

At our house, it seems to us to be a waste of gas to keep the water at 120 to 140 degrees F 24 hours a day. My husband and I keep the water heater set on "warm" most of the time. "Warm" provides us a perfect temperature for showers. When we need small amounts of hot water for kitchen and various other uses, we heat it in a kettle on a surface burner on the range.

When we run the dishwasher several times a week, we turn the water heater to a higher setting. When the dishwasher has finished washing and rinsing, we turn the water heater back to "warm." When we have house guests, we turn the water heater to a higher setting.

61.   To minimize heat loss through the hot water pipes, locate your water heater as closely as possible to where most of the hot water will be needed.

62.   Install the water heater in a place where it will be least exposed to cold weather. The cold weather will cause the water heater to have to work harder to keep the water hot; therefore, the water heater will cost more to operate.

63.   Insulate (wrap) the outside of your water heater with a "water heater blanket." Follow the installation instructions carefully, or get professional help. Also, wrap the pipes going from the water heater. Insulating the water heater and the pipes should save you between $8 and $20 a year on your energy bill.[15]

64.   Repair leaky hot water faucets promptly, because they waste money by requiring the water heater to use energy to replace the hot water which is being lost.

65.   Use water from the cold water tap for doing as many of your household tasks as possible. Heating water costs money.

66.   Drain the sediment (about one gallon of water) from the bottom of your water heater at least twice a year. Screw a garden hose to the water heater faucet which is near the bottom of the tank, and run the hose to the outside of the house. Then, open the faucet to run off the water. Sediment reduces the efficiency of the water heater.

67. If you have to replace your water heater, check to see if a gas or an electric water heater would be cheaper to operate in your area. Take the cost of operation into consideration when shopping for your new water heater.

68. Consider installing a solar water heater. Properly designed systems can save 60 to 70 percent of the costs of heating water by conventional fuels.[16]

You will need, however, to take into consideration how many years it will take to recover your initial investment in the solar system to determine if a solar system will be cost effective for you.

Check out the possibility of a solar system by talking with several experts in the field of solar energy, dealers who sell solar equipment, and your County Extension Service personnel. Also, read about solar water heaters at the library.

WAYS TO SAVE IN THE KITCHEN

69. Ask yourself, "Do I really need a freezer?" "Would the freezer compartment of my refrigerator be sufficient for my needs?" Roughly 12 percent of the energy used in the average home goes for running the refrigerator and the freezer.[17] If you could really do without a freezer, then do so, and save the energy required to run it.

70. Buy a refrigerator and freezer only as large as you actually need. In general, the larger the capacity, the more energy required for operation.

71. If you plan to buy a refrigerator and/or a freezer, consider manual-defrosting models rather than self-defrosting models. The manuals use less energy. When the ice (frost) builds up to more than one-fourth inch, however, the greater energy efficiency of the manuals begins to decline.[18] So be sure to defrost at least when the frost builds up to one-fourth inch.

72.   Keep the coils clean on the backs of your refrigerator and freezer. Dusty coils require the appliances to work harder and, thus, use more energy.

73.   Place your refrigerator in the coolest part of the kitchen and as far away as possible from the range. Follow similar rules for your freezer, or put it in another "cool" place if there isn't room enough in the kitchen or if you don't want it in the kitchen. Heat (such as that from the range, sunshine, and water heater) causes the refrigerator and freezer to work harder; and, as a result, they use additional energy.

74.   Don't store such items as sugar, flour, spaghetti, and dry cereals in your refrigerator or freezer. Such foods don't require refrigeration or freezing, and it is a waste of space and energy to keep them there.

75.   Don't keep your refrigerator any colder than recommended--38 to 40 degrees F for the fresh food compartment and 5 degrees F for the freezer compartment.   If you have a separate freezer for long-term storage, it should be kept at 0 degrees F. Use an ordinary thermometer (not a medical one) for checking the temperatures. It is a waste of money to keep these appliances colder than really needed.

76.   Open the doors to the refrigerator and freezer only when really necessary. The appliances have to use additional energy to recool the interiors when the doors are opened.

77.   When you open the doors to the freezer and refrigerator, get out at that time all of the items you will require for a particular recipe, for the meal which you are about to serve, and for other short-term needs. The more times the doors are opened, the more electricity the appliances use. Use similar rules for returning items to the freezer and the refrigerator.

78.   Avoid opening the refrigerator door throughout the day to get cold water. Keep cold water in an insulated container on the kitchen counter. Each time the refrigerator door is opened, the more energy the refrigerator requires for cooling.

79.   Allow hot food to cool down some before putting it in the refrigerator or freezer. If you put hot food in these appliances, they will have to work harder and will have to use more energy to cool the food. However, don't allow the food to remain outside the refrigerator or freezer long enough to deteriorate or spoil--carefully use your good judgement.

80.   Make sure that the refrigerator and freezer doors are always tightly shut. If the doors are not tightly closed, cool air can escape. Then the appliances will have to use more energy for cooling.

81.   If you are going to be away from home for an extended length of time, plan in advance to use all of the food in your refrigerator (including the freezer section) before you leave. Then unplug the refrigerator, clean the inside well, and leave the door open. You can save the cost of the electricity the refrigerator would have used if you had left it on while you were away. (If possible, do the same thing with your separate freezer, if you have one.)

82.   Run your dishwasher only when it is full (but not over-loaded). The same amount of hot water will be needed for a partial load as for a full load, so it would be a waste of energy (thus, money) to wash less than a full load.

83.   If dishes are only lightly soiled, run them on the "short" cycle on the dishwasher. The "short" cycle will use less electricity and less water.

84.   If dishes really do need rinsing before being put into the dishwasher, use water from the cold water faucet--not from the hot water faucet. Heating water costs money, and cold water is sufficient for this rinsing.

85. Open your dishwasher after the final rinse cycle and let the dishes air dry naturally. Save the electricity required to operate the drying cycle.

86. When you buy your first dishwasher or when the one you have needs replacing, buy one with its own internal water heating element to boost the temperature of the water to the proper temperature needed for washing. Therefore, you will not need to keep your water heater temperature set at 140 degrees F. As a result, you should save money on the cost of heating water.

87. Put most food scraps in the garbage or a compost rather than use the garbage disposer all the time. The operation of a garbage disposer requires electricity.

88. Use water from the cold water tap rather than from the hot water tap when operating the garbage disposer. Not only does the cold water save the energy needed to heat the water, but the cold water aids in getting rid of grease. The grease solidifies in cold water and can be ground up and washed away. (Manufacturers of garbage disposers recommend cold water.)

89. If you are replacing your range, check to see if a gas or an electric range would be cheaper to operate in your area. Take this into consideration when shopping for a range.

90. When you plan to purchase a gas range, look for one with an automatic (electronic) ignition system instead of pilot lights. You will save on your gas use--up to 41 percent in the oven and up to 53 percent on the top burners--with an automatic ignition system.[19]

91. If you have a gas range with pilot lights, have them checked and correctly adjusted by a professional service person to make sure they are burning efficiently.

92. If you have a microwave oven, use it rather than the conventional oven for some of your cooking. Generally, the microwave oven does not use as much electricity as the conventional oven to warm up or cook small quantities of food, and it puts only a very insignificant amount of heat out into the kitchen. (As an example of how low the purchase price can be for a microwave, in 1990 I saw a small capacity, new microwave oven advertised for less than $70.)

93. In general, thaw frozen food before cooking it, and less energy will be required for cooking the food. (Note: Thaw meat, poultry, and fish in the refrigerator. It is unwise to thaw these foods on the kitchen counter; bacteria can multiply rapidly in the thawed outer area while the food is still frozen in the center.)

94. Don't overcook food. Overcooking wastes energy.

95. When you are cooking food in the conventional oven, use a timer, watch the clock, or, if necessary, look through the glass in the oven door to see if the food is done. Don't continually open the door to check the food. Heat escapes every time you open the door, and your cooking will require more energy.

96. When you are using the conventional oven, cook as many dishes of food as the oven will accommodate at one time. Then, while the oven is still on, cook another oven full of food--maybe even a third and fourth oven full. Once the oven has reached the desired temperature, little electricity or gas is needed to maintain the temperature. The extra foods can be refrigerated or frozen for later use.

97. Turn your conventional oven off several minutes before the food is done. The oven will stay sufficiently warm for completing the cooking of the food. Experiment with your own oven and various types of foods you cook in it to determine at what point in the cooking process of particular foods you can turn off the oven and still get a desirable product. The earlier you can turn off the oven, the more energy you can save.

98. Don't turn the range surface burner on until you put the pan on it. Otherwise, energy which could be used for cooking will be wasted.

99. When food begins to boil, turn the range surface burner down as low as possible to maintain the boiling. The lower you turn the heat, the less energy will be used.

100. Turn the electric range surface burners off a few minutes before the food is done. Burners will remain sufficiently hot for several minutes to finish cooking the food. Turning off the burners a few minutes early will save some of the energy used for cooking.

101. Use a pressure cooker (not a pressure canner) to reduce the cooking time of foods. Less cooking time means less energy used. Less energy used means a lower utility bill.

102. Cut potatoes into very small pieces before boiling them for mashed potatoes. Because small pieces will cook quicker than large pieces, you can save energy.

103. Use pots and pans with flat bottoms on the range surface burners. Less heat will be lost because the flat bottoms will make direct contact with the burners and, therefore, will make as much use of the heat as possible and cook the food in a shorter time. If flat bottom pots and pans are not used, more of the heat from the burners will be lost to the surrounding air.

104. On the range surface burners, use cooking utensils which have tight-fitting lids. Keep the lids on until the food is done. Food will cook in less time, and you will use less energy. Of course, some foods may need to be stirred occasionally during cooking. Also, a few foods will require almost constant stirring while they are cooking. Follow the instructions in the recipes and also use your own judgement.

105. Don't continually take the lid off a pan of food cooking on the range surface burner unless there is a valid reason for doing so. Each time you remove the lid, heat escapes; and more energy will be required to complete the cooking of the food.

106.   Use the appropriate size range surface burner to fit the particular size pan you are using. For example, if you use a small pan on a large burner, much of the heat is lost (wasted) to the surrounding air.

107.   Cook food in as little water as possible. The more water you use in the pan on the range surface burner, the more energy required.

108.   Keep the reflector drip pans under the range surface burners clean so that the pans will do a better job of reflecting the heat up to the cooking utensils--therefore, energy will be saved. You might want to line stained or dull drip pans with aluminum foil to reflect the heat and cook the food more efficiently.

109.   In the summer, whenever possible, do your cooking early in the morning and/or late in the evening when the outside temperature is lower, rather than during the heat of the day. Cooking during the early morning and/or late evening should not necessitate the use of as much mechanical cooling for the kitchen as might be needed during the hottest part of the day.

110.   During the summer, do some of your cooking outside on the grill. Using the outdoor grill doesn't heat up the kitchen. A hot kitchen requires more mechanical cooling.

111.   If you need water (but not hot water) from the tap, get it from the cold water tap and not the hot water tap. When you turn on the hot water faucet, you are causing hot water to be drawn out of the water heater; the water heater must use energy to replace this hot water.

112. When heating water, heat only the amount you need. For example, if you are going to make one cup of instant coffee, it is a waste of energy to boil enough water to make three cups.

113. When you need a small amount of hot water for cooking or other uses in the kitchen, and possibly other parts of the house, heat it in a kettle (such as the "whistling kettle") rather than draw hot water from the tap. Cool water will have to be run off before the hot water is available at the tap; this is a waste of energy as well as water.

114. Never boil water in an uncovered pan. Water will come to a boil quicker and use less energy in a covered pan or a kettle (such as the "whistling kettle").

115. Make "sun tea" when you make tea for iced tea. By using the sun to heat the water, you save the expense of heating it by conventional methods.

116. After you have drunk all the coffee you want for the present time and will not drink more coffee for several hours, then turn off the coffee maker. If you have a microwave oven, reheat the next cup in the microwave. Leaving the coffee maker on for hours without a real need is a waste of energy.

117. Install an aerator(s) in your kitchen sink faucet(s) to reduce the flow of water. In the case of hot water, the less used, the less needed to be heated by your water heater to replace it, which will save energy.

WAYS TO SAVE ON LIGHTING

118. Turn off any lights not being used. Burning lights when not necessary is wasting energy. More than 16 percent of the electricity used in the home goes for lighting.[20]

Incandescent lights also give off heat, so turning these lights off decreases the amount of heat to be removed from the house. (Fluorescent lights give off almost no heat.)

119.   Use outside, natural light whenever possible instead of turning on lights inside the house. Natural light is free.

120.   Use fluorescent rather than incandescent light bulbs wherever possible. Fluorescent lights use less electricity than incandescent bulbs. They give off around three times more lumens per watt than incandescent bulbs, and they last about 10 times longer. (Lumen is the measurement of the amount of light produced by a bulb.)   Check individual light bulb packages for specific information.

Fluorescent replacement bulbs are available for conventional lamps and ceiling light fixtures. Other areas where you might consider using fluorescent lights are over the kitchen sink, under the upper kitchen cabinets to illuminate countertops, and in the "workshop."

121.   Check the lumens (measurement of the amount of light produced by a bulb) listed on the incandescent light bulb package to get the best lumen to wattage ratio for your money. (The watts indicate how much energy the bulb uses, not how much light it gives off.)

122.   Use one large wattage incandescent light bulb rather than several small ones in a particular area. For example, one 100-watt bulb gives off more light but uses less energy than two 60-watt bulbs.

123.   If you are buying a new electric lamp, consider one with a three-way switch. Incandescent bulbs are available in several different combinations of wattages--50, 100, and 150, for example. You use the switch on the lamp to select the proper wattage for a particular activity. When only low intensity is needed, switch to the lower wattage and save energy. Use the two higher intensities for reading and various other activities that require more light. Use no higher intensity than is really necessary.

124. Always turn a three-way bulb to a lower lighting level when you are watching television. The lower level not only saves energy but also reduces glare.

125. Use light bulbs (incandescent and fluorescent) with as low wattage as possible but not so low as to cause a personal fall or accident or damage to your eyes. Try replacing the bulbs throughout your house with smaller wattage bulbs, and see if you still have adequate lighting. For example, do you really need a 100-watt incandescent bulb in the hallway? Also, if some of your light fixtures accommodate several incandescent bulbs, remove all but one of them and replace those with burned-out bulbs. If the one good bulb doesn't give sufficient light, replace it with a larger wattage incandescent bulb; or replace it, if possible, with a fluorescent bulb. (See numbers 120 and 122 above for additional information.)

126. Use night lights, whenever possible, rather than larger wattage light bulbs. Use the four-watt rather than the seven-watt when possible. Also, the clear four-watt bulb gives off about as much light as the seven-watt frosted bulb but uses only about half as much energy. These three suggestions will help you save on the energy used for lighting.

127. Try 25-watt reflector floodbulbs in high-intensity portable lamps. They give about the same amount of light (but use less energy) as the 40-watt bulbs that usually come with these lamps.[21]

128. Try 50-watt reflector floodlights in directional lamps. A 50-watt floodlight provides about the same amount of light as the standard 100-watt incandescent bulb but at one-half the cost of operation.[22]

129. Use area lighting whenever and wherever possible. For example, if you are reading, then generally you will need on only the lamp where you are sitting. Make sure the light sufficiently illuminates the reading material. If you are washing and rinsing dishes, usually you will need on only the light above the sink. (Even better would be to have a window at the sink for natural light during the day.)

If you are working at your desk, you probably will need on only a lamp on your desk to sufficiently illuminate the desk area. Area lighting should help you save a significant amount on the energy used for lighting.

130. Install dimmer switches. If you already have them, use them. Dimmers make it easy to reduce the lighting intensity in a room and, therefore, save energy.

131. Use clear rather than frosted light bulbs. Frosted bulbs give off less light per watt than clear bulbs.

132. Keep all lamps, lamp shades, light covers, light fixtures, and bulbs clean so that you can get as much illumination as possible from the bulbs--in other words, as much light for your lighting dollars as possible.

133. Use long-life incandescent bulbs only in very hard-to-reach places. They are less energy efficient than ordinary incandescent bulbs.[23]

134. Use your outdoor lighting only when needed, for example, for deterring burglars, for lighting your walkway if you have to be out after dark, and for outside entertaining at night. Remember to turn off the lights during the day. Using outdoor lighting when unnecessary wastes energy.

135. If you are going to be away from home overnight and want some of your lights to burn at night inside and/or outside your home while you are gone, buy and screw inexpensive light-sensitive units into the appropriate light sockets. When it gets dark enough outside, the units will automatically turn on those lights. When daylight comes, those lights will turn off automatically. These units allow you to save the expense of burning your lights 24 hours a day while you are gone.

136. Consider whether it would be cheaper to use electric outside lights when needed, rather than gas lights which normally burn 24 hours a day.

137. Make sure your lamp shades are white or light-colored and translucent in order to get the most use of the light produced by the bulbs in the lamps.

138. Light-colored walls, ceilings, rugs, draperies, and furniture reflect light and, therefore, reduce the amount of artificial lighting needed.

139. Remember that Christmas lights use energy.

WAYS TO SAVE IN THE LAUNDRY

140. Wash clothes and other items only when they really need to be washed. Washing them merely because they have been worn or used once is wasting energy dollars. For example, perhaps some clothes can be worn a second or third time before they need to be washed.

141. Wash only full loads (but don't overload) in the clothes washer if you want to get the greatest benefit from the electricity being used. For example, the same amount of electricity is needed to run half loads as it takes to run full loads. Half loads must go through the same series of operations as full loads.

If you are using hot water, however, not as much electricity is required to heat the amount of water used for small and medium loads (if your machine has water level settings) as for large loads.

142. When washing heavily soiled garments or other items, pre-soak them in the sink, a tub, or other container or use the soak cycle on your clothes washer. Pre-soaking could prevent you from having to wash the clothes a second time to get them clean.

143. Wash most of your laundry in cold water. Use warm or hot water only when really necessary. Always rinse in cold water. If you use warm or hot water, the water heater will have to use energy to replace the hot water taken from the water heater.

144. If there are children in your home, have them change from school or dress clothes into play clothes when they get home from school or dress-up activities. By changing clothes, "clean" school and dress clothes can be worn again before being washed. Adults should follow similar rules.

145. Use your clothes dryer only when really necessary. Line-dry laundry, when possible, either outside or inside your home depending upon the particular items to be dried, the outside weather conditions, and your own physical condition. Line-drying will save the energy which would have been used by the clothes dryer. (Sunlight can fade colored clothes and other colored items, however.)

146. Separate your drying loads into lightweight items and heavyweight items. Since lightweight items will dry quicker than heavyweight items, the dryer will not have to run as long to dry lightweight loads. If lightweight items and heavyweight items are mixed, the dryer will have to continue to run in order to dry the heavyweight items, even though the lightweight items have already dried. Mixing the items wastes energy.

147. Dry only full loads in the dryer, but don't overload the dryer. Drying full loads is more energy efficient than drying small loads.

148. As soon as you remove one load of laundry from the dryer, put in the next load. If you let the dryer cool down between loads, additional energy will be required to heat it up again.

149. Remove clothes that will need ironing from the dryer while they are still slightly damp. Iron them right away. Energy is wasted if you completely dry clothes that will have to be redampened or steamed for ironing. However, after you have ironed these clothes, don't put them away until they are completely dry; otherwise, they will be susceptible to mildew.

150. If your dryer has an automatic drying cycle, use it. When the load of laundry is dry, the dryer will cut off. Otherwise, if you are not attentive enough and you allow the dryer to continue to run after the load is dry, you are wasting energy.

151. Keep the lint screen in the dryer clean by removing the lint after each load. Lint buildup interferes with the flow of air in the dryer and causes the dryer to use more energy.

152. Vent your clothes dryer to the outside of your home so that unwanted heat will not be blown into the house. During the summer, the heat will increase the need for mechanical cooling.

153. Keep the outside exhaust vent for your clothes dryer clean. A clogged vent will lengthen the drying time and increase the amount of energy used.

154. If you are going to replace your clothes dryer, check to see whether a gas or an electric dryer would be cheaper to operate in your area. Consider the operating costs of each when shopping for your clothes dryer.

155. When doing laundry during the summer, keep the laundry room doors closed if the laundry room is within the house. Otherwise, the heat given off by the washer and dryer will escape into the house, and additional energy will be required for cooling the house.

156. When ironing, continue steadily until all ironing is finished, rather than iron a few items, turn off the iron, wait a while, turn the iron back on, iron a few more items, and so on. Heating up a cold iron takes additional energy.

157. Iron clothes which require the lowest heat setting first, and end up with the ones requiring the hottest setting. Otherwise, you will have to turn the setting up and down, depending on the heat needed for the particular item; and this wastes energy.

158. Turn off your iron a few minutes before you finish ironing, and use the heat left in the iron soleplate to finish. (If you are using the steam setting, however, be careful that you stop ironing before the steam begins to "spot" your clothes. Experiment with your own iron.) Turning off the iron a few minutes early will save energy, even if it is only a small amount. A small amount over many years can mean significant savings.

159. When you purchase garments and fabric, try to choose those that require little or no ironing. You can save electricity.

160. Wrinkles in some clothes can be removed by hanging the clothes in the bathroom while taking a bath or shower and letting the warm moisture remove them. Experiment with your clothes. If this method works on some of your clothes, it will save you the electricity which would have been used to iron the clothes. (Be careful about using this method of wrinkle removal on any clothes which might be damaged by the moisture.)

WAYS TO SAVE IN THE BATHROOM

161.   Install a showerhead flow restrictor or a low-flow showerhead. Either of these can reduce the flow of water from six to eight gallons per minute for a conventional showerhead down to two to three gallons per minute.[24] The less hot water used, the less energy used.

162.   Install a cutoff mechanism on the showerhead so that after you have wet down, you can turn off the water at the showerhead while you soap down. Then, reopen the shower-head for rinsing. Follow the same procedure when washing your hair in the shower. Many gallons of hot water will be saved; as a result, the water heater will use less energy.

163.   If you don't have a special device on your showerhead for reducing or stopping the flow of water at the showerhead, then, after you have wet down, turn off the shower at the tap. Soap down. Then, turn the shower back on for rinsing. Use the same procedure for washing your hair. This method will save many gallons of hot water and require less energy.

164.   Take shorter showers. Less hot water will be used; thus, less energy will be consumed.

165.   When you take a tub bath, run as little water as possible. Is it really necessary to have a tub half-full or even one-fourth full for a bath? Less hot water used means a lower utility bill.

166.   Take showers and baths at the lowest acceptable water temperature. A reduction in the temperature should mean a lower utility bill.

167.   Use aerators on faucets to minimize the flow of hot water. When less hot water is used, your utility bill will be less.

WAYS TO SAVE ON THE OPERATION OF
ENTERTAINMENT EQUIPMENT

168.   Turn off televisions not being watched, and energy will be saved.

169.   Turn off radios, tape players, record players, etc. when no one is listening to them, and save energy.

WAYS TO SAVE ON YARD CARE AND
THROUGH PROPER LANDSCAPING

170.   To help protect your house from winter winds and, thus, save on heating bills, consider planting a windbreak. Call your County Extension Service for specific information on how to correctly design your windbreak (such as how far trees should be from your house and what kind of trees to plant). In certain areas of the U.S., actual fuel savings from windbreak protection can be about 18 to 27 percent.[25]

171.   Using plant materials wisely can help reduce your energy costs. Winter heating bills may be reduced as much as 15 percent while the energy needed for summer cooling may be cut 50 percent or more.[26]

Check with your County Extension Service for information on energy efficient landscaping (such as proper placement of deciduous and evergreen trees and shrubs in relation to your house).

172.   Rather than let gasoline-powered yard equipment idle for long periods, turn it off until you are ready to use it again; and you will save gasoline.

173.   Keep the cutting edges sharp on gasoline and electric-powered yard equipment. The equipment will cut more efficiently and, therefore, use less energy.

174. Use "hand" lawn mowers, pruners, clippers, and other yard tools whenever possible rather than gasoline or electric-powered ones. "Hand" tools consume only your physical energy.

WAYS TO SAVE BY TAKING ADVANTAGE OF SPECIAL UTILITY COMPANY RATES AND PROGRAMS

175. Check with your electric utility company about "off-peak" or "time-of-day" residential electric rates. If your electric company does have such a program, sign up for it. Then, whenever possible, restrict the use of such things as your dishwasher, clothes washer, dryer, and electric oven to the times when the rates are the cheapest. Your electric bill will be less.

176. Check with your electric utility company to see if it installs, free of charge, energy switches on residential central air-conditioners. The program will save you money on your electric bill during the three or four hottest months of the year because the electric company will give you a credit of a certain dollar amount on your bill for each of these months.

My husband and I participate in the program and receive a $10 credit on our June, July, August, and September bills--a total saving of $40 a year. That's $400 in ten years.

177. Call your utility company to see if it offers its customers a Home Energy Audit. The audit will show you where you can make changes in your home to save on utility bills.

178. Check with your utility company and/or the appropriate government agency to see if you are eligible to receive financial assistance with your utility bills.

179. Check to see if you qualify for financial assistance (such as a grant or low-interest loan) for weatherizing your home.

Call your utility company for additional information. Weatherizing can decrease your utility bills.

WAYS TO SAVE THROUGH THE USE OF ALTERNATIVE SOURCES OF ENERGY

180. Use a wood-burning heater. When installing the heater, be sure to install it correctly, for example, the correct distance away from combustible materials to prevent a fire from radiated heat. Get expert advice on properly installing the heater and stovepipe.

181. While you are using a wood-burning heater in your home, use the top surface for cooking; and save the expense of using your range.

182. Buy heating wood in the "off" season (spring and early summer), and you usually will get a lower price. Also, buying at this time will allow the wood time to "season" before winter. Wood that has seasoned for at least six months will give off more heat.

183. Different species of wood give off different amounts of heat. Check with knowledgeable individuals, including the agents at your County Extension Service, to find out what woods available in your area give off the greatest amount of heat; and take this into consideration when cutting or buying firewood.

184. Check to see if you can cut a certain amount of firewood free on some State and Federal lands. Call the State and the U.S. Forest Services for more information. Getting free firewood will save you money on heating costs.

185. The U.S. Department of Energy says:

Fireplaces are at best poor heaters. The volatile gases are drawn up the chimney before they adequately release their energy to the surrounding room. The draft created by the fire draws room air up the chimney along with the burning gases, sometimes resulting in a net heat loss for the whole house. Additional heat is lost if the damper is left open after the fire dies out. A typical masonry fireplace has about 10 percent or less efficiency. The fireplace is not an efficient heating device even with extensive modifications.[27]

186. When there is no fire in the fireplace, close the damper. (See number 185 above.)

187. Check with your electric utility company on price comparisons between wood and electric heating to see if wood heating would be cheaper than electric heating where you live (assuming you are having to buy your wood).

188. Check into the possibility of solar heating for your home. Talk with experts, and do some reading on solar heating at the library.

189. If you live in an area with sufficient wind to operate a windmill, you might consider the purchase of a wind-driven generator for electricity. Check out the cost effectiveness. Talk with experts, and do some reading at the library.

MISCELLANEOUS WAYS TO SAVE ON ENERGY COSTS

190. Before buying such items as a furnace, room air-conditioner, water heater, refrigerator, refrigerator-freezer, freezer, dishwasher, or clothes washer, compare the energy consumption of similar models to determine which model is the most energy efficient. The information will be listed on the black-and-yellow Energy Guide label attached to each model. The most energy-efficient model will be cheaper to operate than the less energy-efficient models.

191. Let your hair dry naturally, and save the electricity needed to run an electric hair dryer.

192. Don't buy motorized equipment or gadgets when hand-operated ones will do the job. Motors use energy.

ENDNOTES

1. U.S. Department of Energy, *Tips for Energy Savers* (Washington, D.C., 1986), p. 1.

2. U.S. Office of Consumer Affairs, *Hypothermia - A Winter Hazard for Older Americans*, by Virginia H. Knauer (Washington, D.C.: Revised November, 1985).

3. U.S. Department of Energy, *Tips for Energy Savers* (Washington, D.C., 1986), p. 1.

4. *Ibid.*, p. 5.

5. *Ibid.*

6. *Ibid.*

7. *Ibid.*, p. 7.

8. *Ibid.*, p. 5.

9. *Ibid.*

10. *Ibid.*

11. *Ibid., p. 9.*

12. U.S. Office of Consumer Affairs and U.S. Department of Energy, *Your Keys to Energy Efficiency* (Washington, D.C., July, 1985), p. 4.

13. U.S. Department of Energy, *Tips for Energy Savers* (Washington, D.C., 1986), p. 2.

14. U.S. Office of Consumer Affairs and U.S. Department of Energy, *Your Keys to Energy Efficiency* (Washington, D.C., July, 1985), p. 10.

15. *Ibid.*, p. 4.

16. Bruce Snead, *Choosing a Solar Water Heater* (Manhattan, Kansas: Cooperative Extension Service, Kansas State University, August, 1983), p. 1.

17. U.S. Department of Energy, *Tips for Energy Savers* (Washington, D.C., 1986), p. 1.

18. U.S. Office of Consumer Affairs and U.S. Department of Energy, *Your Keys to Energy Efficiency* (Washington, D.C., July, 1985), p. 5.

19. U.S. Department of Energy, *Tips for Energy Savers* (Washington, D.C., 1986), p. 11.

20. *Ibid.*, p. 17.

21. *Ibid.*, p. 18.

22. *Ibid.*

23. *Ibid.*, p. 17.

24. U.S. Office of Consumer Affairs and U.S. Department of Energy, *Your Keys to Energy Efficiency* (Washington, D.C., July, 1985), p. 5.

25. William L. Loucks, *Windbreaks and Home Energy Conservation* (Manhattan, Kansas: Cooperative Extension Service, Kansas State University, May, 1984).

26. Gustaaf A. van der Hoeven, *Energy Efficient Landscaping* (Manhattan, Kansas: Cooperative Extension Service, Kansas State University, November, 1982), p. 1.

27. U.S. Department of Energy, *Heating With Wood* (Washington, D.C., May, 1980), p. 11.

CHAPTER 7

HOW TO SAVE ON YOUR ENTERTAINMENT EXPENSES

*Beware of little expenses: a small
leak will sink a great ship*
                                    Franklin

INTRODUCTION

For most people, entertainment is a necessary part of living. However, many people spend disproportionate amounts of their income on entertainment and wonder why they don't have more money left over at the end of the month or larger balances in their savings accounts.

Entertainment need not be expensive to be enjoyable and wholesome. This chapter offers some suggestions that can help you cut your entertainment costs yet still allow you to receive pleasure and satisfaction from your activities.

WAYS TO SAVE THROUGH AT-HOME ACTIVITIES

1.   Talk with family members. Conversations with the family are not only free but, hopefully, they will produce happier, more positive, and more satisfying relations within the family.

2.   Encourage your children to perform plays or provide other entertainment for the adult members of the family. Assist them in their preparations. Not only could the entertainment cost nothing, but it could also foster a closer and warmer relationship among family members.

3.   Have a family backyard cookout. You and your family must eat, so why not make it a special, fun-time activity? Let all family members have a part in planning and conducting the activity. Such a cookout could take the place of an expensive evening out.

4.   Plant a small, backyard vegetable garden. Encourage all family members to participate in planning, tending, and harvesting the produce. You might want to let each family member have his or her own section of the garden. Having a garden should be fun; and you will probably get your financial investment, and maybe more, back from the money you save by not having to buy all of your vegetables. You might even have some extra vegetables to share with others or sell.

5.   Play cards and other "table" games. Sometimes, you can find used games and playing cards at garage sales. I purchased several new packs of playing cards at a garage sale for 10 cents a pack. Your initial investment normally will be your only expense, and the games or cards can be used over and over many times.

6.   Listen to the radio. This is a relatively inexpensive form of entertainment which can be quite satisfying. Many radio stations offer continuous music ranging from "hard rock" to "classical." In addition to music, radio offers news and programs on current events and special interest topics.

7. Watch television. If you use some discrimination in choosing programs, television can be quite enjoyable and educational and can be a less expensive type of entertainment than many other types. A small, portable black and white television set can be purchased for around $50. I paid $45 plus tax for a new one several years ago, and it still works perfectly.

8. Watch televised sports and save the cost of tickets. You often have a better view of the activities than you would have occupying a box seat at the event itself.

9. Don't have cable TV. Although you would have access to many more stations, cable TV is an added monthly expense. Ask yourself if it is really necessary.

10. If you own a video tape player, rent a movie instead of going to the movie theater. Tapes of good movies can be rented for as low as $1.00 for one evening. If it is your time to entertain friends, invite them over to watch the movie with you.

11. Check with your public library to see if it has compact discs, video tapes, audio tapes, and records for loan at no charge. Getting them from the library will save you the expense of buying or renting them.

12. Work crossword puzzles for inexpensive entertainment. You can buy a book of 100 puzzles for the cost of two soft drinks. Begin with "easy" puzzles first; then work up to more difficult ones.

13. Read for entertainment. Check out free books at your public library rather than buy them, unless they are books you will refer to almost daily, such as this book.

14. If you buy books, try to find used ones. Check such places as garage sales, thrift shops, and used book stores. For example, often you can purchase used copies of current "best sellers" for a fraction of the price you would have to pay for new copies.

15. If you buy new books, buy paperbacks instead of hard-covers. Paperbacks usually are much cheaper.

16. If you own and play a musical instrument, entertain yourself, your family, and your friends by playing it. Excluding the purchase price of the instrument, this form of entertainment should be free or very inexpensive.

17. Your family or you and a few close friends could spend an evening or some time on the weekend decorating the Christmas tree or preparing and decorating for other holidays and special occasions. Decorations and other preparations need not be expensive to provide an enjoyable time together. (Decorations should be saved for reuse, if possible.)

18. Have friends over (after dinner) to play cards or participate in other inexpensive activities. Serve a few appetizing, but inexpensive, snacks; and the evening's entertainment should not put a strain on your pocketbook.

19. Contact some friends and organize regular get-togethers. Activities could include such things as exercising; doing crafts; playing musical instruments; singing; or discussing books, investments, politics, current events, or how to save money. Inexpensive snacks could be served. The group meetings could be rotated from home to home.   One of the organizing objectives of the group meetings could be to keep the get-togethers as inexpensive as possible.

20. When you have guests to your home for dinner or cock-tails, table decorations need not be expensive or elaborate. Use flowers and greenery from your own yard or garden rather than purchase expensive cut flowers or arrangements. Note: For additional suggestions on ways to save money when you entertain others, see the section on "Ways to Save on Enter-taining Others" in chapter 8.

WAYS TO SAVE THROUGH PARTICIPATING IN "PUBLIC" ACTIVITIES

21. Always keep your eyes open for free or inexpensive entertainment. Such activities might include a lecture on the "heavenly bodies," a demonstration on cake decorating, a talk on the latest computer technology, a training workshop on ways to save on your income taxes, a presentation on nuclear energy, or a program on investment strategies.

Dozens of free and low-cost activities are normally available at any given time. They may be offered by various organizations, clubs, or groups; colleges and universities; government agencies; individuals; and businesses. The less you pay for entertainment, the more money you will have to spend for other items or to put in the bank.

22. See free exhibits in shopping malls. For example, this week there may be an exhibit on solar energy. Next week, local kitchen dealers might have an exhibit of contemporary kitchens. Another week, fishing boats may be on display.

23. Participate in free or inexpensive activities conducted in shopping malls. For example, this week local beauticians may be holding free personal makeup consultations. Next week, graphologists may be giving free individual handwriting analyses.

24. Go window-shopping. It is not only free, but it can be fun, also. Window-shopping can help you keep informed on such things as the latest clothing fashions, current trends in home decorating, and new innovations in home office equipment. For example, information gained through the above window-shopping will give you ideas on how to update your present wardrobe, how to modernize the furnishings in your home, and how to change your home office for more efficiency.

25. Spend time at your local library. You can read books, magazines, and newspapers; listen to cassette tapes and records;

and watch video tapes without having to buy them. Check with your local public library to see what free services it provides. Some public libraries may not provide all of the above services, while others may provide these and many more.

26. Participate in various free activities at your public library. For example, some libraries provide "storytime" for young children and lectures for adults. Check with your local library to see what activities are available, ask to be placed on the library's mailing list to receive activity announcements, or watch your local newspaper for such announcements.

27. Visit public art galleries. Admissions normally are free or relatively low in price. If there is no admission charge, most art galleries provide a container in which you may place a donation to help defray operating costs. A modest donation is all that is necessary.

28. Visit public museums. Admission normally is free, or only a small admission fee is charged. If no fee is charged, you may wish to drop a small donation in the container provided to help with operating expenses.

29. Go to open houses and grand openings. For example, there may be an open house conducted by the local historical society offering free admission to the history museum and free refreshments; or a new furniture store may be having a grand opening with free gifts, door prizes, and free refreshments.

30. Tour new and used homes which are for sale by going to free residential open houses held by owners or real estate agents.

31. See the exhibits at your county and state fairs. There are usually commercial, home economics, agricultural, and 4-H Club exhibits, in addition to various other exhibits. Normally a small admission fee to the fairgrounds entitles you to see all of these exhibits.

32. Exhibit, free of charge, your own items (such as flowers and vegetables you have grown, clothes you have made, furniture you have refinished, and pictures you have painted) at county and state fairs. Contact your County Extension Service or the county and state Fair Boards for details. You might even win ribbons or money on your exhibits.

33. Visit your State Capitol. Admission is free. Most state capitols have various permanent and temporary exhibits. Guided tours and informational literature are available at some state capitols. Visit the U.S. Capitol whenever you have the opportunity.

34. Tour a fire station, factory, radio station, television station, winery, police station, and other interesting places if such tours are possible. The tours usually are free. Some of the places may even provide free souvenirs and/or refreshments. Call the place you wish to visit in advance to find out when such a tour can be arranged.

35. Go to the movie theater when the tickets are less than full price. For example, tickets usually are cheaper for the matinee. Also, some theaters reduce the price of admission on one designated night of the week. Take advantage of these "specials."

36. If you plan to attend a concert, symphony, or ballet, where different priced tickets are available based on the location of the seat, buy the least expensive ticket. In addition, tickets may be cheaper for matinees and for certain nights of the performance. Also, ask about special discounts for senior citizens, students, and groups.

37. Play tennis on free or low-cost public courts. Check to see if reservations are required or recommended.

38. Attend church activities. Some churches sponsor potluck dinners; picnics and various other outings; educational classes on a wide range of topics; plays; movies; musical performances;

special activities for youth, singles, and senior citizens; and classes for widows, widowers, and divorced persons.

Many churches may have several activities going on at the same time. You can make your own selection. Normally, there is no charge for participating in most of these activities. If there is a fee, it usually will be low.

39. Utilize church recreational facilities such as basketball courts, indoor gymnasiums, tennis courts, swimming pools, bowling alleys, and baseball fields. Usually, these facilities may be used by church members at no cost.

40. Join several clubs and attend club meetings and various other inexpensive club activities. Limit yourself to clubs with low membership fees.

41. If a public beach is nearby, visit it. You could go swimming or wading, lie in the sun, picnic on the sand, look for seashells, or just walk along the beach. (Caution: Based on the results of research on the relationship between sun exposure and premature wrinkling of the skin and skin cancer, many medical experts recommend that people apply a sunscreen when they are outdoors.)

42. Visit community, city, state, and national parks. Some may be free, while others may charge relatively low entrance and/or activity fees.

43. Check with the National Park Service or Forest Service for information on the following special, free or low-cost permits to visit historical sites, parks, monuments, and recreational areas administered by the federal government:

a. Golden Eagle Passport (for persons under 62 years of age).

b. Golden Age Passport (for persons 62 years of age and older).

c. Golden Access Passport (for blind and disabled persons).

44. Visit the zoo. Some zoos provide free admission on certain days of the week or at certain times of the day.

45. Go on a picnic. You must eat anyway, so why not make the occasion an enjoyable, inexpensive form of entertainment?

46. Go on a hike. If carefully planned, a hike can be very inexpensive or even free if you already own your hiking equipment. It can also be exciting and enjoyable.

47. Take a nature walk. Not only can it be inexpensive or free, but it can be a lot of fun.

48. Participate in free or low-cost trips offered by various organizations, groups, clubs, churches, and colleges.

49. Check out possible savings on "off-season" travel, hotels, and tourist attractions. Check with your travel agency or directly with the airlines, hotels, etc.

50. When planning any entertainment activity which requires the outlay of money, always ask about special fees and discounts for senior citizens, students, children, disabled persons, families, and groups. You may not be told if you don't ask. You could save on your entertainment expenses.

WAYS TO SAVE THROUGH HOBBIES

51. Start a hobby which costs relatively little or no money such as: making dried arrangements from plants you grow or collect and dry yourself; singing; doing volunteer work; writing; cooking (you and your family must eat anyway); working in the yard; reading; collecting such things as matchbook covers, paper napkins and menus from restaurants, Christmas and other used greeting cards, newspaper clippings, free calendars from businesses, recipes, used stamps, rocks, seashells, beverage cans, and business cards; or starting a miscellaneous insect collection or a collection of only one type of insect such as butterflies. Try to think of other hobbies you could start which would be free or inexpensive.

52. Select hobbies which will do the following: make you money, produce gifts to give to your family and friends, and/or produce things you need yourself. For example, couponing and refunding could be financially rewarding hobbies--see Chapter 4.

MISCELLANEOUS WAYS TO SAVE ON ENTERTAINMENT EXPENSES

53. Visit nearby friends. This form of entertainment should be quite inexpensive and can be very enjoyable, rewarding, rejuvenating, and inspiring.

54. Play sports games with friends. Organize a softball game in the park, a backyard badminton or horseshoe game, or a tennis match at the public tennis courts. These and other economical games should help you save on your entertainment expenses.

55. Cut down on the cost of entertaining others. Others may have a good time, but you are the one who must pay the bills. When you do entertain others, do so as frugally as possible. Activities do not have to be expensive to be in good taste and to be enjoyable.

56. Ride a bicycle. If you have a bicycle already, this activity will cost you nothing but a little physical exertion. (Ride where it is safe.)

57. Enter free contests. Pick up forms wherever you go. You never know when you may come out a "winner."

58. Drastically limit your purchases of records, audio cassettes, video tapes, and compact discs. If you bought just one audio cassette per week at a conservative price of $7, that would amount to $364 in one year and $3,640 over a period of 10 years. Instead, listen to your radio or listen to records, tapes, and CDs at the library (or, if possible, borrow them from your library for home use).

If you do want to buy some records, tapes and CDs, check out the garage sales, thrift shops, and some used book stores. Some of my husband's favorite audio cassettes came from thrift shops. You could also trade records, tapes and CDs with friends.

59. Discontinue subscriptions to magazines which you do not find time to read. Better yet, discontinue all subscriptions and read the magazines at the library. Also, check the thrift shops for used magazines. I have purchased dozens of fairly current magazines at thrift shops for as little as 15 cents each--a sizable saving over the new rack prices.

60. When you must buy books, try to find used ones. Used books will be much cheaper than new ones, and used paperbacks generally will be cheaper than used books with hard covers.

61. Trade magazines and books with others. Once you have finished reading a magazine or book, and you don't wish to retain it for future reference, trade it. By trading, you should be able to cut down on your magazine and book expenses.

62. Read magazines and brochures available in the following and other places while you are waiting for or receiving service: stockbroker's, doctor's, dentist's, lawyer's, insurance agent's, financial advisor's, and accountant's offices; beauty shops; barber shops; hospitals; banks; automobile garages; repair shops; and carwashes. By reading these publications while you are waiting, you can keep yourself informed without having to pay for the information.

63. Shop for used sheet music and music books at thrift shops, garage sales, used book stores, and other places. These items can be relatively expensive if purchased new. When my husband started, as an adult, learning to play the piano, we bought beginning books for 5 to 15 cents each at a thrift shop.

64. When you are buying new entertainment items, such as musical instruments, games, and sports equipment, always shop around for the best prices. Hopefully, you can wait and purchase the items when they are on sale at the lowest prices.

65. Ask about and compare warranties when you are shopping for new entertainment items. Some warranties may be better than others. If all other things are fairly equal among the various brands, choose the brand with the best warranty.

66. Whenever possible, buy good, used entertainment items rather than new ones. You should be able to save a substantial amount of money. Shop the garage sales and thrift shops. You also might want to put an advertisement in the newspaper. For example, your ad might read: "Wanted. A good, used set of women's golf clubs. Call-------."

67. If you have entertainment items you haven't used in several years and doubt that you will ever use again, consider selling them. Put an advertisement in the newspaper and notes on various bulletin boards. Your ad and notes might read: "For Sale. Good, used two-person aluminum fishing boat and trailer. Call-------." You might also let your friends and neighbors know, by word-of-mouth, that you are interested in selling your boat and trailer.

68. Make your own costumes for Halloween, masquerade parties, and other occasions instead of buying or renting them. Use inexpensive materials around the house and save money.

CHAPTER 8

HOW TO SAVE ON YOUR FOOD COSTS

He will always be a slave who does
not know how to live upon a little
                                    Horace

INTRODUCTION

Food is the second largest expense item for many people. It is a basic need, so it is certainly a necessary expense. However, there is a wide range in the amount of the monthly income spent by people for food--both food eaten at home and food eaten "out."

The suggestions in this chapter will show you how to lower your food expenditures by a considerable amount.

WAYS TO SAVE ON FOOD PURCHASES

1.   Plan your weekly menus around grocery store "specials." Whenever possible, limit most of your food purchases to only the "specials." Check out the "specials" listed in circulars and in the food section of your newspaper. You should not have to pay full price for very many food items if you plan well. Most

food items normally will be on sale sometime during a period of several months. By concentrating on the "specials," you should be able to save a sizable amount on your weekly grocery bill.

In addition to concentrating on the "specials" when you are planning menus, take into consideration the manufacturers' cents-off store coupons and refund forms you have on hand. An ideal situation would be one in which your grocery list includes only "specials," you have coupons on these items, and you have refund forms for them for partial or complete refunds of the purchase prices. You may not be able to achieve this situation on all the items you must buy; but, by very careful planning, you should be able to accomplish this goal quite often--each time you can, you will lower your grocery expenses.

2.   Make sure "specials" or "sale" items are really bargains. In fact, the "sale" prices of some of these food items may be even more than their regular prices.   I actually have seen such situations. Make sure you know what the regular prices are before you fill your grocery cart with "specials."

3.   Prepare a written shopping list before you go to the grocery store. A shopping list should help you to avoid unwise impulse buying. Buy only what is on your grocery list unless you find outstanding, unadvertised "specials" on items which you can use (this is wise impulse buying) and cheaper substitutions for items on your list.

4.   In general, shop for groceries at grocery stores where regular prices are the lowest. The regular prices on identical items can vary a great deal from store to store. By routinely observing the regular prices of a variety of food items in different grocery stores, you will soon know which stores have the lowest prices on particular items. Also, shopping at two or more grocery stores for the "specials" can make a big difference in the amount of money you save on your overall grocery bill.

5.   Check out the grocery stores where you sack and carry out your own groceries. The regular prices (and perhaps prices of "specials") are usually lower here than at full-service grocery stores.

6.   Are there retail grocery "warehouses" in your area which sell in bulk and large containers but at considerable savings over the purchase of single items and small containers at the conventional grocery stores? These are usually no-frills stores, and the foods may be displayed in their own cases.   The buildings may be located in lower-rent areas of town.   You probably will have to carry out your own purchases. The stores may accept only cash.

7.   Some general, discount-type department stores stock a limited variety of food items, which are often cheaper than in the grocery stores. For example, I have found ready-to-eat cereals to be cheaper and spices to be much cheaper at one particular chain, discount department store.

8.   Get a group of friends together, and form an informal or a formal food co-op. You can buy in large quantities at some retail (and maybe wholesale) establishments, and save money on food purchases. For example, perhaps four of the members could split a 100-pound bag of onions; and each could contribute one-fourth of the purchase price.

9.   Limit your food purchases at convenience stores. There is usually a wide gap between the prices on most food items here as compared to the prices at traditional grocery stores.

10.   When shopping several stores for food items, consider how far the stores are from each other and whether you would still save money over the cost per mile of owning and operating your automobile. (See the "Introduction" to Chapter 1.)

11.   If the grocery stores where you shop do not put prices on individual containers, write the prices on the containers for your own information so that when you are checking the cash register tapes against your purchases when you get home, you can see if the computers were programmed with the correct prices. If the prices were not correctly programmed on some items, pick up the money due you or return the money due the stores the next time you are in the stores.

Make sure you save the cash register tapes and take them with you when you go to collect or pay your money. Also, if prices are manually rung up on the cash register, check your cash register tapes when you get home. Cashiers can make mistakes.

12. Before going into the grocery store, check the front windows for "specials" which were not advertised in the newspaper. Sometimes, you will find some good buys.

13. When you go into the grocery store, pick up a store circular (usually displayed near the door). It may contain some good specials. It, also, sometimes contains store coupons and refund forms.

14. When you go into the grocery store, keep your eyes open for a cart of bent cans, crushed boxes, cans with missing labels, and outdated but acceptable food items. You can usually find super bargains. Of course, you don't want to buy a package whose contents are exposed, a can of which you do not know the contents, or a can which might be punctured. I have gotten some "steals" from these carts, such as a half dozen two-pound bags of good, but slightly hardened powdered sugar for 10 cents each and boxes of ready-to-eat cereal from which someone had torn the boxtops for one-half price. (The inner packages of the cereal were still securely sealed.)

15. When choosing a particular item off the grocery store shelf, check all of the identical cans or packages of that item. Sometimes, some of the identical containers of the item will have lower prices on them--prices marked before a new shipment at higher prices came in or, perhaps, incorrectly marked prices. You could save 10 to 50 cents or more on a can or package. I occasionally find this situation and save on my grocery bill.

16. Compare the prices of national brands, store brands, "off" brands, and generic (no-name) labels of a particular food. Buy the cheapest one (which is usually the generic label) unless you have a manufacturer's cents-off store coupon on a more expensive one and will end up paying less than the price of the cheapest one. Don't just assume that the most expensive brand is necessarily the best. For example, the food inside the generic container could be identical in quality to the food in the container carrying the national brand name. Or, some companies may distribute their product under their brand name and also under a generic label.

17. If you buy only national brands and intend to continue buying only national brands, then compare the prices of the different national brands. Even with national brands, prices differ among the different brands.

18. When buying foods which have "open dating" on them, in general choose the cartons, cans, packages, bags, jars, or other containers with the most recent dates. Products with the latest dates should be the freshest. The dates may be the freshness dates, pull or sell dates, packing dates, or expiration dates.

Usually the dates will be accompanied by relevant wording to inform you what the dates mean, such as "sell by 4-1-91" or "best if used by 6-19-91." For example, if you are buying a carton of a specific food item, and some of the identical cartons have the notations, "best before 11-4-91," and some, "best before 10-1-91," you would ordinarily choose the carton with the date of 11-4-91. The fresher the product, the better buy you should be getting for your money.

19. Take advantage of "buy one, get one free" in the grocery store if you can use the items and if the prices are within your price range.

20.   Take advantage of special deals like "free five-pound bag of sugar with a $10 purchase" if you need $10 worth of groceries anyway and have already planned to spend at least $10.

21.   When you find food items on sale at very good prices (maybe even half-price), stock up. You might even want to purchase a year's supply if you have adequate storage space, if you can use the items in a year's time, and if they will maintain acceptable quality for a year. My husband and I are still eating corn and various kinds of peas and beans which we bought at four cans for $1.00 over a year ago.

If bargains are exceptionally good ones, you can probably realize more from investing some of your money in these food items than you can draw in interest at the bank--a rate of return of 25 to 50 percent or more on your food dollar is extremely good. Don't stock up on food which is not a good buy unless you have a very good reason for doing so.

22.   When you buy items on sale, group them all together and put them on the checkout counter first. Watch and make sure the cashier rings up the sale prices and not the regular prices.

23.   If stores sell out of the advertised specials, ask the managers if comparable items are being substituted, and, if not, ask for rainchecks. Most stores will either substitute or give rainchecks, so be sure to ask.

24.   Check to see if buying in bulk would be cheaper for you than buying the same items singly. For example, you might be able to get a 15 percent discount on a case of canned tuna. On the other hand, if you wait for the tuna to be put on sale, you might save more than 15 percent. Consider all relevant things before buying in bulk. (See number 21 above).

25.   In general, severely limit your purchases of expensive foods. Rather, buy cheaper foods. For example, a steady diet of asparagus, salmon, oysters, shrimp, exotic fruits, T-Bone steaks, and other relatively expensive foods could put your food budget in serious trouble.

26. Limit your purchases of convenience foods if they cost more than the expenses of preparing the foods from scratch at home. Some convenience foods are cheaper to buy than to make at home. For example, frozen orange juice concentrate is usually cheaper than fresh home-squeezed orange juice. However, instant potatoes are usually more expensive than fresh whole potatoes. You can usually make pizzas cheaper than you can buy comparable frozen ones; and most canned sandwich spreads are more expensive to buy than to make.

Figure out for yourself the cost of preparing a particular food from scratch (excluding the value of your time). Then compare this cost with the purchase price of the convenience food. Buy accordingly.

27. Unless you have a medical problem which requires you to buy certain, special "diet" foods, limit your purchases of these foods. They are almost always more expensive than "ordinary" foods.

28. As a general rule, limit your purchases of foods from the grocery store delicatessen. Most deli foods are more expensive than similar non-deli foods.

29. Cut back on traditional snack items such as potato chips and candy bars. In comparison to many other foods, traditional snack foods normally are more expensive. Buy cheaper snack foods.

30. Limit your purchases of "junk" foods. Relative to necessary nutrients, "junk" foods usually provide a limited return on your money.

31. Cut back on the purchases of expensive condiments such as some spices. Although condiments do enhance the flavors of many foods, some can be quite expensive. Try to stick to the less expensive ones.

32. To help you get the most food for your food dollars, compare the ingredients listed on cans, boxes, and other containers. The first item listed on a U.S. food container is the major ingredient, by weight, followed by the other ingredients listed in descending order by weight. For example, if two different brands of canned vegetable soup have the same weight designations, and their prices are comparable, but water is listed first on one of the cans and second on the other, you would ordinarily want to buy the one with water listed second. This can would contain more food and less water. Therefore, you would get more food for your money.

33. When you are comparing the cost of different food items, brands, forms of foods, kinds of containers, etc., compare the price per unit to see which is the best buy. The unit price may be, for example, the price per pound, ounce, count (such as paper cups), quart, pint, or square foot. Always take a small, inexpensive pocket calculator with you to the grocery store to figure the cost per unit if the store doesn't display that information on the shelves with the products. Divide the price of the item by the number of ounces, etc. to get the unit price.

Also, use the unit price when you are trying to decide if the largest container of a particular item is the best buy. The largest size may not always be the best deal. Sometimes, two smaller sizes, totaling the same weight or quantity as the one larger size, will be cheaper. By comparing unit prices, I sometimes have found the larger size to be even higher in price per unit.

By using unit pricing to make price comparisons, you can choose the most food for your money. At the same time you are comparing price per unit, take into consideration the list of ingredients. (See number 32 above for additional information on comparing ingredients.)

34. Compare the prices of a particular food fresh, versus frozen, versus canned, versus dried; and, in general, buy the cheapest. Don't assume that just because one version of a food was cheaper one or two months ago that it is still cheaper today. Prices do change from season to season, from the beginning of the season to the end of the season, and for other reasons such as weather conditions and strikes. For example, I have noticed that during fresh strawberry season, frozen strawberries are often on sale at drastically reduced prices. This is the time to stock up on frozen strawberries.

35. If you find an identical food (such as sugar, cookies, cereal, popcorn, coconut, and raisins) available in jars, cans, boxes, bags, or other types of containers, buy the cheapest type of container. For example, a bag of popcorn will normally be much cheaper per ounce than a jar of popcorn. Always compare the prices per unit. (See number 33 above.)

36. Buy the cheapest cut or form of a particular food which will meet your needs. For example, if you are making spaghetti sauce, a can of tomato pieces, tomato paste, or tomato sauce, rather than a can of whole tomatoes, might be sufficient and should save you money.

37. When you are buying groceries, make the refrigerated and frozen food sections your last stops. This plan will allow the food to stay cold or frozen until the last possible moment. If you put the refrigerated and frozen foods in your shopping cart at the beginning of your shopping, they may become warm or thawed by the time you reach the checkout counter. By keeping the foods at their optimum temperatures, the longer the quality of the foods can be maintained. The better the quality, the better the return on your food dollars.

38. When you purchase frozen foods, make sure they are firm (well frozen). If they are not well frozen, you are spending your money for foods which may have already started to decline in quality.

39. When you buy foods, make sure the containers are well sealed. Foods in well-sealed containers should maintain their freshness longer; therefore, you get a better product for your money.

40. Purchase meats, poultry, and fish by "cost per serving." Consider how much wastage (bone, fat, gristle) there will be. In other words, how many edible servings can you get from one pound of the particular meat, poultry, or fish you are considering? Figuring the "cost per serving" will help you to get the most edible food at the lowest price.

41. Buy whole chickens rather than cut-up chickens if cut-up chickens are more expensive per pound. (They normally are.) Cut them up yourself and save money.

42. Use poultry and fish (if less expensive per edible serving than meat) at some meals.

43. Buy less expensive cuts of meat.

44. Use ground beef. It usually is one of your best beef buys.

45. Buy a whole or half ham and have it sliced rather than buy the more expensive prepackaged, sliced ham.

46. Buy bacon in boxes of "ends and pieces" rather than buy the more expensive packages of "regular," uniform strips.

47. Buy "family packs" of meat, poultry, and fish if you can use that large a quantity and if it is cheaper per pound (which it usually is) than small packages. For example, a "family pack" containing a dozen chicken breasts should be cheaper per pound than a package of two breasts. Also, a ten-pound "family pack" of ground beef should be less per pound than a two-pound package.

48.   When buying shrimp, the smaller-sized shrimp are usually less expensive per pound than the larger-sized shrimp. Buy the small ones and save money. (However, see number 40 above.)

49.   When you find meat, poultry, and fish on sale at very good prices, buy several packages if the items are within your price range and if you have sufficient storage space.   There should be little need to ever pay full price for these foods. Grocery stores usually will have a different one on "special" every week.   Shop for these "specials" as early in the day as possible for the best selection.   Later in the day, these items usually will have been "picked over" and the selection may not be as good.

50.   Before you merely assume that you can save money on your meat bill by buying, for example, a half of a beef, figure carefully if you could buy the equal net amount of beef on sale throughout the coming months at the grocery store for less than you would pay for half a beef. Get out a piece of paper, and do some figuring to determine which of the two alternatives would be the least expensive for you.

51.   Use alternates (substitutes), such as dry beans and peas, cheese, peanut butter, nuts, and eggs, at some meals instead of always serving meat, poultry, or fish. These protein alternates are usually less expensive per serving.

52.   Limit your purchases of fresh fruits and vegetables during their off seasons because they usually are much more expensive than when they are in season. For example, a particular fresh vegetable may be four pounds for $1.00 during its peak growing season, but 99 cents or higher per pound in its off season.

53.   Don't buy fresh fruits and vegetables at the beginning of their seasons. Wait several weeks until the prices come down sharply.

54.   Pick around for the largest oranges, apples, heads of lettuce, and other fruits and vegetables when making purchases if the items are priced individually (and if all items in a specific category are the same price--such as all heads of lettuce at 79 cents a head). Generally, the larger the individual item, the more you are getting for your money.

55.   Buy less than the top grades of most fruits and vegetables, since the top grades are the most expensive. Would lower grades serve your purposes equally as well?

56.   Buy rolled oats for use as a breakfast food sometimes. Eat them cooked or uncooked. I prefer them uncooked with milk and sugar over them. My husband prefers them cooked. Oats are inexpensive compared to many ready-to-eat breakfast cereals.

57.   Buy large boxes of ready-to-eat cereals rather than packages of assorted single-serving boxes, which are usually much more expensive per unit. (See number 33 above.)

58.   At the grocery store, buy "day-old" bread and other bakery products, which are cheaper than "fresh" bakery items.

59.   Buy bread and other bakery products at one of the bread company retail outlets. The products may be several days old, and some may be slightly broken (such as cookies in a bag); but the products are cheaper, and I have always found them to be very acceptable.

60.   Use powdered (dry) milk if it is cheaper than fluid milk.

61.   If cheaper per pound (which is usually the case), buy blocks of cheese rather than prepackaged sliced or grated cheese.

62.   Cut down on the consumption of carbonated soft drinks. Two soft drinks per day at 30 to 70 cents each (depending on whether you have the drinks at home or "out") cost roughly $18 to $42 per month, $216 to $504 in a year, and $2,160 to $5,040 in ten years.

63. Buy large containers of carbonated soft drinks if they can be consumed before they go "flat," rather than small cans and bottles; and you usually will save money. (However, check their unit prices before buying them to make sure they are the cheapest per ounce in this particular situation. See number 33 above.)

64. Purchase carbonated soft drinks in returnable bottles if they are cheaper than those in throw-away bottles and cans. Be sure you return the bottles for refunds or exchange; otherwise, your original purchase price for the drinks will, in reality, include the amount of your deposit on the bottles.

65. Drink less expensive soft beverages. Would fruit flavored drink mixes and iced tea be cheaper than canned or bottled carbonated soft drinks?

66. Cut back on coffee from the vending machine at work. Two cups per workday at 40 cents per cup would cost approximately $17 a month, $204 per year, and $2,040 in 10 years. If you want coffee, take a container of hot coffee to work with you or make it yourself at the office--either should save you a significant amount on expenses for coffee at work.

67. If you drink alcoholic beverages and/or serve them at parties or meals, keep your eyes open for sales on them. Stock up if the sale prices are good ones. Buy large sizes, or even cases if the savings warrant it and if you can use the large quantity.

68. In general, grocery shop no more than once each week. You'll save gasoline. You probably will also save some money on groceries because you normally will not buy as much in one trip as you will in two or more trips to the grocery store. You will also be in a better position to take advantage of "specials" such as "free dozen of large eggs with a $10 purchase" or "free one-pound can of ground coffee with a $30 purchase." For example, if you went to the grocery store four times during the week and spent $9 each time, you would not be able to get the free coffee you could have gotten if you had concentrated your purchases into one trip.

69.   Grocery shop alone. Spouses, roommates, and especially children may influence you to buy one or more additional items. Or, you may be distracted by the person with you and not concentrate as much on saving on the grocery bill. There-fore, you may spend more money than you might have if you had shopped alone.

70.   Try to avoid shopping for groceries when you are tired. If you are tired, you will concentrate less on getting the most for your food dollar.

71.   Don't shop for groceries when you are in a hurry. It takes time to compare prices and to get the most for your money.

72.   Don't shop for groceries when you are hungry. You usually will buy more food items, including snack items, when you are hungry.

73.   Try to shop for groceries when the store is not crowded. You will feel more relaxed and be in a better position to make wiser economical decisions.

74.   Buy at farmers' markets, at roadside stands, out of the backs of the farmers' trucks located wherever, and from farmers selling around in your neighborhood. Usually (but not always) you can buy the fruits and vegetables cheaper than you can buy them at grocery stores.

75.   Watch the newspaper for advertisements for "pick-your-own" fruits and vegetables. You should be able to get them cheaper by picking them yourself.

WAYS TO SAVE THROUGH COUPONING

(See Chapter 4, "How to Save Money Through Couponing and Refunding," for additional detailed information.)

76.   Use manufacturers' cents-off store coupons whenever and wherever possible. Coupons lower the amount of money you must spend on food.

77.   Buy a copy of the newspaper on the day manufacturers' cents-off store coupons appear. If the coupons are ones which you can use, consider buying several copies of that issue of the newspaper if you can save more than the cost of the newspapers. Using coupons should enable you to realize a large saving on your grocery bill.

78.   Always sort out and put in a separate envelope the manufacturers' cents-off store coupons you plan to use on your trip to the grocery store. The more convenient the coupons are, the more apt you are to make use of them in the store. Also, always take along all of your other store coupons so that you can take advantage of good, unadvertised grocery store "specials."

79.   In general, shop only at grocery stores which double or triple manufacturers' cents-off store coupons (unless the prices are so much higher that you would end up paying more than you would pay at stores which deduct only the face values of the coupons). Shopping at these stores will double or triple your savings if prices are comparable to those in other grocery stores.

80.   If the grocery stores don't double or triple coupons each day of the week, then, in general, shop only on double or triple coupon days. You should shop on other days only if there is a good reason for doing so. When you shop on other days, you are losing money on your manufacturers' cents-off store coupons.

81. Look for "Specially Marked Packages" with coupons and/or refund forms on the outsides or insides of the packages. Sometimes the values of the coupons and/or the refunds will equal or exceed your cost for the products. If you can use the products and the coupons on the packages and take advantage of the refund offers, these should be extremely good purchases.

WAYS TO SAVE THROUGH FOOD PREPARATION

82. Don't overcook meat. Meat "shrinks" with cooking; thus, your food dollar "shrinks."

83. "Extend" or "stretch" meat, poultry, and fish by using them in casseroles, stews, soups, and other dishes. By making these items go a little further, you can cut back some on the purchases of them, which will save you money. These items are usually more expensive than vegetables, spaghetti, and most other foods you would normally use in casseroles, etc.

84. Make ground beef go further by adding bread crumbs, rolled oats, cooked rice, cereals, and commercial extenders--you can decrease your purchase of ground beef.

85. Prepare and cook less tender cuts of meat in such ways as to tenderize the meat, such as cooking it in a pressure cooker, cooking it in a slow cooker, adding a commercial tenderizer to it, pounding it, or marinating it. Less tender cuts are usually less expensive.

86. Fill in your meals with lower cost foods such as potatoes, rice, dried beans and peas, macaroni, spaghetti, and bread.

87. Substitute less expensive foods for more expensive ones. For example, the following are usually cheaper substitutes: toasted oats in place of nuts, all-purpose flour for cornstarch, bouillon cubes for canned beef and chicken broth, margarine or shortening for butter, bottled lemon juice for fresh-squeezed lemon juice, and fresh onions for dehydrated onions.

88.   Prepare most foods from scratch.   Most, but not all, convenience foods are more expensive. (See number 26 above for additional information on convenience foods.)

89.   Make baby food in your blender, and you can usually save money.   Follow the instructions that come with your blender and those in your other recipe books.

90.   Instead of throwing it away, use overripe (not spoiled) fruit in cobblers, puddings, congealed desserts, cakes, and pies. Throwing away food is throwing away money.

91.   Instead of discarding wilted lettuce and other wilted raw vegetables, try soaking them in cold water to restore crispness. Throwing them away is wasting money.

92.   Put very small amounts of leftover cooked vegetables, meat, poultry, and fish together in a container in the freezer. When you have accumulated enough food, make a soup, stew, or casserole.   Saving even tiny bits of leftovers is making use of every penny's worth of your food.

93.   Save stale (not spoiled) bread for bread crumbs.   Using the stale bread saves you the expense of buying bread crumbs or using "fresh" bread which could have been used for other purposes.

94.   Save leftover vegetable, meat, and poultry juices for possible later use.   Refrigerate or freeze the juices, depending on how soon you plan to use them.   Using these juices could save you money on your grocery bills.   For example, saving chicken broth could save you the expense of buying canned broth.

95.   Save leftover juices and syrups from canned fruits for later use.   These juices and syrups can be used for drinking, for making punches and congealed salads, and in preparing other dishes; this will save you the expense of buying such juices and syrups.

WAYS TO SAVE THROUGH PROPER FOOD STORAGE

Don't allow any of your food to reach the point that it has to be thrown away. Throwing away food is just like throwing money out the window. I don't think you would deliberately toss away your hard-earned money.

96. Use fresh fruits and vegetables before they begin to deteriorate so that you can get all the freshness for which you paid.

97. Store dry foods such as dry beans and peas, rice, cereal, and spaghetti in such a manner that insects will not get to them. Foods infested with insects must be thrown away.

98. Store canned foods where the cans will not be susceptible to rusting. Normally, if cans rust through to the inside, they must be thrown away if there is a possibility that the contents are spoiled, such as with vegetables and meats. (However, some canned foods, such as popcorn, peanuts, and ground coffee, can probably be salvaged.)

99. Don't store foods under sinks. Pipes may leak, heat may be given off when hot water runs through the pipes, and insects might get in around openings through which the pipes pass. Leaks, heat, and insects are all potentially harmful to food.

100. Don't store foods over the range or near the water heater. The excessive heat may speed up the deterioration of the foods.

101. Return foods which should be refrigerated to the refrigerator as quickly as possible. For example, don't leave leftover foods sitting on the dining table while you clear away and wash the dishes. Foods left out of the refrigerator too long could spoil and would have to be thrown away.

102. Put away foods which need to be refrigerated or frozen as soon as you get home from the grocery store. Leaving them out could shorten their lives and even cause them to spoil if the lapse of time is too long between the time you took them from the frozen or refrigerated sections at the grocery store and put them in your home freezer or refrigerator.

103. Wrap foods properly for the freezer so they will not become freezer-burned and have to be discarded.

104. Date foods as you put them in your freezer, so you will be able to determine the oldest foods and use them first. Always rotate the oldest ones to the front of an upright freezer or the top of a chest freezer. Not dating and rotating the foods might cause older foods to be overlooked beyond the time when their quality is optimum for human consumption; therefore, those foods probably would be thrown away.

105. A separate freezer should be set at 0 degrees F. A higher temperature could cause premature deterioration of the foods in the freezer.

106. Rotate the foods in your cabinets as you buy new foods. For example, if you have four cans of corn in the cabinet and buy six new cans, put the six new cans behind the four older cans. Use the same procedure with foods in your refrigerator.

WAYS TO SAVE ON EATING OUT

107. Eat fewer meals out. You should be able to save a considerable amount of money on your food expenditures by eating most of your meals at home.

108. Take your lunch to work rather that eat lunch out. For example, a $3.50 lunch (which is conservative) eaten out each workday costs approximately $75 a month, $900 a year, and $9,000 in 10 years. A $5.00 lunch out (which might be closer to what the average working person spends) would amount to about $108 a month, $1,296 a year, and $12,960 in 10 years.

Simple, yet nutritious, sack lunches which you prepare at home should cost you only a small fraction of these amounts.

109.   When you are eating out and you are paying for your own meal, don't order the most expensive item on the menu. Rather, order one of the less expensive items.

110.   If you plan to eat out, consider lunch rather than dinner, since an identical dish can be several dollars less during lunchtime. In addition, some restaurants even add a salad, dip, or other item to lunch entrees at no extra cost; the added item would cost extra at dinnertime.

111.   Avoid "high-class" restaurants where, it seems, you are expected to tip nearly every employee in the restaurant. This type of tipping could add a large amount to the overall cost of your meal.

112.   Eat at places where you normally are not expected to tip or, if so, certainly not as large a percentage as at full-service restaurants. Some of these places might include steak houses and other similar establishments where you go through the "line" and place your order, picking up some of your food as you go through; traditional cafeterias; and fast food places. (Some eating establishments even display signs: "No Tipping, Please.")

113.   Go to restaurants where you can order half-orders or individual items if you are a light eater. Otherwise, unless you ask that your leftovers be put in a doggie bag, you are wasting money.

114.   Some restaurants have separate carry-out establishments attached to them or located next door. The identical restaurant foods are sold there but are available at cheaper prices. Getting the carry-outs will save you money.

115. Watch for opening specials offered by new restaurants and other types of food establishments and save on your costs of eating out.

116. Whenever possible, use coupons to help reduce your costs when eating out.

117. Take advantage of offers such as "buy one, get one free," "two for one," "all you can eat," and "one-half price from four to six p.m. on Tuesdays and Thursdays," and save a sizable amount on eating out.

118. Ask restaurants, fast food places, cafeterias, and carry-out places if discounts for senior citizens, students, and children are available. Discounts help reduce your costs.

119. When eating out, be aware of special deals for senior citizens offered by some food establishments, such as a free soft drink with the purchase of a sandwich.

120. If children are with you when you eat out, ask if a children's menu is available. The prices are cheaper.

121. If you have sufficient food left on your plate, and if it seems appropriate to do so, ask the waiter or waitress to put it in a doggie bag for you. You are wasting your money if the leftovers are thrown away.

122. In general, when eating out, don't offer to pay the checks of others at your table. Let each person pay his or her own bill in most instances. Paying others' checks could put your food budget in serious trouble. Exceptions to this rule, of course, will arise occasionally.

123. If your eating companion insists on picking up your tab, then, by all means, let the person do so, but be prepared to reciprocate on a future occasion.

124.   Just drink the water brought to your table in the restaurant or ask for a glass of water if water is not routinely brought, rather than order a soft beverage. A carbonated soft drink, a glass of iced tea, or a cup of coffee could easily cost over $1.00, maybe closer to $2.00, so save yourself this expense.

125.   Limit the number of alcoholic beverages you have in a restaurant or eliminate them there entirely, since they can run your restaurant bill up quite a lot. Having your drinks at home will be less expensive. (Don't drive if you have been drinking!)

126.   Go to happy hours where free snacks are served. Buy one drink (alcoholic or nonalcoholic) and make your meal on snacks. It is almost unbelievable at the array of snacks some places offer. A meal for the price of one drink would be a fairly inexpensive way of eating out. (Don't drive if you have had alcoholic beverages!)

127.   Attend open houses, grand openings, and other free activities where free refreshments are served, and save on your food expenditures.

128.   Have your children take their lunches to school if this seems appropriate and is cheaper than eating in the school cafeteria or eating out.

WAYS TO SAVE ON ENTERTAINING OTHERS

129.   Have guests for meals only to the extent you can really afford them. Don't go into debt just so you can entertain others. Others may have a good time, but you may have to struggle to pay the food bills.

130.   Have guests for meals at your home rather than take them out to eat. Eating at home should be cheaper.

131.   When you have guests for meals at your home, stick to less expensive menus, for example, green beans rather than asparagus, a lettuce and tomato salad rather than a salad with mushrooms and avocados, a chicken casserole rather than T-bones, and an inexpensive dessert.

132.   When you have guests to your home for meals, and you want to serve hors d'oeuvres before the meals, serve simple, inexpensive ones. A couple should be sufficient. When you are serving meals, you don't expect your guests to fill up on hors d'oeuvres.

133.   Have potlucks sometimes when you have guests for meals. Feeding a lot of people can be expensive; but if all guests share in the expenses by contributing a dish or two of food, your expenses can be kept to a minimum. Maybe you and some close friends could even organize a potluck club, and get together once a month.

134.   Cut down on serving meals when you entertain--rather, serve snacks or maybe just desserts. Snacks or desserts can be much less expensive than complete meals.

135.   If you are having a cocktail party, let the guests help themselves to snacks rather than your continuously circulating among them with trays of food. They probably will waste less if you let them serve themselves. The less wasted, the less should be your expenses for the party.

136.   If you owe a number of people because they have had you to cocktail parties or meals at their homes, or if you don't owe them but just want to have them over for cocktails or a meal, consider having them all over at one time, if you have enough room. If you don't have sufficient room for all of them at one time, have half on one evening and half the next evening.

It should be cheaper to do either of the above rather than have the events weeks apart. You can buy larger cans, packages, etc. (usually cheaper per unit) and prepare all the food at one time; buy larger containers of beverages (which should be cheaper than a lot of small containers); and use the same decorations, such as floral arrangements. Also, the house will still be clean should you have to split the group into two consecutive evenings.

WAYS TO SAVE THROUGH GROWING YOUR OWN VEGETABLES

Plant a garden if you can grow food cheaper than you can buy it. Add up all of your anticipated expenses of growing the food, and then compare this figure with the expected cost of buying the food fresh, frozen, canned, or dried. You will then have the necessary information to decide if planting a garden would be cheaper for you. On the average, a home garden should save money on grocery bills; however, this may not be true for everyone. If you do decide you will plant some vegetables, see the suggestions below.

137. If you have room enough in your backyard, consider planting your garden there.

138. If you don't want to plant a full-fledged garden, plant vegetables in your flower beds.

139. If you don't have any ground space (maybe you live in a high-rise apartment), then plant vegetables in flower pots, window boxes, and other suitable containers.

140. Check to see if community garden plots are available where you live. They may be free or very inexpensive--around $10 to $20 per plot. In some instances, the sponsor (a community organization, the county government, or other group) will even plow the plots at the beginning of the planting season free of charge.

141. Before planting a garden for the first time, you probably should seek free expert advice from the Agricultural Agent at your County Extension Service.

WAYS TO SAVE THROUGH PRESERVING YOUR OWN FOODS

142. Consider canning and freezing fresh foods if this is cheaper than buying them already canned and frozen. Whether you grow your own fruits and vegetables or buy them for canning and freezing, you cannot just assume that you will automatically save money doing your own canning and freezing. Figure how much your total cost will be for growing or buying the foods plus the expenses of canning and freezing them, and then check to see what the total price of comparable canned and frozen items would be at the grocery store. Now you have the facts to show which alternative would be cheaper for you.

143. Wash and save various kinds of suitable, used plastic cartons and other containers for freezing foods. The fewer you must buy, the less money you will need to spend for containers.

144. Wash and save used plastic freezer bags and other appropriate bags for freezing food. Reusing bags cuts down on the expense of buying bags.

145. Save jar rings to be used over and over again in canning and, thereby, save on your canning expenses.

146. Try to buy used canning jars. I have seen these jars advertised for sale in the classified sections of newspapers. You may even want to place an ad in the paper worded, "I want to buy good, used canning jars, such as Ball and Kerr. Call-------." Used jars should cost much less than new ones.

147. If you need a pressure canner, try to find a good, used one rather than buy a new one. Put an advertisement in the newspaper. The ad might read, "I want to buy a good, used pressure canner. Call-------." You might also consider purchasing a canner with a friend with each of you paying one-half of the purchase price. Either of these options will save you money on the cost of a canner.

148.   Consider if you really need a freezer. Would owning a freezer be cost-effective for you? Consider how much you would actually use it. If you are thinking about buying one, read the labels on the freezers to see how much the estimated yearly cost of operation would be. Also, take into consideration the purchase price. Consider how long it would take you to recover the purchase price, taking into account how and to what extent you would use the freezer.

Considering all expenses involved, how much do you estimate you could actually save by growing your own foods, buying fresh foods, and/or buying frozen foods on sale and storing them in your freezer? Don't just assume that a home freezer will automatically save you money on your food bill when all related expenses are taken into consideration.

If you already own a freezer, also consider the above. Would it be to your advantage to sell your freezer? Take all things into consideration before buying one or before selling the one you have. Do some figuring and also do some reading at your public library before making a final decision.

WAYS TO SAVE BY TAKING ADVANTAGE OF GOVERNMENT AND OTHER FOOD PROGRAMS

149.   Check with the school(s) which your children attend to see if your children are eligible for free or reduced-price lunches through the School Meal Program. Some schools even provide breakfast.

150.   If you are a senior citizen, check with the nearest Office on Aging about possible free or low-cost meals.

151.   Check to see if you qualify to receive food stamps under the Food Stamp Program. Call your local Human Services Office and ask where you should apply.

152. Check to see if you qualify for the Women, Infant, and Child Nutrition Program (WIC). The program provides certain food items to pregnant and nursing women and to infants and small children who meet the program requirements. Call your local public Health Department for additional information.

153. Check to see if you are eligible to receive free surplus foods periodically distributed under the Commodity Food Distribution Program. Check with your local Human Services Office for further information.

154. Check with local food banks to see if you are eligible to receive free food from them. Check the telephone directory or ask at your local Human Services Office for information.

155. Some nonprofit organizations and other groups provide free meals. Ask at the local Human Services Office and local churches for information about free meals.

156. Some churches provide free meals. Check with the local churches or ministerial alliances.

MISCELLANEOUS WAYS TO SAVE ON FOOD COSTS

157. Don't overeat. Overeating is an unnecessary expense, and dieting to lose the excess weight which you gain can be expensive.

158. Instead of large servings, take small servings of food on your plate, see that your children take small servings, and put very small servings on the plates of children who are not old enough to serve their own plates. If you or family members eat the small servings and still are hungry, you or they can always have additional small servings. If large servings are initially put on plates, some of the food may end up being thrown away. Throwing away food is throwing away money.

159. Scrape or drain the last bit of food (such as mayonnaise, mustard, ketchup, steak sauces, salad dressings, jellies, and jams) from containers. Even small amounts of food can make a difference over the years in your outlay of money for groceries.

160. Take advantage of refunding. Refunding can return to you some of the money you have spent for food. (See Chapter 4 on "How to Save Money Through Couponing and Refunding" for additional information.)

161. Fish for food. One of my husband's and my favorite foods is fried crappie. When they are biting well, we find that it is relatively easy to stock up with several months' supply. Fishing can be relatively inexpensive and can save you some or all of the expense of buying fish.

162. Gather wild nuts, berries, and other wild foods and save some money on your grocery bills. Be sure you know which wild foods are safe to eat and which ones are unsafe--some are poisonous!

163. Cut down on the number of cookbooks you buy. Right now, get all of your cookbooks out and estimate how much money you have invested in them. Are you surprised? How many of your cookbooks have generally the same recipes?

CHAPTER 9

HOW TO SAVE ON FUNERAL AND BURIAL EXPENSES AND HOW TO DEAL WITH RELATED ITEMS

Death takes no bribes
Franklin

INTRODUCTION

Americans arrange for more than two million funerals for their families and friends each year. Some people spend more for a funeral than for any other single "item" they buy. Costing around $2,000 and up, a funeral may be the third most expensive purchase for many other people after a home and a car.[1]

This chapter offers some suggestions for cutting funeral and burial costs while maintaining the dignity and spirit of the occasion. It also gives suggestions of other things to check on before and after a death occurs.

WHAT TO DO BEFORE A DEATH OCCURS

1.   Have a will written.   Having a will should save your survivors unnecessary expenses, frustration, work, and problems in getting your estate settled.   Also, you could be assured that your assets will be distributed as you desire (within certain limits of the law), not as the State desires.   See a lawyer as soon as possible and discuss your will.   It is a sad fact that seven out of ten Americans die without a will.[2]

2.   Write out a list of your important papers and various other personal information and always keep the list up-to-date.   This list could save your survivors the expense of trying to locate such papers and information.   You might include such items as the following:

a.   names and addresses of all of your life insurance and accidental death insurance companies (include policy numbers, amounts payable, and names and addresses of beneficiaries)

b.   names and addresses of banks, savings and loan associations, credit unions, and other financial institutions where you have checking and savings accounts, certificates of deposit, share accounts, and other accounts (include account numbers)

c.   names and addresses of companies in which you have stocks (include account numbers and number of shares you hold)

d.   names and addresses of companies or institutions in which you have pension/retirement plans (include plan or contract number and names and addresses of beneficiaries)

e.   a list of all of your credit cards, including names and addresses of issuers and account numbers

f. names and addresses of companies with whom you have medical/health, disability, and long-term care insurance (include policy or identification numbers)

g. a list showing where all your important papers are kept (For example, what is kept in your bank safe deposit box, in your home files, with your lawyer, with your accountant, or at other locations?)

h. names and addresses of companies with whom you have your automobile, home, and other items insured (include policy numbers)

i. names and addresses of organizations in which you hold membership (include membership numbers)

j. your Social Security number, post office box number, and any other important numbers

k. location of your bank safe deposit box, the box number, and location of the keys; and location of keys to other important things, such as the lake house

l. emergency information, such as who should be contacted in case of death (include addresses and telephone numbers), your birthplace, your birth date, and instructions on the type of funeral and burial you desire (include plot number and location of cemetery, name and address of funeral home with which you have made previous arrangements, clothes in which you wish to be buried, and instructions for disposition of vital organs if you have made arrangements to donate them)

m. names and locations of businesses you own

n. names, addresses, and telephone numbers of companies with which you have burial policies (include policy numbers and the amounts payable)

o. names and addresses of individuals, banks, and businesses you owe and those who owe you (include the amount owed and account numbers if applicable)

p. names and addresses of companies where you own bonds along with identification numbers

q. names, addresses, and telephone numbers of your lawyer, accountant, stockbroker, insurance agent, physician, and others

r. location of the original copy of your will

s. list of your real estate and locations

t. list of your personal property located at places other than your principal residence

u. anything else which might be of help to your survivors

3. Check with local memorial and funeral societies about membership. These societies are nonprofit organizations and can provide guidance on funerals, burials, and cremation; advance planning of arrangements; and ways to minimize costs. Some societies have agreements with funeral directors for lower-priced disposition of the body than can usually be arranged by nonmembers. In addition, the societies can give moral support. Membership fees are very low.

Write to: The Continental Association of Funeral and Memorial Societies, 2001 South Street, N. W., Suite 630, Washington, D.C. 20009 for a free informational brochure entitled *The Memorial Society* and a free *Directory of Member Societies.*

4. Check with the nearest Veteran's Affairs office to determine what benefits are available to veterans, their spouses, and their dependent children. Such benefits could include burial in a national cemetery, payment of some funeral and burial expenses, a headstone or a grave marker, an American flag, and survivor's benefits.

5.   Check with your local Social Security office to see if you are eligible for the lump-sum death benefit. (If so, the benefit will go to your appropriate survivor upon your death.)

6.   Check with your present and all previous employers and determine what, if any, death benefits are available to your survivors in the event of your death.   Such benefits might include life insurance, pensions which might be paid to your spouse upon your death or when your spouse reaches the required age, and accidental death benefits.

7.   Check with your labor union and determine if it will provide death benefits for your survivors. For example, does it provide any financial assistance with funeral and burial expenses?

8.   Plan and make arrangements for your funeral, burial, or cremation yourself. You can make more rational and informed decisions about such arrangements than your survivors will be able to make in their time of bereavement and emotional stress. Do as much preplanning and prearranging (not necessarily prepaying) as possible.

Since you are more apt to be thinking much more clearly before your death than your survivors after your death, you should be able to choose more wisely with economy in mind. Such preplanning could save your survivors 50 percent or more on the cost of your funeral and burial.   Often, bereaved families spend much more for funerals and burials than they can afford.

If you decide to prepay for funeral and burial arrangements, be sure to obtain a valid contract with set prices. Prices could escalate, and you could leave your survivors with another bill to be paid. However, don't rush into prepaying for funerals and burials. There are some possible pitfalls. For example, the funeral home could go out of business or go bankrupt, or you might move too far away from your present location for your survivors to readily take advantage of the arrangements for which you have paid.

Before prepaying funeral and burial expenses, carefully check out the funeral home offering the services. Make sure it has a reputation for honesty, reliability, and good quality goods and services. Ask the funeral director what happens to the money you prepay to him or her. For instance, does it go into a special fund protected under state law?

Even if you do not choose to make prearrangements for your funeral and burial, at least write down your wishes in as much detail as possible so that your survivors will be spared the strain and frustration of making such decisions during their bereavement.

9. Shop around for the best prices. Because prices can vary from funeral home to funeral home, check with several funeral directors and compare prices. For a start, call them on the telephone. Ask for prices for individual goods and services and for prices for the entire "package" of goods and services.

If you do not plan to prepay for funeral and burial arrangements, ask about terms just in case your survivors may be unable to pay for all the goods and services immediately following your death. Also ask the funeral directors about any items for which your survivors may be required to pay in advance, such as flowers and obituary notices.

After getting the initial information over the telephone, arrange to visit selected funeral homes personally to examine their goods, meet the directors, tour selected areas of the funeral homes (such as the chapel and viewing rooms), and further discuss goods, services, and prices.

10. When you visit funeral homes personally, ask each director for a written, itemized price list of individual goods

and services as well as the price of "package" deals. The written price lists from several funeral homes will enable you to compare prices and make an economical decision.

11. Ask the funeral directors which of their goods and services are required by law. For example, what are the requirements regarding embalming? After you determine which items are required by law, you can decide which, if any, of the optional goods and services you want. The more options you choose, the more the funeral and burial will cost.

12. When you visit funeral homes, ask to see caskets and vaults in all price ranges--from the least expensive to the most expensive. Decide which you want and can really afford.

13. When you are checking with funeral homes on prices, ask if rental caskets are available for the funeral. If they are, consider renting an "expensive" casket for the funeral and buy a less expensive one for the actual burial.

14. Check with funeral homes on costs for cremation as opposed to the traditional funeral and burial. The cost of cremation should be considerably less than that for the traditional funeral and burial.

15. Consider donating your body to a medical school. Check with several medical schools and ask for details on how to arrange for such a donation and what, if any, expenses would be incurred by you or your survivors. The expenses should be quite small or nothing.

16. Check on the availability, location, price, and cost of upkeep of cemetery plots. You may wish to consider choosing one and purchasing it. Take into consideration whether you plan to continue living in the area or, if not, whether you still would wish to be buried there. Also, ask if the plot could be "exchanged" for a plot in another part of the country should you wish to do so at a later date. Compare costs and choose the least expensive plot that will meet your needs.

17.   Look at sample grave markers and compare prices of the different types.   Make your choice and inform your family of that choice.   Making this choice could save your survivors a considerable amount of money.

WHAT TO DO AFTER A DEATH OCCURS

18.   If you do not know whether the deceased had made and paid in advance for funeral and burial arrangements, call local and nearby funeral homes and ask if they have any record of such arrangements.   Be sure to examine all papers of the deceased and look for funeral and burial contracts.   Neglecting to check out the possibility of such arrangements could result in unnecessary expenditures for survivors.

19.   If the deceased and the family of the deceased are extremely poor, check with the local county government to see what financial assistance for burial might be available.

20.   If the deceased lived at your address, think about having someone "house-sit" for you while you are at the funeral. Burglars take advantage of such absences to break into houses. They learn where the deceased lived and the time and date of the funeral by reading the obituary column.   They assume that no one will be at home and plan their break in.   A house-sitter could prevent loss of your personal property.

21.   If the deceased was a veteran, the spouse of a veteran, or a dependent child of a veteran, check immediately after death with the nearest Veteran's Affairs office to determine (if you don't know already) whether the deceased is eligible for burial in a National Cemetery.   Check also on what payments are available for funeral and burial expenses.   In addition, ask if a grave marker or headstone is provided.   Generally, a survivor is eligible to receive an American Flag to use in the funeral and to keep afterwards.   If you are the surviving spouse or a dependent child of a veteran, ask about survivor's benefits.

22. If the deceased was a participant in the Social Security System, contact your nearest Social Security office as soon as possible after the death and apply for any benefits that might be payable to eligible survivors. Also, apply for the lump-sum death benefit.

23. Contact all life insurance companies with which the deceased had policies and file claims for payment.

24. Collect from insurers any funeral/burial/death benefits payable to survivors.

25. Check with the deceased's present and all previous employers to determine what benefits, if any, might be payable to survivors. Such benefits might include life insurance, accidental death insurance, pension benefits, and payments under Worker's Compensation Insurance. Also, be sure to collect pay for any vacation and applicable sick leave accumulated but not taken by the deceased.

26. Contact the deceased's employee's labor union and collect any death or survivor's benefits due. For example, ask whether the labor union provides for any financial assistance with funeral and burial expenses for the deceased or with living or educational expenses of the survivors.

27. Check with the company with which the deceased carried medical/health insurance. Free accidental death and dismemberment insurance is sometimes provided to those participating in group medical/health plans. The death and dismemberment insurance might be sponsored and administered by an organization other than the medical/health insurance company, such as that sponsored and administered by the National Association of Government Employees. If the death was an accident, normally the payment will be made to a designated beneficiary.

28. File for any pension/retirement benefits due the survivors of the deceased.

29. Check with community credit unions, credit unions at all places where the deceased has been employed, and possibly other credit unions to see whether he or she had deposits or life insurance there. If so, discuss payment of the money in the accounts and apply for insurance benefits.

30. Check with insurance companies with which the deceased had automobile insurance and homeowners insurance to determine whether any death benefits, such as payment of funeral and burial expenses, are payable under the policies.

31. Check with the deceased's automobile club to see if any life insurance or other benefits are due the survivors.

32. Check with all credit card companies with which the deceased held credit cards and apply for any death benefits that are due. For example, some credit card companies automatically carry accident life insurance on cardholders. The insurance may be collected by survivors, for example, if the cardholder had charged his or her airline ticket on the credit card and was subsequently killed in a crash of the aircraft or died within a specified time following the accident.

33. If the deceased died in an accident on a trip arranged by a travel agency, survivors may be eligible for payment of death benefits from the agency. Some travel agencies automatically provide accident life insurance coverage to persons who purchase airline tickets through the agency. Check with the agency to see whether the deceased was covered by such a policy. If so, apply for benefits.

34. Submit any medical claims for the deceased to health insurance companies and/or Medicare for payment or reimbursement.

35. Collect any death benefits due survivors from various organizations, associations, clubs, and other groups to which the deceased belonged. Some of these may have provided free or inexpensive life insurance on the deceased as a membership benefit.

36. Check on all debts of the deceased. Some debts may carry credit life insurance that will pay the outstanding balance of the debts.

37. Notify the deceased's insurance companies of the death; cancel policies, if appropriate (or remove the name of the deceased from the policy, if appropriate); and request refunds of premiums. Such insurance may include automobile, personal property, medical, disability, homeowners, and others. Discuss the above with the deceased's insurance agent(s) before taking any action.

38. Cancel orders for unwanted goods and services ordered by the deceased and collect any applicable refunds.

39. Turn in season tickets that were held by the deceased (for sports events, symphonies, ballets, etc.) and request refunds.

40. Cancel unwanted magazine and newspaper subscriptions and book club memberships held by the deceased and request refunds.

41. Cancel memberships in clubs and organizations to which the deceased belonged and request refunds.

42. Cancel hotel reservations, trip and tour reservations, and airline reservations for the deceased and request applicable refunds.

43. If the deceased was a college student, cancel enrollment and request refunds of prepayments for such things as tuition, room and board, laboratory fees, and activity fees.

44. Cancel medical and dental appointments for the deceased. Some members of the medical and dental profession charge patients even if they do not show up for their scheduled appointments. Even though you surely could have the charges cancelled, cancelling the appointments will prevent your having to further deal with the situation.

45. If the deceased was renting living accommodations for himself or herself only, contact the landlord and cancel the lease. Ask for any applicable refunds, such as the security deposit and rent paid in advance.

46. Check copies of income tax returns filed recently by the deceased to determine whether refunds are due. If the refunds are not received, you will know to follow up. (Check with your lawyer, tax accountant, IRS, and State Tax Office for instructions on filing final tax returns for the deceased.)

47. If the death of the deceased was the fault of someone else, check on the possibility of benefits payable under liability insurance carried by the person at fault. Also, consider whether a lawsuit should be brought against the responsible party. Consult your lawyer.

48. Collect the total amount or accept periodical payments for debts owed to the deceased.

49. Be cautious of strangers offering help during your bereavement, particularly those wanting to help you handle or invest your money. Put off making major financial decisions (if at all possible) until your mental state will allow you to think clearly and logically.

50. If the deceased was your spouse, check with all appropriate sources of survivor's benefits to determine whether you would lose your benefits if you remarry. After receiving the necessary information, you can, in time, make an informed decision on remarriage.

SOURCE FOR ADDITIONAL INFORMATION

51. Write to the Conference of Funeral Service Examining Boards of the United States, 520 E. Van Trees Street, P. O. Box 497, Washington, Indiana 47501 for information on the laws related to funerals and burials in the various states. This association represents the licensing boards of 47 states and will respond to consumer inquiries or complaints about funeral providers.

ENDNOTES

1. Federal Trade Commission, Bureau of Consumer Protection, *Consumer Guide to the FTC Funeral Rule* (Washington, D.C., April, 1984).

2. Mary J. Stephenson, *Writing Wills in Maryland, Fact Sheet 283* (College Park, Maryland: Cooperative Extension Service, The University of Maryland, 1983-84).

CHAPTER 10

HOW TO SAVE MONEY ON GIFTS, GIFT WRAPPING, GREETING CARDS, AND DECORATIONS

Take care of the pence, and the pounds
will take care of themselves
                    William Lowndes

INTRODUCTION

Giving gifts, sending greeting cards, and decorating for various holidays and special activities are probably not vital to your survival and well-being; but they are fun, and have become a part of the American tradition. However, some people spend too much of their disposable income on these three things. Most people have family members, friends, and acquaintances who are having birthdays; having wedding anniversaries; getting married; getting divorced; graduating from kindergarten, grade school, high school, or college; having babies; getting promotions; retiring; not feeling well; and spending time in the hospital.

Then, there are holidays such as Christmas, New Year's Day, Easter, St. Valentine's Day, Independence Day, Thanksgiving Day, Halloween, Flag Day, St. Patrick's Day, Veterans Day,

Memorial Day, and Labor Day. Don't forget about Mother's Day, Father's Day, Grandparents' Day, Mothers-in-Law Day, Bosses' Day, and Secretaries' Day. Responding to all of the above occasions could really take a big bite out of your bank account. By using the suggestions in this chapter, you should be able to keep your expenses for gifts, cards, and decorations to a minimum.

WAYS TO SAVE ON GIFTS

1.   Limit gift-giving, both in the number of people to whom you give gifts and in the cost of the gifts. Otherwise, you could find yourself spending a disproportionate amount of your income on gift-giving. Other people may enjoy your generosity, but it is you who will have to pay the bills.

2.   Always keep an assortment of gifts on hand for gift-giving. Buy gift items when they are on sale (preferably when they are 75 percent or more off) and save them until the appropriate occasions arise. Usually, you will pay much more (probably full price) for gifts if you wait and buy them immediately prior to the times you need them.

3.   Give gift vouchers to immediate family members and other relatives, to neighbors, and to friends. The recipients can exchange these vouchers for the items listed on them. Some examples are: A child could give his or her working mother a voucher reading "dishes from one meal washed"; a wife could give her husband one which says "one breakfast in bed"; a husband could give one to his wife saying "one outside grilled dinner for the family"; you could give to an elderly neighbor a voucher which says "one free lawn mowing"; and to a friend who seldom goes out because she can't afford a baby-sitter, you could give a voucher which reads "one night of free baby-sitting." These gifts need not cost anything extra and could be unique and fun.

4. Make gifts. Use your talents and imagination to make attractive gifts for less than you could purchase satisfactory gifts. (Numbers 5 through 11 below are just a few examples of gift items which could be made.) Think--"what gifts could I make?"

5. Make cookies, cakes, and candies to give to family members, friends, co-workers, and neighbors.

6. Make and give jams, jellies, and preserves as gifts.

7. Write out your favorite recipes on cards, place them in recipe file boxes, and give them to people you know who take particular pride in their own cooking.

8. Compose a poem for a friend or family member who would appreciate such a gift. Your only cost should be a few sheets of paper.

9. Plant a flower bed for a special person as a gift. An acquaintance of mine planted a large bed of marigolds for her elderly mother and father at their duplex. Her parents thought the flower bed was a perfect gift. The only cost was for two packages of flower seed.

10. Start some potted plants yourself from seeds or cuttings and give them as gifts. By using inexpensive, but suitable, pots, your costs should be minimal.

11. Learn to make floral arrangements using flowers and greenery from your own yard. These can be given to friends and family members in the hospital or on special occasions. Such arrangements might be one rose in a simple bud vase, six or eight flowers tied with a pretty ribbon (which the recipient could place in his or her own container), or a large container of greenery and dozens of flowers. Floral arrangements you make yourself usually are much less expensive than those purchased at the florist.

12. Purchase potted plants from a nursery, grocery store, or discount store to give as gifts. Generally, the cost will be less than the price of the same plants purchased at the florist.

13. If someone wants to give you a gift with no commitments on your part, accept it. Not having to buy that particular item will save you money.

14. If you receive a gift which you cannot use or you have a sufficient number of similar items already, save it and give it as a gift to someone else for whom it would be appropriate. Giving this item will save you the expense of purchasing a gift.

15. If you win items or receive free merchandise which you cannot use, put them in your gift inventory. The fewer gifts you have to buy, the more money you will save.

16. Get free gifts by saving and sending in boxtops, labels, and other proofs-of-purchase. (See chapter 4 on "How To Save Money Through Couponing and Refunding.") Place these gifts in your gift inventory and use them on appropriate occasions.

17. Get free gifts for your gift inventory by hosting parties offered by home-party plans such as Tupperware. The gifts you receive usually are based on the dollar amount of orders you are able to sell. Getting free gifts saves you money.

18. Be on the lookout for new items suitable for gifts when you go to garage sales. The items normally will be only a fraction of the cost of similar items purchased in a store.

19. When you receive a gift and think you might want or need to exchange it, be sure to save the box, wrapping paper, and any labels and tags which will identify the store from which the gift was purchased. Take all of these with you when you go to exchange the gift and present them to the salesperson as evidence that the gift was purchased at that store. Being able to exchange an unusable gift will allow you to exchange it for something you would ordinarily have to buy yourself.

WAYS TO SAVE ON GIFT WRAPPING

20. Save and reuse gift-wrap paper. The more you can reuse, the less you will have to buy.

21. Buy gift-wrap paper on sale (up to 75 percent off) following Christmas and other holidays for use next year. If you wait until just prior to the holidays to buy the paper, you will likely have to pay full price.

22. Check to see if rolls of gift-wrap paper are cheaper per unit (square inch, square foot, or square yard) than sheets of gift-wrap paper. Buy the type that offers the most for the money.

23. Use black-and-white and colored sheets of newspaper for some of your gift wrapping. It's cheap and chic.

24. Wrap your gifts yourself, rather than pay to have them wrapped, unless, of course, having them wrapped is cheaper than wrapping them yourself. If free gift wrapping is offered, by all means take advantage of the service.

25. Save and reuse bows and ribbons. The more of these you reuse, the fewer you will have to purchase.

26. Whenever you purchase items which you are not going to use as gifts, always ask for free gift boxes, anyway. Save the boxes for later gift-giving. Gift boxes can be expensive if you have to purchase them, and this adds to the cost of the gifts.

27. Save suitable, miscellaneous boxes for use as gift boxes. Keep a supply on hand at all times.

WAYS TO SAVE ON GREETING CARDS

28. Buy boxes of greeting cards (birthday, Christmas, anniversary, Easter, Valentine, get well, and sympathy) rather than individual cards. The cost per card normally is much less if you buy them in boxes. Boxes of cards often can be found on sale, giving you even greater savings.

29.   Buy Christmas cards on sale following Christmas. You can expect to save up to 75 percent over the price charged before Christmas. Keep the cards until next year and use them.

WAYS TO SAVE ON HOLIDAY DECORATIONS

30.   Buy holiday decorations on sale following particular holidays (especially Christmas) for use next year. Buying decorations after specific holidays can mean savings of 50 to 75 percent or more over pre-holiday prices.

31.   Put an advertisement in the newspaper for buying used holiday decorations. The ad might read: "I want to buy a good, used eight-foot green artificial Christmas tree. Call-------." Used decorations should cost only a fraction of the price for new decorations. Use a newspaper ad, also, if you have decorations to sell.

32.   Check at garage sales for used holiday decorations. You may be able to find new or nearly new decorations at almost "giveaway" prices.

33.   Make your own holiday decorations. Use your talents and imagination to make decorations cheaper than you can buy them.

34.   Save holiday decorations for use again next year. The longer you can use them, the longer you can postpone purchasing ones to replace them.

35.   Save used greeting cards for use in decorating for various holidays. For example, cutouts from used Christmas cards make excellent decorations for your Christmas tree and dining table.

36. Buy an artificial Christmas tree which can be used year after year rather than buy an expensive live tree every year. A $20 live tree each year over a ten-year period would amount to $200. By shopping carefully and after Christmas, you should be able to buy an artificial tree for a small fraction of that $200.

37. Cut your own Christmas tree. It should be cheaper than buying one already cut. Maybe you have a friend who lives in the country and has an ample supply of wild, suitable evergreen trees. Ask if you might cut one for your Christmas tree. Some Christmas tree farms will give you a discount if you cut your own tree from their plantation.

CHAPTER 11

HOW TO SAVE ON YOUR HEALTH CARE COSTS

For age and want save while you may;
no morning sun lasts a whole day
                                    Franklin

INTRODUCTION

In 1984, Americans spent more than seven times as much on health care as they did in 1964. The estimated personal health care expenditure for an individual was approximately $1,680 in 1984.[1] Costs have increased considerably since then.

The suggestions in this chapter can help you reduce your health care costs by hundreds of dollars each year. **However, these suggestions are not intended as a substitute for professional medical, dental, and other health care.**

WAYS TO SAVE ON MEDICINES

1. Ask your physician to prescribe generic drugs (if available in your prescriptions) rather than brand-name drugs or to indicate on your prescriptions that the generic equivalents may be substituted. However, follow your physician's advice. Your

physician should know whether to prescribe generics or insist on brand names for your particular medications and in your specific situation.

The following is an example of the difference in the price of the brand-name drug Inderal and its generic equivalent (Propranolol): At the pharmacy in one of the national chain grocery stores in Denton, Texas, the price for 100 of the 40 mg. Inderal tablets was $25.99 in 1990. The Propranolol was $13.07 at the same store. If the consumer required one tablet per day, purchasing the generic drug would have resulted in a saving of $47.16 per year on just this one prescription.

The average savings from using generic drugs over brand-name drugs normally is between 30 and 40 percent but could be as much as 80 percent in some cases.[2]

Each drug has a generic name. Generic refers to the complex chemical name of the drug, rather than the manufacturer or brand name. Many generic versions of brand-name drugs come on the market after the patents for the brand-name drugs held by the original manufacturers have expired.[3] (Generic equivalents are not presently available for all brand-name drugs.)

All of the 50 states have laws allowing, and in some cases requiring, pharmacists to substitute a generic drug (if one is available) for a brand-name one unless the prescribing physician insists that the brand-name drug be used.[4]

2. If the prescription tablets you must take are available in dosages twice the amount you require, can accurately be broken in half, and can be purchased for less than twice the price of two of the ones containing the exact dosage you need, ask your physician about prescribing the double dosage sizes.

For example, in January, 1990, at the Walmart pharmacy in Denton, Texas, the Hydrochlorothiazide tablets (the generic of the brand-name Hydrodiuril) were priced at $2.38 for 100 of the 25 mg. tablets and also $2.38 for 100 of the 50 mg. tablets. The Hydrodiuril tablets were $11.39 for the 25 mg. tablets and $16.47 for the 50 mg. tablets. By purchasing the 50 mg. Hydrochlorothiazide tablets and breaking them in half, you would get 100 extra dosages free. One hundred extra dosages of the Hydrodiuril tablets would cost just $5.08.

There is even on the market a device for splitting tablets in half. It sells for approximately $5.00 and should pay for itself in a relatively short time through savings on your drug bills. By all means, follow the advice of your physician concerning whether or not your particular medication can be accurately divided into two equal dosages.

3. If your physician prescribes medicine for a short-term condition, ask if he or she has free samples from drug companies which he or she would be willing to give you to treat your condition. If so, you could save your money.

4. Use a low-cost, mail-order service for your prescriptions, over-the-counter medications, and various health aids. For example, if you are 50 years old or older, employed or retired, you can join the American Association of Retired Persons (AARP), 1909 K Street, NW, Washington, D. C. 20049, for a small annual membership fee. One of the benefits of membership is the use of the mail-order AARP Pharmacy. Also, some health insurance policies provide for prescription drugs to be ordered from mail-order drug companies at significant savings.

Perhaps you can join AARP or another organization, switch your health insurance policy, or take some other necessary action that would qualify you to order prescription medicines, etc. cheaper than you can buy them at your local drugstore. Check out the possibility of such mail-order services. (NOTE: Be extremely cautious about switching your health insurance policy just so you can have access to a mail-order drug service. Get professional advice before you switch.)

5. If your physician prescribes a drug for you, and if you use a low-cost, mail-order drug company for your drug needs, ask your physician if he or she has enough free samples (given to him or her by the drug companies) of the drug to give to you to last until you receive your supply through the mail. Getting the free samples will save you the expense of having to buy a small supply of the drug locally at a price higher than the mail-order company charges.

6. Before having your drug prescriptions filled, call at least six different pharmacies at traditional drugstores and at other stores offering prescription drug service and compare the costs of filling the particular prescriptions. The prices could vary by a considerable amount from pharmacy to pharmacy. Also, ask about any discounts that may be available. For example, many pharmacies give discounts to senior citizens.

7. Consider buying generic over-the-counter medicines and medical items. Generics should be much cheaper than brand names.

8. Shop around for the best prices on your over-the-counter drugs (such as medicines for headaches and the common cold) and medical items (such as plastic adhesive bandages). The prices could vary substantially among drugstores, discount stores, and various other stores. Buy them where they are the cheapest.

WAYS TO SAVE ON PHYSICIANS' CHARGES

9. If you are enrolled in Medicare, ask your physician if he or she accepts "assignment," which means that your physician agrees to charge you no more than the amount "approved" by Medicare for covered services and supplies. Refer to your copy of *The Medicare Handbook* for details.

10. Consider doing some do-it-yourself medical testing, checking, and examining. For example:

    a. Take your own and your family's temperatures

    b. Take your own and your family's blood pressures

    c. Examine your own breasts monthly for lumps

    d. Use over-the-counter test kits, such as those for:

        1). Detecting pregnancy
        2). Detecting hidden blood in the stool
        3). Checking for blood glucose in diabetics

By taking care of some of your own medical needs yourself, you could save the cost of having your physician handle them. Some of the above should, however, be conducted in close conjunction with medical guidance. Medical self-testing, etc. is not meant to replace medical exams, advice, and guidance from your physician and other qualified medical professionals. For example, your physician might advise you to check your own blood pressure at home between visits to his or her office.

11. Shop around for a physician. Some may be more reasonably priced because of their locations in areas of lower overhead, because they are general practitioners (GPs) rather than specialists, and because of various other acceptable and legitimate reasons. Also, ask your friends, co-workers, and others what physicians they use and whether or not they have ever used "Dr. So-and-So." If you can locate a competent, reputable, and lower-priced physician, you could save a substantial amount of money on your office visits, etc.

12. In general, ask your pharmacist to recommend medicines available without prescriptions for the relief of relatively simple medical conditions such as the common cold, sore throat, mild headache, mild menstrual pain, corns, and dandruff. If your pharmacist can adequately handle some of your medicine needs, you should be able to decrease the number of office visits to your physician. Be sure to tell the pharmacist what other medicines you are taking. However, your pharmacist is not meant to take the place of your physician. If your condition warrants seeing your physician, by all means do so.

WAYS TO SAVE ON HOSPITAL AND OUTPATIENT CARE COSTS

13. Ask your physician if your medical problem can be handled just as adequately on a "home health care" basis as it can in the hospital. If it can, you should, in general, realize sizable savings over the cost of hospital care.

14. If your present physician recommends surgery, consider getting a second and maybe a third opinion from other physicians before undergoing nonemergency surgery. Make sure, however, that a short delay will not be harmful to you. Many health insurance policies cover the cost of a second and even a third opinion from other physicians. Some policies require a second opinion on some types of surgery; otherwise, the insurance companies will decrease the percentage of payments for the surgery and related hospital and other charges. Also, the second and third physicians might suggest satisfactory alternatives to surgery. Read your health insurance policy carefully.

Discuss the entire matter with your present physician. The above suggestions could decrease the amount of money you will have to pay out of your pocket.

15. If your medical problem (for example, tests or minor surgery) can be handled just as safely and satisfactorily as a hospital outpatient, in the physician's office, or at a "surgicenter" (specializing in one-day surgery) as it can be as a hospital inpatient, then consider choosing one of these first three options.

The difference in charges between the first three options and that of checking into the hospital as a regular patient could mean considerable savings for you. Also, some insurance policies will pay a larger percentage of the costs incurred as an outpatient as compared to a hospital inpatient. Check your health insurance policy. Discuss the three options with your physician and ask for his or her advice.

16. If you must be hospitalized for surgery, for example, ask your physician if some or all of the preliminary tests can be done prior to hospital admission. Not only can the preadmission testing probably cut a day or two off the length of your stay in the hospital, but it uses fewer of your allotted "hospital" days so you will have more days left when you really need them.

If testing can be conducted prior to admission, then read your health insurance policy carefully before you make a final decision to make sure your policy will pay for preadmission testing and under what conditions. Spending fewer days in the hospital normally will lower your hospital bill.

17. If your physician is on the staff of more than one hospital, if he or she says that the quality of care offered by the hospitals is equal, and if your physician has no preference of one hospital over another, then call the hospitals' business offices to ask the costs of rooms and various other items and services. In general, consider choosing the least expensive hospital. Be sure you talk with your physician in detail about this situation.

18. Prior to checking into the hospital, tell your physician that you prefer a semiprivate room, which is cheaper than a private room. Most health insurance policies will not pay for the difference in the price of a semiprivate room and a private room, except under certain circumstances. (If your policy does pay the full price of a private room, then choose the private room.)

You may even want to choose a ward if your health insurance doesn't pay enough to cover even a semiprivate room or if you don't have health insurance and will have to be personally responsible for all of your hospital charges. Wards usually are cheaper than semiprivate rooms. However, all hospitals may not have wards. Some do not even have semiprivate rooms. Call the various hospitals for information.

19. Before you check into the hospital, call the hospital business office and ask what items are not included in the cost of a room, possibly items such as a television, telephone, and cot and meals for someone sitting with you. Usually, such items are not covered by your health insurance if they are itemized separately on your bill. Decide whether you want the extras if you have to pay for them yourself. Read your insurance policy carefully to determine what items are not covered.

20. Think twice before checking into a hospital on a Friday or Saturday. Unless it is for an emergency, for a scheduled weekend surgery, or in relation to childbirth, most health insurance policies will not pay the charges for hospital admission on Friday or Saturday. Usually, testing will not occur until Monday; so you could save yourself the cost of one or two extra days in the hospital. Examine your policy, and discuss all of the above with your physician.

21. Don't stay in the hospital any longer than you really need to. Another day of hospital confinement means a higher bill. Confer with your physician for his or her advice.

22. Hospitals usually have set check-out times, after which patients are billed for an additional day's stay. Find out what the check-out time is, and plan to leave by that time. Also, ask about check-in times. Knowing and abiding by check-in and check-out times could save you money.

23. Go over your hospital bill or outpatient bill and other related bills carefully and don't pay charges for services, medicine, or supplies you did not receive. There is always a chance that charges incurred by other patients could have been erroneously posted to your account.

WAYS TO SAVE ON DENTAL BILLS

24. Shop around for the best prices on dental care. Ask people you know what dentists they use. Call these (and others, too) and ask for their prices for the work you need to have done on your teeth. The prices could vary a great deal among dentists. If you can locate a low-priced, yet reputable and competent, dentist, you could save a considerable amount of money on your dental bills. For example, dentists in small towns may have lower overhead than those in large cities and may be able to charge lower prices.

25. Check to see if "discount" dentists are available where you live. They usually are much cheaper than "regular" dentists. Check your telephone directory and, also, ask around. For instance, a "discount" dentist may be able to charge less if some of the dental work is performed by other trained people in the office and not done solely by the dentist.

WAYS TO SAVE ON EYEGLASSES AND EYE CARE COSTS

26. After you get your written prescription for eyeglasses, shop around for the best price for filling the prescription. Call six to eight different opticians and optometrists for prices. Also, watch the newspaper for specials at various optical shops. There could be a wide spread in prices from place to place. Make sure the place you choose has a good reputation--ask friends, etc.

27. If you need eyeglasses only for reading and/or close-up work, consider purchasing inexpensive magnification eyeglasses available at various stores, such as K-Mart and Walmart. Simply go to the stores and try on glasses until you find a pair that gives you the needed magnification. The prices range from approximately $9.00 to $15 a pair. Some stores stock these eyeglasses in very stylish frames. My husband has several pairs of such glasses.

28. When you are not wearing your eyeglasses, always keep them in a protective case to minimize scratching the lenses and breaking the frames. If you keep them in good shape, you could delay buying new ones until you need a different prescription.

29. Consider some do-it-yourself eye testing, and you possibly can save yourself the costs of some office visits. I secured a free "Adult Home Eye Screening" kit developed by the Minnesota Society for the Prevention of Blindness and Preservation of Hearing. In addition to testing visual acuity, the kit also contains a test for early indication of macular degeneration and a list of questions to determine if a person is at risk of developing glaucoma.

The tests in the kit are not meant, however, to take the place of thorough professional eye examinations. They are only meant to provide you with a clue to the health of your eyes. Self-testing could alert you to possible problems between regular professional exams.

WAYS TO SAVE ON HEARING AIDS COSTS

30. After you get your prescription for your hearing aid(s), shop around for the best price for the particular type of hearing aid you need. The prices do vary from place to place. Also, ask about the details of the trial period, refund procedures, and warranties. For example, some companies will permit you to "try out" the hearing aid for 30 days before you pay for it. Then, if it doesn't meet your needs by the end of the trial period, you can return it; and you are under no obligation to buy it.

31. Remove the battery from your hearing aid when it is not in use, and the battery normally will last nearly twice as long as it would if left in the hearing aid even if the hearing aid is turned off. Thus, you should be able to cut your hearing aid battery costs by about 50 percent. Also, prices of batteries vary from store to store, so shop around for the best price on the type of battery you use.

WAYS TO SAVE THROUGH FREE AND LOW-COST MEDICAL/HEALTH SERVICES

32. If your employer makes available certain free medical care and medicines to employees (and maybe spouses and dependent children) through a "Company" nurse or doctor, then take full advantage of this benefit. You could cut your medical expenses by a tidy sum.

33. If you are a veteran, find out what medical benefits you could be eligible to receive. Call or write the nearest Veteran's Affairs office for information. The benefits might make a big difference in how much money you must be out for medical care.

34. If you are a college student, take advantage of free or low-cost medical care and prescription medicines offered by the campus student health services.

35. Check to see if you or your family qualify for Medicaid (a free medical assistance program). Call or go to your local Social Services Office for information.

36. Call or visit your county and/or city Health Department to see what services are offered free or at a reduced cost. Some services which may be offered are medical examinations, immunizations, well-baby care, prenatal care, and TB (Tuberculosis) testing. If the services you need are not provided by the Health Department, ask where you might receive the care at the least cost.

37. See if you qualify for free or low-cost medical services from various charitable organizations, government offices, and other groups. Call your county or city Health Department, local office on aging, and local Social Services Office and ask for information on where you should go for the particular help you need.

38. Contact the business offices of your local hospitals to see if you are eligible to receive free medical care. Some hospitals are required to offer a certain amount of free care, for example, for indigent persons.

39. Take advantage of free tests. For example, the local office of the American Cancer Society usually provides free colorectal cancer testing. Some national chain department stores offer free hearing tests at various times throughout the year. Some pharmacies located in national chain grocery stores provide equipment within the stores for free, do-it-yourself blood pressure tests. Getting free tests cuts down on your outlay.

40. Watch the newspaper for upcoming Health Fairs and similar public events where a variety of free tests, screening, and information may be available. The following are a few examples of what might be offered: information on alcohol and other drugs; birth control information, blood pressure checks; dental screening; fitness testing; glaucoma screening; nutritional information; stress management information; vision screening; and hearing exams. Not having to pay for these will lower your medical/health expenditures.

41. If you, a family member, or a friend has a drinking problem, call Alcoholics Anonymous for free help. Locate the number in your telephone directory.

42. If you are unsure of where to turn for free and low-cost medical help, call or visit several local churches. The ministers and other church personnel usually will be able to direct you to appropriate places which provide the help you need.

43. Check with your local Health Department and Social Services Office for information on where you can obtain free or low-cost mental health counseling.

44. Inquire at your community Mental Health Services to see if you are eligible for free or reduced-cost mental health counseling. Charges usually are made on a sliding scale.

45. Talk with your minister to see if he or she provides mental health counseling. Such counseling normally will be free.

46. If you are a college student, check with the Psychology Department, Counseling Center, or other appropriate department or office to see if mental health counseling is offered free or at a low cost to students.

WAYS TO SAVE THROUGH PRACTICING PREVENTIVE MEDICINE/DENTISTRY

47. The U.S. Department of Agriculture, in conjunction with the U.S. Department of Health and Human Services, suggests the following dietary guidelines for Americans who are already healthy to help them stay healthy: Eat a variety of foods; maintain desirable weight; avoid too much fat, saturated fat, and cholesterol; eat foods with adequate starch and fiber; avoid too much sugar; avoid too much sodium; and if you drink alcoholic beverages, do so in moderation.[5] Staying as healthy as you possibly can should keep your medical expenses to a minimum.

48. Follow your physician's medical advice. By doing so, it is possible that you could decrease your need, thus costs, for future medical care.

49. Stay as physically active as advisable based on your medical and physical conditions and age. Consult your physician first on the correct amount and kind of exercise for you. "Keeping fit" could reduce your expenses for medical care.

50. If you don't eat properly, ask your physician if you should take a vitamin and/or mineral supplement. Getting the right kinds and amounts of vitamins and minerals could help in maintaining your health and could lower your medical and dental expenditures.

51. Get enough rest. Sufficient rest helps to maintain good health. Healthy people may not need as much medical care as unhealthy people. Less medical care usually means fewer expenses.

52. Don't smoke. This advice is given by many knowledgeable professionals as one way to help maintain good health, since some adverse medical conditions are linked to smoking. The healthier you stay, the less should be your medical expenditures.

53. Stay mentally active. "Exercise" your mind by doing such things as reading, completing crossword puzzles, and doing other "mind" stimulating activities. Being mentally active should help you stay healthier. The healthier you are, the less you should expect to have to spend on medical care.

54. Follow safety rules to help prevent personal accidents. Accidents could necessitate your having to spend additional money on medical care.

55. Brush, floss, and care for your teeth as advised by your dentist. Properly caring for your teeth should mean fewer dental bills.

MISCELLANEOUS WAYS TO SAVE ON HEALTH CARE COSTS

56. Have as good a health insurance policy as you can possibly afford. Without adequate insurance coverage, you could end up paying a large percentage of your health care expenses out of your own pocket. If you must do without some nonessentials to pay the premiums, do so.

57.   Be sure to file insurance claims for all applicable bills for medical, dental, eye, ear, and psychological care. Getting these bills fully or partially paid or reimbursed by your insurance company takes all or some of the financial burden off of you.

58.   If you have health insurance and you have already met the deductibles for the calendar year, then consider doing such things as the following before the end of the calendar year (if they are covered by your policy):

a. Get prescriptions refilled, if you are going to continue taking the medicines.

b. Have needed checkups.

c. Have needed tests.

d. Have other needed medical care.

e. Have needed dental work done.

Once your deductibles are met, the costs out of your pocket should be less, maybe nothing. For example, if you have already met the $50 deductible for dental care, then speak to your dentist about going ahead and having those two bad teeth filled (that is, if your policy covers fillings). If you wait until January, you may have to satisfy another $50 calendar-year deductible. Read your policy carefully before making final decisions.

59.   If you have an accident while driving your automobile or are a passenger in a vehicle involved in an accident, check your automobile policy to see what medical expenses of yours it covers. Also, ask the driver of the car in which you were a passenger what medical expenses of yours are covered under his or her auto insurance policy. Being able to recover all or part of your medical expenses related to the accident could ease your financial burden.

60. If you and/or family members become disabled, check with your nearest Social Security Office to see if you and/or they are eligible for Social Security disability benefits.

61. Check with your employer and/or previous employers if you are suffering from a job-related injury, disability, disease, or illness to see what benefits may be payable to you under Workers' Compensation. If you are the survivor of a worker, inquire about any possible benefits payable to you.

62. Become a member of a blood bank and donate blood regularly. Then, if you and/or your family members need blood, it normally will be free. Check with your local hospital, in your telephone directory, and with your employer for information on blood banks.

63. If you need to purchase medical equipment, consider putting an advertisement in the newspaper. The ad might read something like this, "Would like to buy a good, used wheelchair. Call-------." Used equipment normally will be considerably cheaper than comparable new equipment.

64. In general, rent medical equipment to be used on a short-term basis if you can rent it for less than you can purchase it. For example, if you need a "hospital" bed for two weeks, renting it probably will be cheaper than purchasing it. Another consideration, however, is that you can sell the equipment you have purchased when you no longer need it. Check out the prices, and decide for yourself.

65. Take advantage of senior citizens' discounts offered by some pharmacies and other stores on medicines and medical products. You may not automatically be told about such discounts, so always inquire about them when you are making such purchases. Getting discounts will cut your costs.

66. Stock up when you find over-the-counter medicines and medical items you routinely use on sale at very good prices. Buying on sale cuts your expenses.

67. Limit your purchases of medicines and medical supplies at convenience food stores. They usually are much more expensive at these stores than at other types of stores.

ENDNOTES

1. Mary J. Stephenson, *Risk Management: Health Insurance and Disability Income Insurance, Fact Sheet 407* (College Park, Maryland: Cooperative Extension Service, University of Maryland, 1984-85).

2. U.S. Department of Health and Human Services, *Generic Drugs: Cutting Costs, Not Corners*, by Bill Rados. HHS Publication No. (FDA) 86-3156 (Washington, D.C.: Government Printing Office, 1987).

3. *Ibid.*

4. *Ibid.*

5. U.S. Department of Agriculture and U.S. Department of Health and Human Services, "Dietary Guidelines for Americans" in *Home and Garden Bulletin No. 232*, Second Edition (Washington, D.C.: Government Printing Office, 1985).

CHAPTER 12

HOW TO SAVE MONEY ON YOUR HOME FURNISHINGS AND RELATED ITEMS

*He who spends all he gets
is on his way to beggary*
Samuel Smiles

INTRODUCTION

At least a minimum amount of furniture; something to cover your windows; some type of floor covering, unless you have nice floors which you don't want to cover; at least one set of sheets, pillowcases, and pillows for each bed; a few bath towels; maybe a few bric-a-brac; and some dishes and cooking utensils usually are essential for most people. Even these basics cost money. However, this chapter can show you how to buy, care for, and repair your household items on a shoestring.

WAYS TO SAVE ON THE PURCHASE, REPAIR, AND CARE OF FURNITURE

1.   When purchasing furniture, consider choosing the fabrics, colors, etc. which will require as little maintenance as possible. The need for more care will require more time and expenses

on your part. For example, a white, fabric sofa in the den will show stains and dirt more readily and, therefore, will require more care than a dark, floral fabric sofa or a vinyl sofa.

2.   When buying a sofa or armchair with upholstered arms, if neither has its own separate, detachable arm covers to protect the upholstery, then purchase a coordinated piece of fabric and make arm covers.   These arm covers will help keep the upholstery from becoming soiled and worn and, thus, will extend the life of the furniture and prevent premature replacement or reupholstering costs.

3.   Buy used furniture rather than new furniture.   Some possible sources are:

a.   Secondhand (used) furniture stores. Look in your telephone directory for names, addresses, and telephone numbers.

b.   "Junk" stores. These stores may be found off the beaten path and are often located in the poorer sections of town where the rent is cheaper. The merchandise might be rather jumbled up and dusty, but you could find just the pieces of furniture you need at reasonable prices.

c.   Garage sales.   Occasionally, you can find furniture--and at favorable prices. If the prices are higher than you think they should be, try to bargain for lower prices.

d.   Advertisements in the newspaper. Usually, there will be ads in the paper listing various pieces of furniture for sale.   Normally, you can find furniture in very good condition for 50 percent (or less) of the original purchase prices. Pieces of furniture in not quite as good shape can be bought at even greater savings. If you don't find the furniture you need, put your own ad in the paper. For example, your ad might be worded, "Wanted: good, used bedroom suite. Cheap. Call-------."

e.   Salvation Army stores and stores run by other charitable organizations and churches. These stores sometimes might have used furniture.

f.   Stores which sell new furniture but take trade-ins. You could get some good buys here.

g.   Community bulletin boards and bulletin boards where you work, live, and shop. A friend of mine once advertised a white fabric sofa for $50 on the bulletin board in her apartment complex. The sofa was sold within a few hours. It was in almost perfect condition. The buyer got a super bargain. If you don't find what you want listed on the bulletin boards, put your own notes on them. State what you would like to buy, and list your telephone number. You may get a super bargain, too.

4.   Check out furniture stores which sell only unfinished furniture. You can stain, paint, or "finish" the furniture in whatever way you wish. This furniture is cheaper than comparable new furniture which is already "finished."

5.   Consider buying slightly damaged new furniture. For example, a floor model dresser may be greatly reduced in price because it has several small scratches on one side.

6.   If you have to end up buying new, "finished," first-quality furniture, by all means wait until the furniture goes on sale. Ordinarily, such furniture will be on sale several times during the year at 30 to 50 percent off the original price. Not waiting for the sales is like throwing your money out the window.

7.   Shop around for interest rates when you are about to buy furniture. The rate offered by the store where you are planning to buy the furniture probably will be higher than the rate you can get at your credit union or bank. Even getting a one percent lower interest rate could make a big difference in the amount of money out of your pocket over the life of your loan.

8.   Make an ottoman or footstool by padding and covering a strong wooden box, a plastic milk crate, or other suitable, sturdy container. You should be able to make one for much less money than you would have to pay for a new one.

9.   Consider reupholstering your own furniture instead of buying comparable new furniture. Since labor is a big part of the upholstering expense, you can do the job yourself for much less. If you don't know how to do upholstering and would like to learn, call your County Extension Service to ask if and when such a course might be offered.

If you don't want to do the job yourself, look under "Upholsterers" in the yellow pages of the telephone directory for places which do upholstering. Call local furniture stores to see if they know of people who do upholstering in their homes. Also, check the classified section of the local newspaper for upholstering ads. You probably can hire someone to reupholster your present furniture cheaper than you can buy comparable new furniture; but you probably can buy good, used similar furniture for less than the cost of paying someone to do the reupholstering.

Weigh the pros and cons of all the options and choose the one that is the most financially advantageous to you.

10.   If your sofa and chairs are in need of reupholstering, but your funds are far too short, then make slipcovers for them from inexpensive fabric. If you can't make slip covers, check the prices for ready-made slipcovers at discount and department stores.

11.   Repair and/or refinish your present furniture instead of buying comparable new furniture. If you would like to tackle the job of refinishing your furniture yourself, the necessary supplies (with instructions) are available at various stores, such as some hardware, building supply, discount, and department stores. You can refinish the furniture yourself for a small part of the cost of paying a professional to do it if you are willing to put the time and elbow grease into the job. I have refinished a number of pieces of my furniture by following the instructions on the can of refinisher.

If you can't do the repairing or refinishing yourself, then consider hiring it done if this would be cheaper than buying comparable new furniture. Check the yellow pages, call local furniture stores, and read the classified section of the newspaper to locate people and businesses which repair and refinish furniture.

12.   Recover your present lampshades yourself instead of buying new shades. You should be able to save a sizable amount of money.

13.   If you can't recover your present lampshades, then replace the shades if this would be cheaper than buying complete new lamps.

14.   When your lampcords become frayed, repair or replace the cords rather than discard the lamps. Repairing or even replacing the cords will cost only a small fraction of the price of new lamps.

15.   Recane worn-out seats of chairs if recaning is cheaper than replacing the chairs. If you don't know how to cane, call your County Extension Service for information.

16.   Buy webbing and reweb your patio chairs yourself rather than buy new chairs. Rewebbing is easy and cheap to do.

17.   Spray your fabric upholstered furniture with an appropriate protector (such as Scotchgard) to help keep it from becoming soiled. Protecting the fabric should extend its life and save you money in the long run. (Carefully follow the instructions on the container of protector.)

18.   Use a special mattress pad or other appropriate covering to help protect your mattress for longer wear and higher resale or trade-in value.

WAYS TO SAVE ON THE PURCHASE OF WINDOW
COVERINGS

19.   Buy used draperies, sheers, shades, blinds, and curtain rods, rather than new ones. Used window coverings and rods will cost you far less. Some places to check are:

> a. Garage sales. Occasionally, used draperies, sheers, and curtain rods can be found here.

> b. Advertisements in the newspapers. Sometimes, you will find ads selling used draperies and other types of window coverings. Consider, also, putting your own ad in the paper for the particular window covering you want to buy.

> c. Bulletin boards where you work and at various places in your community and around town. There is a possibility that notes offering draperies and other window coverings might be posted at these places. Also, post your own note stating your phone number and what you want to buy.

20.   Make your draperies yourself instead of buying them ready-made if you can save money. If you don't have the expertise needed to make them, compare the cost of hiring someone to make them with the cost of buying comparable new ones. In general, choose the less expensive route.

21.   If you have to resort to buying new window coverings, try to wait until they are on sale. Put sheets or something else over your windows in the meantime. By waiting, you could save up to 50 percent--or maybe even more.

WAYS TO SAVE ON THE PURCHASE AND
CARE OF FLOOR COVERING

22. If possible, wait and buy floor covering when it is on sale. Since most floor coverings normally will be reduced in price one or more times throughout the year, you should rarely ever need to pay full price.

23. Purchase discontinued and closeout floor covering rather than the regular stock. You should be able to get a good deal. Try to bargain with the merchant for even a lower price than the one being offered.

24. Buy floor covering in "squares" if the price of the total number of "squares" you need is cheaper than one piece of wall-to-wall floor covering and install them yourself.

25. If you can't afford to buy wall-to-wall carpeting, buy a less expensive room-size rug.

26. If you can't afford to buy wall-to-wall carpeting and your floors look reasonably good, consider inexpensive area rugs or no rugs at all.

27. Purchase remnants if they are large enough for your needs. Maybe a store has just the amount you need left over from a large floor-covering job. Remnants should be substantially cheaper than the same amount of floor covering cut directly from a roll. Make sure, however, that you are not really being charged the regular price.

28. Shop around for good, used carpet. Check the advertisements in the newspaper, go to garage sales, ask at carpet stores, and call remodeling and construction companies. For example, you may find some good, used carpet taken out of a residence simply because the new owners wanted to change the color scheme throughout. There should be a very wide gap between the price of new carpet and that of used carpet.

29. When buying carpet or rugs, buy colors which will not easily show spots, stains, and dirt; therefore, the carpet and rugs shouldn't need to be cleaned or replaced as soon. As a result, you can delay the time when you will need to spend additional money.

30. If your carpeting or rugs need cleaning, check with several carpet-cleaning establishments for their prices. Also, call rental stores and other stores (such as some drugstores) which rent carpet-cleaning equipment and ask for the cost of renting such equipment and the cost of the carpet-cleaning solution. You should be able to save money by renting the equipment and doing the cleaning yourself. If so, consider that option.

WAYS TO SAVE ON THE PURCHASE OF SHEETS, TOWELS, AND TABLECLOTHS

31. Buy such items as sheets, pillowcases, towels, bathcloths, tablecloths, and fabric napkins only when they are on sale. The "white sales" can save you money. Watch for the ads in the newspaper. Also, at other times throughout the year, you might find such items reduced in price. In addition, sometimes you can find discontinued or soiled "linens" at great savings. Rare should be the occasion when you will need to pay full price for these items. Paying full price is wasting your money.

32. Purchase slightly "irregular" sheets, pillowcases, towels, and other similar items. Many times, the flaws are almost impossible to detect; and the items should cost a great deal less.

33. Go to garage sales. I have bought very good, used sheets, pillowcases, bathcloths, tablecloths, and beach towels at these sales at mere fractions of the prices of new ones.

34. Check out the advertisements in the newspapers. You may be able to find, for example, good, used bedspreads and sheets at low prices. Also, consider putting your own ad in the newspaper. Your ad might state, "I want to buy a good, used brown floral king-size bedspread. Cheap. Call-------."

35. Make your own bedspreads instead of buying them if they are cheaper to make. You could buy new fabric or use such things as old draperies. Compare the prices of buying them and making them. Choose the option which is the lightest on your pocketbook.

36. Make tablecloths and napkins instead of buying them ready-made if you can make them for less. Compare the costs and choose the less expensive alternative.

37. Cut out and sew pillowcases from the good parts of overly worn sheets. Usually, certain areas of sheets wear out while other areas may have several years of use left in them. Salvaging these sheets saves you the expense of buying pillowcases.

38. Use the good parts of excessively worn bathtowels to make bathcloths and dishcloths. Making them saves you the cost of buying them.

39. Use scraps of leftover fabric, and fashion a "patchwork" quilt. A quilt not only can keep you warm, but it also could be attractive enough to use as a bedspread. Making your own quilt will save you an enormous amount of money. In general, buying a quilt is very expensive.

WAYS TO SAVE ON INTERIOR DECORATING AND ACCESSORIES

40. Some stores offer "free" interior decorating advice. Take advantage of these services if you are not obligating yourself to buy furniture and accessories from the stores or if you do already plan to buy some items from the stores. The stores offer their services because they hope you will buy some items from them.

41.   Read magazines and books on interior decorating at the library, and then do your own interior decorating rather than hire it done. Interior decorators can be expensive.

42.   Check out the latest trends in home furnishings by going to various stores. Then, go home and see what you can do with what you already own to bring them up-to-date with a minimum amount of money. For example, if pillows are the talk of the town, could you sew up some to toss around? If prints are popular, could you make a slipcover for your old sofa? If nature is in, could you collect some driftwood, pine cones, seashells, and dried wild foliage for your house?

43.   Don't buy an extremely large number of bric-a-brac to just sit around and collect dust. Bric-a-brac can cost a lot of money. If you aren't careful, before you know it, you could have many dollars tied up in them. The money you spent for them could have been collecting interest, not dust.

44.   In general, never pay full price for accessories. Since accessories normally are not absolutely essential, wait until they are on sale. Why pay full price for nonessential things?

45.   Put an advertisement in your local newspaper for accessories such as potted plants, wall hangings, and various bric-a-brac. An ad such as the following could get you some cheap plants: "I want to buy potted house plants, two to five feet high. Call-------."

46.   Go to garage sales, flea markets, thrift shops, "junk" stores, and auctions to look for inexpensive items to decorate your home.

47.   Decorate the interior of your house or apartment with free or inexpensive things such as seashells; stones and rocks of interesting shapes and colors; baskets; throw-pillows made from scraps of fabric; driftwood; used books and magazines; jars containing various things from beans to sand; candles; pine cones; posters; dried gourds, pods, red peppers, and Indian corn; and cotton bolls.   Use your imagination to think of dozens of other items.

48.   Use live plants grown from your and friends' slips (cuttings) and seeds in your house, apartment, or room.   Plant them in various containers you already have on hand. Starting your own plants could cost you very little, if any, money.

49.   Learn to make floral arrangements using fresh flowers and greenery from your own yard and from nature to use in decorating.   Making your own will be much cheaper than buying arrangements from the florist.   Check out books on floral arrangements from the library.

50.   Gather dry flowers, leaves, grasses, cones, seeds, and other vegetation from your own yard and from the "wild" and make your own dried arrangements to use in your home. Making them is less expensive than buying them.

WAYS TO SAVE ON COOKING UTENSILS, DISHES, AND PAPER, PLASTIC, AND ALUMINUM PRODUCTS

51.   In general, buy 9 x 11 inch paper towels instead of the 11 x 13 inch size.   Normally, you will get more paper towels for your money with the 9 x 11 size; and for most jobs, this size should be large enough.   (Compare the unit prices of each before making a final decision.)

52.   Buy such things as paper plates, paper towels, and paper dinner napkins on sale rather than pay full price.   If the sale prices are unusually good bargains, consider buying a year's supply if you have enough money and adequate storage space.

53.   Check out the garage sales for used pots, pans, dishes, glasses, flatware, and microwave cooking utensils.   If you can find such items, you should be able to buy them for a very small amount of money.

54.   You may be able to locate used dishes, pots, and pans through advertisements found in your local newspaper. If not, put your own ad in the paper. Buying used items should save you a great deal of money. Your ad could be worded, "I want to buy several used pots and pans. Cheap. Call-------."

55.   Use glass and ceramic dishes and dishes made of other suitable materials you already have on hand rather than buy a lot of special microwave cooking dishes.

56.   If you can't locate used cooking, serving, and eating utensils, and must buy new ones, then wait until they are on sale. It usually will just be a matter of time until they are reduced in price.

57.   Save and wash out good, used plastic bags for use again. Every one saved means one less to buy.

58.   Save and reuse sheets of aluminum foil and various foil containers whenever possible. Reusing them saves you money.

59.   Wash and reuse plastic dinnerwear, containers, forks, spoons, and knives if possible. The more use you can get from them, the less money you will have to expend.

60.   Save plastic and paper grocery bags for lining garbage and wastepaper containers rather than buy liners. Liners cost money.

MISCELLANEOUS WAYS TO SAVE ON HOME FURNISHINGS AND RELATED ITEMS

61.   Ask yourself, "Is it absolutely essential to my survival and well-being to buy this particular item I am thinking of buying?" A "no" answer will save you money.

62.   Shop around for the best prices. Simply put, getting the best deals possible on your purchases decreases your outlay.

63. Be careful about buying on impulse. Impulsive buying can leave you short of money.

64. When appropriate, ask about the warranty on the item you are about to purchase. Always get the warranty in writing. All other things being equal, you generally should choose the brand, etc. with the best warranty. The extent of your warranty could mean the difference in your putting out no money, a little money, or a big chunk of money if the particular item you purchase turns out to be faulty.

65. Follow the use-and-care instructions which come with your furniture, linens, draperies, and other household items. Following the instructions could extend the lives of the items. The longer their lives, the longer you can delay the expense of repairing or replacing them.

66. Whenever possible, take your purchases home yourself and save the delivery charges (unless delivery is free).

67. Limit your purchases of household items which must be dry-cleaned. Dry cleaning is expensive and adds to the overall costs of the items. However, if items you buy require dry cleaning, be sure you do have them dry-cleaned. Washing them might shrink or damage them. Then, you will have the financial burden of replacing or repairing them.

68. In general, do as many of your repairs yourself as you can. Hiring people to make the repairs will cost you more money.

69. Remove stains from carpeting, fabric upholstery, and draperies correctly and as soon as possible before the stains "set," possibly necessitating replacement of the items. Replacements cost money.

70. Use coasters under legs of furniture to help protect floors and/or floor covering. Damage could occur over time without such protection.

71.　If you have items you haven't used for several years and don't anticipate using, consider selling them.　You could put an advertisement in the newspaper and notes on the bulletin boards at work and other places.　Turning unused items into money could be a wise decision.

72.　Don't throw away anything potentially useful.　A cup without a handle; a pan without a lid; an empty coffee can, jar, or margarine container; egg cartons; trays from cookie packages; and dozens of other seemingly useless things have uses. Think about how something can be put to use before discarding it; or, at least keep it around for a reasonable length of time before getting rid of it--you might find a use for it.

CHAPTER 13

HOW TO SAVE MONEY ON YOUR HOUSEHOLD APPLIANCES

Spare and have is better
than spend and crave
                    Franklin

INTRODUCTION

Although major household appliances usually last for many years, the initial purchase can take a large amount of your money at one time if you pay cash. If you finance the purchase, you will have monthly payments (including interest) for an extended period of time. You will have monthly operating costs (utility bills) to pay also. Most appliances will require servicing occasionally, and repairs can be expensive.

This chapter suggests some ways to help keep the costs of purchase, operation, and repair of your appliances at the lowest possible level.

WAYS TO SAVE ON PURCHASING HOUSEHOLD APPLIANCES

1. Ask yourself: "Do I really need the particular appliance I am thinking about buying?" "Do I really need a freezer, an automatic dishwasher, a clothes dryer, or a trash compactor?" "Could I use the money I don't spend on the appliance for something I need more?" For example, if you are thinking about buying a freezer, consider such things as the initial cost of the freezer, the cost of electricity to operate the freezer, how full you realistically think you will keep it, how much you could save by purchasing items on sale if you had a freezer in which to store them, how much you could save on the cost of food by buying fresh fruits and vegetables and freezing them yourself, and how much you could save by buying in bulk if you had a freezer.

Don't just assume that a home freezer will save you money on your food bill. Think about how much and what kind of use you will make of the freezer. Do some indepth reading on freezers at your library before you rush out and buy one.

2. Sometimes replacing a particular appliance will be cheaper in the long run than having it repaired. Make the decision which will give you the greatest financial advantage. (See number 28 in this chapter.)

3. Never be afraid or embarrassed to haggle for the best price possible on appliances. You may be surprised at the discount the dealer will be willing to give you.

4. Buy on sale rather than pay full price for appliances. Usually, most appliances will be on sale sometime or several times throughout the year. You could save from 10 to 25 percent or more of the original price.

5. When you are comparing prices, ask how much trade-in allowance you can receive for your used appliance. If you can

get more for it by selling it yourself rather than trading it in, you may wish to sell it.

6. Be careful about buying on impulse. Appliances are expensive, so considerable thinking and planning should be done prior to purchasing in order that you may buy exactly what you need at the lowest possible price.

7. Don't look first at the most expensive models of the appliance you need. Look first at the bottom-of-the-line models. These basic models, without all the "extras," may fit your needs perfectly. If they don't, then examine the next price level models and so on until you find the appliance with the "extras" you feel you simply cannot do without. If you start with the top-of-the-line models, you may be tempted to buy one which has features you really could do without; and you will pay more for it.

8. When looking for a new or used appliance, shop around and compare prices at a half-dozen or more different places, such as appliance stores, furniture stores which sell appliances, department stores, rental shops, furniture and appliance warehouses, home remodeling businesses, thrift shops, auctions, garage sales, and bulletin boards at your place of work and in your community. Also, ask acquaintances if they know of someone who has a particular appliance for sale. The more places you look, the greater the likelihood you will find what you want at a price you are willing to pay.

9. When shopping for new home appliances, read the information listed on the required Energy Guide labels found on such items as room air-conditioners, clothes washers, dishwashers, freezers, refrigerators, refrigerator-freezers, furnaces, and water heaters. The label on each of these appliances shows the estimated annual operating cost of that particular appliance. Compare different makes and models of the particular appliance you need and determine which would be cheaper to operate. The savings in operating costs could be considerable over the life of the appliance. Those savings could be drawing interest for you if invested.

Also, you should take into account the purchase prices of the various makes and models of the appliances you are comparing. For example, is the purchase price of the most energy efficient 18 cu. ft. self-defrosting refrigerator-freezer greater than the one that is less energy efficient? Will the savings in operating costs over the life of the piece of equipment be more than the difference in the purchase price? In general, select the make and model that will give you the greatest overall financial advantage.

10. When trying to decide between a gas and an electric model of a particular appliance, calculate the annual operating costs using local gas and electric rates. Take these costs into consideration when making your final decision to purchase.

You should consider, also, the initial purchase price and estimated cost of upkeep for both the gas and electric makes and models as well as the cost of converting to gas if your home is not already equipped to handle gas appliances.

11. Don't buy an appliance with a capacity larger than you really need. For example, if you are planning to cool one small room, you probably don't need an 18,000 BTU window air-conditioner. In general, the larger the capacity, the more expensive the appliance. Why waste your money paying for more capacity than you need?

12. When buying appliances, don't buy models with features you probably will never use. Ask yourself, "Do I really need those added options?" Buy appliances with only the options you really need and plan to use. For example, if you never use liquid fabric softener in the clothes washer, would it not be a waste of your money to pay extra for an automatic dispenser for liquid fabric softener?

13. Buy white, rather than colored new appliances, if white ones are cheaper. At some stores, colored appliances are a little more expensive.

14. Buy this year's models of appliances on sale at the end of the year. Often, you can find some excellent buys because business establishments normally try to sell as many "old" models as possible to make room for "new" models.

15. Check around for floor-models when shopping for new appliances. Often, you can purchase such models at drastically reduced prices. My husband and I bought a floor-model electric clothes dryer at considerable savings (probably below cost). It was perfect, with the exception of a tiny scratch on one side; and it carried the same warranty as the nonfloor-models. If you purchase a floor-model, insist on the new model full warranty.

16. Consider buying good, used appliances rather than new ones. Following are some possible ways to locate used appliances:

> a. Place an ad in the local newspaper. The ad might read, "I would like to buy a good, used, small electric range. Call-------."

> b. Watch the ads in the newspaper. For example, some people who are moving out-of-town may not wish to move their large appliances and will offer them at prices considerably below their real value.

> c. Shop the garage sales. Occasionally, home appliances are available.

> d. Check with new appliance and furniture dealers to see if they have good, used appliances for sale which they have taken as trade-ins.

> e. Check out used stores that sell appliances.

Regardless of where you shop for used appliances, be very careful when buying them. You could be buying the problems of the previous owner. Be sure the appliance you buy is in good working condition and get a warranty if possible.

17. Consider buying "rebuilt" household appliances. "Rebuilt" appliances have been checked and repaired and are in working order. One of these may meet your needs as well as a new appliance and, generally, it will be much less expensive. Some "rebuilt" appliances may carry a store warranty for a short period of time--maybe 30 to 90 days.

18. Consider buying certain household equipment with others and sharing the purchase price, upkeep, and use of it. This type of arrangement is best suited to equipment that is used infrequently. For example, you might make a joint purchase of a pressure canner, a floor polisher, or a rug shampooer. Buying equipment with others will cut your initial cash outlay and reduce your costs for repairs and general maintenance. Put your share-purchase, repair, and maintenance agreement in writing, and see that each purchaser has a copy.

19. Take advantage of free items. For example: You need an electric range. An appliance store is offering a free, small microwave oven with the purchase of an electric range. Other appliance stores are offering nothing free with such a purchase. If the prices, models, quality, and various other conditions are the same or very close to the same, buy the range at the store where you can get the free microwave. If you already have a microwave, save the new one and give it as a gift and save yourself some money. Or, place an ad in the newspaper and sell it. The proceeds you receive will reduce the cost of your new range.

20. Ask about, read, and make sure you understand the warranties on any appliances you are considering buying. Compare warranties of various makes and models. All other things being equal, choose the makes and models offering the best warranties. The better the warranties, the greater the potential financial benefits for you.

21. Before you purchase an appliance, make sure service will be available near where you live. For example, if you plan to buy a particular brand in a city 60 miles from your home, check to see if that brand can be serviced locally. Also, if you plan to buy a certain brand locally, be sure that it can be serviced locally. Don't just assume that a particular brand can be serviced near where you live. The farther you or the repair person has to travel, the higher the overall expenses will be.

22. If you have the necessary transportation and the help required to unload and set up, deliver your own appliances, unless delivery is free. Delivery charges increase your costs for the appliances you purchase.

23. If you are "handy" with tools, install your own appliances, unless installation is free. In general, don't pay for something you can do yourself.

24. When buying an appliance, try to get terms of 30, 60, or 90 days with no interest charges, rather than pay cash or finance it with interest charges. By getting "same-as-cash" terms--for example, "90 days same-as-cash"--your money can be drawing interest for 90 days. The interest you earn on your money will, in a manner of speaking, reduce the purchase price of the appliance. Also, you will pay no interest on the purchase.

WAYS TO SAVE ON APPLIANCE REPAIRS

25. Always follow the instructions in the owner's use-and-care manual for the proper care and operation of your appliance to help ensure long service and minimize the need for repairs. The longer you can use an appliance before having to repair or replace it, the more money you will save.

26. After the warranty on an appliance has expired, do as many of the required repairs as you can yourself rather than take it to the repair shop or call a service person to come to your home. Do not repair or attempt to repair an appliance yourself while it is still under warranty. Doing so could void your warranty. Read your warranty to be sure.

If you do not have the necessary skill or expertise to do your own repairs, consider taking an introductory course in household appliance repair which might be offered at a nearby college, high school, vocational school or technical institute, or by the County Extension Service. Such courses normally are relatively inexpensive. You should be able to do your own repairs for less than the cost of hiring someone to do them.

27. Before you call a service person to come to your home to repair an appliance, read the section on "problems" in the owner's use-and-care manual which came with the appliance. It will list some things to check. For example, is the appliance plugged in? Do the batteries need replacing? Is the appliance turned on? Has a fuse blown or has the circuit breaker tripped? Does a button on the appliance need to be pressed? Does a knob on the appliance need to be turned? Reading the use-and-care manual could save you the cost of a service call.

28. If you have an old appliance which needs repairing, consider how much the repairs will cost. Also, consider the age and overall mechanical condition of the appliance. Ask a reputable, reliable service person his or her professional opinion regarding whether you should have it repaired or replaced. Based on all the facts you have, make the decision that will be to your financial advantage in the long run.

29. Check with relatives, friends, neighbors, and co-workers for their recommendations of reputable, reliable, honest, and reasonably-priced appliance repair persons. Using a repair person without these attributes could cost you more money now and in the long run.

WAYS TO SAVE ON PURCHASING TELEVISIONS

30. Buy a black-and-white television instead of a color set. Normally, black-and-white sets are much cheaper.

31. Consider buying a portable television set rather than a console. A portable should be much cheaper. A portable can be more easily taken to the repair shop if repairs are needed, thus saving yourself the cost of a home service call or a pick-up and delivery charge.

32. Check on the cost of a floor-model/demonstration television set versus a new one. You could save a considerable amount of money. Ask about the warranty. Insist on the full warranty which is offered on new sets. Keep in mind, however, that some floor-models are left running continually throughout the store hours. Ask the salesperson about this. You should have to pay much less for a set that has run continually over a period of time than you would pay for one turned on only occasionally.

33. Consider buying a good, used television rather than a new one. Some sources are hotel/motel chains that are replacing their sets, advertisements in the newspaper, television repair shops, appliance stores, rental shops, garage sales, and furniture stores which sell television sets. The purchase price of a used television set should be much less than that for a new set. If you do purchase a used set, be sure it is in good working order and get a written warranty if possible.

34. If you decide to purchase a new television set, trade in your used set if trading it is more profitable than selling it yourself. Ask the dealer how much he or she can allow you for the set as a trade-in. Then place an ad in the newspaper and see if you can sell it for more than the dealer will allow. Any amount you can realize over what the dealer will allow will reduce the cost of the new set.

35.   Ask about, understand, and compare warranties when shopping for a television set--new or used. With all other things being equal, choose the set offering the best warranty. The better the warranty, the less money you potentially will be out for repairs.

36.   If you have suitable transportation and adequate help to unload it, deliver your television to your home yourself and save delivery charges. If delivery is free, let the store deliver it.

37.   When you are purchasing a television set, ask if the store offers "30, 60, or 90 days same-as-cash." If it does, take advantage of the free credit. You can let your money draw interest until the bill is due.

38.   Before you buy a television set, determine if you can obtain service near where you live. The longer the distance you or the repair person must travel to get your set repaired, the greater will be the overall cost of repairs. Someone must pay for the cost of travel. Usually it will be you.

WAYS TO SAVE ON TELEVISION REPAIRS

39.   Always follow the instructions in the owner's use-and-care manual which came with your television set. The manual instructs you on the proper care and operation of the set. Following the instructions should extend the life of your television and minimize the need for repairs and, thus, save you money.

40.   Ask people you know for recommendations on where to have your television set repaired. Their past experiences could save you money and problems.

41.   Before you call a television repair person to come to your home or before you take your set to a repair shop, read carefully the "problems" section in your owner's use-and-care manual. It will list some things to check. For example: Is your set plugged in? Is it turned on? Is the antenna wire connected to the television and to the antenna? Does a knob on the set need adjusting? You just might save yourself the cost of a service call or a pick-up and delivery charge.

42. Take your television set to the repair shop yourself if possible. Save the cost of a home service call or a pick-up and delivery charge.

MISCELLANY

43. Turn off all television sets, radios, and tape players if no one is watching or listening to them. The more they are used, the sooner they have to be repaired or replaced--and this takes money out of your pocket (if they are no longer under warranty).

44. Think twice before purchasing service contracts on your major home appliances and television sets. The contracts are expensive. Ask yourself if the purchase of such a contract would really save you money in the long run. As the appliances and televisions become older, the higher the annual contract premiums.

It may be to your advantage not to purchase the contracts and to place the amount of money you normally would pay for the service contracts each year into a savings account. Your money could be earning interest. If repairs are required, take money from the account to pay for them. If it is not necessary to use all the money in the account for repairs, you can use the remaining amount toward the purchase of a replacement appliance or television set when the need arises. Consider all the pros and cons when making the final decision.

45. When you purchase a sewing machine, select one with only the attachments, stitches, and options you really need. Why pay for features you probably will never use? For example, if you need a machine only for occasional mending, buy a basic, inexpensive one. Also, consider buying a portable machine rather than a cabinet model. A portable usually is cheaper. Consider a used machine. I bought a basic, used portable one 20 years ago; and it still serves my needs. Regardless of what machine you do buy, ask about and understand the warranty. Use and care for your machine according to the instructions in your owner's use-and-care manual to extend its useful life and cut repair bills.

46. If you plan to finance the purchase of your appliance, television, or sewing machine, shop around for the best interest rate available. The rate offered by the store where you plan to make the purchase may well be higher than the rate at your credit union or bank. A saving of just one percent in the interest rate can be worth your efforts in shopping around.

47. If you have not used particular pieces of household equipment for several years, consider selling them. You could place ads in the newspaper or notes on various bulletin boards. The money you receive from the sale of idle equipment can be placed in your savings account or used for everyday expenses.

48. Before you purchase a household appliance, television set, or sewing machine, go to your local library and consult *Consumer Reports* and *Consumers' Research Magazine*. Read about different makes, models, and options. Being informed should help you make a better financial decision.

CHAPTER 14

HOW TO SAVE ON YOUR HOUSING COSTS

*Resolve not to be poor: whatever
you have, spend less*
                    Samuel Johnson

INTRODUCTION

For many people, housing is their biggest, single monthly expense; and some people spend a disproportionate amount of their income on housing. Some are trying to keep up with the Joneses, some are trying to fulfill the American dream of owning their own home, some see a nice home as a status or success symbol, while others just want a place to live and to which to retreat after a hard day at work. Whatever your reason, this chapter gives you some suggestions for saving money on your housing expenses.

WAYS TO SAVE ON BUYING A HOME

1. Calculate if renovating your present residence would be cheaper than selling it and buying another one. Get .estimates from several remodeling companies, and check out the costs of

homes on the market. Compare these figures, and choose the option most financially advantageous to you now and in the long run.

2.   When you are planning to buy a home, choose a reliable, reputable, and competent real estate agent to assist you. He or she should be able to advise you on the following: The best locations for future appreciation of housing values and locations which are "questionable"; current home prices; interest rates and availability and variety of financing options; quality of construction and physical and mechanical conditions of various homes; negotiating for the best purchase price; and the many other aspects of buying a home.

However, don't blindly follow all of his or her suggestions. Understand that the agent is trying to make a living. When looking for an agent, ask your friends, people with whom you work, relatives, your banker, your lawyer, and others for recommendations. A carefully chosen agent could save you money now and in the future.

3.   You might be able to buy a home at a lower price during the coldest months of the year when fewer people are out looking for a place. Also, try the hottest months of the year. If you are the only viable prospect a seller has had in a few months, and depending upon his or her urgency to sell, the seller may be willing to accept your reduced offer.

4.   When considering the purchase of a dwelling, make sure you definitely want a particular home before you put down your earnest money. You probably will not be able to get the money back if you simply decide you don't want that place.

5.   Ask about written warranties when you are looking at new homes. Some builders guarantee the homes they build against certain defects for 10 years. Also, if you are looking at homes less than 10 years old, ask the present owners if the homes have written warranties on them which are transferable to the new owners. Having such a warranty on the new or used

dwelling you buy could save you money on repairs should the home have defects or develop problems during the warranty period.

6. Buy living quarters only as large as you really need. For example, if you are single with no children, do you really need a two-story four-bedroom house? Generally, the larger the house, the higher the purchase price, property taxes, utility bills, homeowners insurance, and expenses for upkeep.

7. When you are shopping for a home to buy, greatly consider the location. For example, even though you can buy a house at a lower price in a certain area, think twice before you do so if the area is deteriorating and if the houses are decreasing or likely to decrease (or not increase) in value. Otherwise, over the years, you could lose money on your investment.

8. Shop around for living accommodations. Look at a number of possibilities. Generally, it might not be financially wise to buy the first and only place you look at. (Of course, there are exceptions to this suggestion.) Shopping around should give you a better understanding of housing prices and could help you negotiate a better deal when you do buy.

9. When looking for a home to buy, be sure to include places for sale by the owner. If you can buy directly from the owner, he or she doesn't have to pay a real estate agent a commission fee and may be willing to pass part of the savings along to you. Negotiate for your part of the savings.

10. If you are considering the purchase of a condominium or townhouse, try to ascertain what the increase in your monthly maintenance fee will be in the years to come. Will a new roof be needed shortly on all of the units? Will the swimming pool need repairing soon? Will the streets within the complex need major repairs within a few years? Will the grounds need considerable work? The expenses of these repairs and replacements will be borne jointly by all the owners of the individual units. If these or other problems are evident, before long you might see a drastic increase in your monthly maintenance fee.

11.   Consider purchasing a new or used mobile home if your finances are low.   Some mobile homes are less expensive than conventional housing.   Shop around for the best price.   Also, check to see how much you will have to pay each month to rent a space to put your mobile home on (or how much you would have to pay to buy your own lot).   What about the costs of "hookups" to water, sewer facilities, electricity, and gas?   Find out the cost of having your mobile home moved and "set up."   What about interest rates on a mobile home loan if you have to finance your purchase?

12.   Consider the possibility of purchasing a duplex.   Live in one side and rent out the other side.   The rent you receive could help in making your monthly mortgage payments.

13.   Check out very carefully and thoroughly the housing you are planning to buy to make sure you are aware of such things as the following:

a. any major structural problems with the floors, walls, ceilings, windows, doors, gutters, etc.

b. plumbing problems

c. adequacy and condition of the electrical wiring

d. existence of termites and/or evidence of termite damage

e. adequacy of and problems with the heating and cooling systems

f. adequacy and condition of the sewage system

g. condition of the garage

h. condition of the appliances

i. adequacy of the insulation

j. condition of the water

k. condition of floor coverings

l. evidence of moisture problems within the house, including the basement

m. condition of the roof

n. condition of the foundation

o. condition of the fireplace

p. adequacy and condition of the lawn, trees, and other plants

q. condition of any outbuildings

This inspection is even more important if you are buying an older home. If you don't have the background and sufficient knowledge to do the inspection yourself, hire a professional housing inspector. The inspection could detect existing and potential problems. If there are problems but you still want to buy the home, point these problems out to the seller. Negotiate for a reduced price of at least enough to cover all or a reasonable part of the repairs and replacements relating to these problems. Such an inspection could save you much more than the cost of the inspection.

14. Don't be afraid to make an offer which is considerably lower than the "asking" price for a home. You can always raise your offer. Negotiate to get the best possible price. Many sellers ask more than they expect to receive in anticipation that potential buyers will offer less. You could save yourself thousands of dollars.

15. When you are buying a home, try to get the seller to pay as many of the closing costs as you can. The more the seller pays, the less you will have to pay.

16. When you are shopping for a home to buy, ask about property taxes on the ones you are serious about. Property taxes normally vary from city to city and usually are lower outside the city limits. Property taxes add to the overall cost of housing.

17. Generally, when you buy a residence, pay as large a down payment as you can afford; and you will save money on interest over the years because you will be financing a smaller loan (assuming that you cannot afford to pay cash for the purchase). Normally, you will also save a large amount of money in interest by financing the home for fewer years, for example, 20 years instead of 30 years.

18. When financing the purchase of your home, shop around for the lowest interest rate. Even one-fourth of one percent could save you thousands of dollars over the life of the loan. Also, ask about the different types of residential mortgage loans available. For example, one of the nontraditional types is the graduated-payment mortgage. One of the nontraditional loans might be suitable for your particular situation. Check with five to ten different financial institutions to compare interest rates and types of mortgage loans.

Are you a veteran? Are you at the low-income level? Are you a first-time buyer? Specific categories of people could qualify for lower interest rates than the current ones. Make sure you understand every word of your loan agreement before you sign it. Is the interest rate subject to change? Is there a substantial penalty for early repayment of the loan? What happens if you are late in making your monthly payments? Knowing the answers to such questions beforehand could save you money.

19. Don't pay excessive interest rates just so you can be a homeowner. Try waiting until the rates come down some. I know personally of one buyer who financed a home purchase at 18 percent in 1981. In 1986, the mortgage rates were down to around nine percent. The higher the interest rates, of course, the higher your monthly payments. However, factors in addition to interest rates must also be considered, for example the annual inflation rate, when you are contemplating postponing a home purchase.

20. If you finance the purchase of your home, try to get a clause put into the loan agreement that you can prepay your loan at any time and not be charged a penalty (or at least, be charged only a minimum penalty). This clause might possibly save you many thousands of dollars. For example, if mortgage interest rates drop (as they did in 1986 to about nine percent, down from 18 percent in 1981), you could borrow money at a lower rate and pay off your present loan taken out at a higher rate.

21. When buying a residence which has a mortgage on it, try to assume the present mortgage if the interest rate is lower on it than the rate would be on a new loan. Some mortgages are transferable with no escalation in interest rates. Finding such a mortgage could save you a considerable amount of money in interest over the life of your loan.

22. When financing the purchase of your home, see if you can get the mortgage loan without a property tax escrow account and a homeowners insurance escrow account. Why let the financial institution store your money (usually without paying you interest) until it is time to pay your real estate taxes and your insurance premium? You could put the amount each month into a savings account and draw interest. (If the lender insists on the escrow accounts, ask that interest be paid to you on them!)

23. If you financed your home at a high interest rate, you may be able to renegotiate for a lower interest rate if rates have gone down, or borrow money at a lower rate and pay off the loan. Check with the financial institution where you financed your purchase and see what options are open to you.

WAYS TO SAVE ON SELLING YOUR HOME

24. Try to sell your home yourself and save the cost of a real estate agent's commission. Agents usually charge around six percent (it can be more) of the selling price. I sold my condominium on my own through an advertisement in the newspaper and saved myself thousands of dollars. I utilized a title company to handle the closing (paperwork and various legal matters).

25. If you choose to place your home with a real estate agent, ask the agent if, under certain, specified conditions, he or she would be willing to accept a rate lower than the usual rate of commission. For example, you might agree to pay six percent commission if your agent sells your house within three months, a reduced commission if selling it takes longer, and even a lower commission if *you* find a buyer for your house. Make this proposal to several reliable real estate agents until you are able to get the terms you want, or near what you want--you could save a great deal of money.

26. If you are selling your dwelling, try to get the buyer to pay as much of the closing costs as you can. The more the buyer pays, the less you will have to pay.

27. Keep records (receipts, invoices, contracts, cash register tapes, and cancelled checks) of all improvements which you make to your home. These records could be financially beneficial, taxwise, when you sell your home--they could possibly lower the amount of income tax you will have to pay on the profit you make on the sale of your home.

WAYS TO SAVE ON RENTING

28. Live in the home of someone rent free in exchange for doing work around the house. Check out the classified section of the newspaper for advertisements offering such arrangements. If you don't find such offers, put your own ad in the newspaper. The ad might state, "Will do work around the house in exchange for free rent. Call-------."

Some ads even offer free rent to someone who is available to be at the person's home overnight to provide a degree of security to the person; no work is required.

29. Rent a room rather than an apartment or house. A room should be much cheaper, plus you usually won't have to pay any part of the utilities and telephone base rate. Often, you will have free use of the washer and dryer and be given cooking and television-viewing privileges. Some landlords even provide the use of sheets and towels to the renter free of charge.

30. Get a roommate and share equally the cost of the rent, utilities, and telephone base rate. You can save 50 percent. Ask your friends, and check the advertisements in the newspaper for someone who would like a roommate. If you can't find a roommate, then put an advertisement in the newspaper yourself. It could read, "Male roommate wanted. Share two-bedroom, furnished apartment. Split rent, utilities, and telephone base rate. Call-------."

31. Rent a house or apartment no larger than you really need. Usually, the larger the accommodation, the higher the rent.

32. If you are currently renting, consider moving to a smaller house or apartment if the one in which you live is larger than you really need. Rent and utilities should be lower for a smaller one.

33.   Continue to live with your parents as long as possible. If you are making enough money, you might want to pay them a specified amount monthly for your room and board.   This amount, generally, should be substantially less than the cost of renting and maintaining an apartment of your own.

34.   Read your lease carefully before you vacate your rented living quarters. If you vacate before your lease expires, you might still be liable for payment of the monthly rent until the end of the lease period or until a new renter for the place is found (whichever comes first). If this is the case, delaying your move until your lease expires could be to your financial advantage. Otherwise, you might be paying rent on this place and your new residence at the same time.

35.   Give the required number of days' notice before vacating your rented living accommodations. Otherwise, you could lose your deposit.

36.   When you vacate your rented housing at the end of your lease, leave it clean and in the shape it was when you moved in. Otherwise, you could lose your deposit; and you might be charged for certain damage you caused and for cleaning which has to be done. For example, you could be billed $20 for cleaning the inside of the oven, $100 for cleaning the carpet, $15 for cleaning the inside of the refrigerator, and the full cost of replacing a broken window.

WAYS TO SAVE ON HOME MAINTENANCE

37.   Do as many of your home repairs yourself as possible rather than hire them done. If you don't have the necessary skills for some tasks, check out the possibility of taking a course in simple home repairs. Call your local vocational-technical school, high school, community college, and County Extension Service for information on if and when such courses might be offered. Doing your own repairs will be cheaper than hiring someone to do the work for you.

38. Don't postpone minor home repair jobs until they become major problems. Major repairs will cost more money. For example, if you have a small leak in the roof on your home, repair the faulty area right away, rather than wait and risk extensive water damage to your home.

39. Clean spots off the walls in your home instead of repainting as often as you normally would. My husband and I have satisfactorily spot-cleaned our walls and delayed the expense of repainting for several years. Postponing periodical painting will save you a sizable amount of money over the years.

40. Paint your own house--inside and outside--and save yourself a large amount of money since most of the cost of the paint job is for labor. If you are not familiar with the different kinds and qualities of paint, get assistance from the salesperson in choosing the correct paint for the job you want to do. Perhaps the store also has information on how to prepare the surface for painting, how to paint, and other important items relating to painting. If the store doesn't, then check at your public library for information.

41. Do your own wallpapering and save yourself the high cost of labor. If you have never wallpapered before, obtain the necessary information to do it properly before starting. Your public library and stores selling wallpaper should be good sources of information.

42. If you live where the temperature reaches freezing, wrap your exposed water pipes to help keep them from freezing and possibly bursting during winter and causing water damage to your home and its contents. This preventive measure could save you a lot of money in the future.

43. In general, you usually should deal only with local, reputable, well-established home repair businesses--not "fly-by-night," "will be in this area only two weeks," "door-to-door," and "working out of the back of the truck" operators. Check these sorts out with your local or state Better Business Bureau, local

Chamber of Commerce, and local or state Consumer Protection Office. Don't let yourself be swindled out of your hard-earned money. (First of all, never open your door to strangers!)

WAYS TO SAVE ON MOVING EXPENSES

44.   Try to get your present employer to pay all or part of the cost of your move if you are moving to a new location with the same company or organization.

45.   If you are changing employers, try to get your new employer to pay all or a reasonable share of your moving expenses.

46.   When you move, borrow a truck (if you don't own one) from a friend or your employer to transport your possessions. Also, get some of your friends to help load your things (and unload them too). The above should be your cheapest way to move.   Be sure to call your homeowners insurance agent concerning coverage of your possessions during the move.

47.   If you can't borrow a truck for your move, the next cheapest way should be to rent a truck, such as a U-Haul or Ryder truck. Do your own packing, loading, unloading, and driving. If you don't have one or two people to help with the loading and unloading, you usually can hire a moving company to load your vehicle at your present residence and unload it at your new residence. If you are moving a considerable distance away, you shouldn't have any problem hiring a different moving company at your destination to unload the truck.

This way of moving will be much less expensive than hiring a professional moving company to do the complete moving job. Before you actually go to rent the truck, talk with your homeowners insurance agent about coverage on your belongings during the move.

48. Get estimates from several different moving companies if you're going to utilize professional movers. Set up a time for them to come to your home to look at your belongings. Rates could vary considerably among moving companies.

49. When you are calling around to compare prices, ask the moving companies if their charges are cheaper during certain months of the year and certain days of the week or month (nonpeak times). Move when the rates are the lowest, if at all possible, and save yourself some money.

50. If you hire a moving company to do your moving, make sure you understand what the company is liable for if some of your possessions are stolen or damaged during the move. If this coverage is insufficient, consider purchasing additional coverage unless your homeowners insurance covers your goods in transit. Not having adequate coverage during your move could cost you money out of your pocket if damage or theft occurs.

51. Do your own packing (if permitted) even if you are going to use movers. Professional movers normally charge extra for packing. However, some professional moving companies might move only what they have packed themselves or assume liability for only the company-packed items.

52. If you hire professional movers to move you, make sure you make a detailed, itemized list for yourself of all of your items to be moved before the movers arrive. A list can more readily alert you to items lost or stolen during the move and help you to avoid forgetting to include such items in your insurance claim.

53. Before you move, sell everything you no longer need or want. Advertise the items in the newspaper, put a note on the bulletin board where you work, and/or have a garage sale. The less you have to move, the less your moving expenses should be.

54.   Carry important papers and documents, jewelry, money, and other small valuable items with you, rather than trust them to the movers. Carrying them with you could save you the cost of replacing them or the hassle of collecting insurance on them (and, maybe, having to shoulder part of the loss yourself, such as the deductible amount).

55.   Remember to arrange beforehand to have your telephone and utilities "disconnected" at your old residence as soon as you vacate it.   It is a waste of your money to continue these services, even for one day, if you are not there to benefit from them (unless there is a valid reason for continuing them).

56.   Be sure to fill out change-of-address cards and send them to all people and businesses from whom you receive mail in time so that your incoming mail will not go to your old address after you have moved. For example, if bills go to your old address first, have to be put back in the mail by the new resident at your old address, and then have to be rerouted to you by the post office, they may not reach you in time for you to pay them in order to avoid late charges.

WAYS TO PROTECT YOUR HOME FROM BURGLARS

Take precautions to protect your home and possessions from burglary. Even if you have homeowners insurance, replacing what is stolen or damaged could cost you a considerable amount of money out of your pocket--maybe more than it would have cost you to do some things to make your home more secure. (However, don't make your home so burglar-proof that you can't get out quickly if you need to.)   This section suggests some things you can do to help protect your home and your belongings. Some of the suggestions will cost you nothing, while others will require only a minimum outlay of money.

57.   Write down the emergency telephone numbers of the local police and county sheriff's office and the numbers of several nearby neighbors. Keep the numbers by your telephone(s). Having the numbers handy can decrease the time it takes you to call for help.

58. If you live in a rural area, don't assume that you are immune from burglaries. You are not.

59. Protect your home during the day as you would at night. Burglaries also occur during daylight hours.

60. Check into the possibility of organizing a Neighborhood Watch where you live. A Neighborhood Watch should help to deter burglaries in your area.

61. Keep the outside doors to your home locked at all times, including when you are at home. Locked doors make it more difficult for burglars to enter your home and might discourage or prevent them from breaking in.

62. Keep your garage door closed at all times. A closed door could help prevent a break in.

63. Keep all gates in the fence around your house locked at all times. Locked gates (especially tall ones and tall fences) might possibly make it harder for a potential intruder to enter your premises. If entrance is too difficult, he or she may give up and move on to an easier target.

64. Don't leave house keys hidden outside your home. A burglar might locate the keys and unlock an outside door to your home.

65. If you store valuables within your home, hide them and do so in the most unlikely places possible. Professional burglars know about most of the ordinary hiding places.

66. Make sure shrubbery and trees don't hide doors and windows. Shielded entrances can provide greater cover for burglars to enter your residence unnoticed by neighbors and passers-by.

67. Don't open your door to a stranger. By opening your door, you could be giving a would-be burglar easy entrance into your home.

68. Don't put your name and residential address on your keyring. If you happen to lose it, a dishonest person could gain entry to your home.

69. Don't make it common knowledge that you are going to be away from your home. Burglars can take advantage of your announced absence to rob your home with more ease.

70. When you are away from your home, don't leave notes on the door such as, "I will return at 4:00 p.m.," or "I will be back in town next Tuesday." Such notes let burglars know their break ins won't be hampered by the residents.

71. If you are going to be gone from home for several days, stop your mail, newspaper, and various other regularly scheduled deliveries. An alternative to stopping deliveries is to ask a friend to pick up such items each day from your house and keep them until you return. A box full of mail and a pile of newspapers alert a potential burglar that the residents probably are not at home and, therefore, that they will not foil an attempt at entry.

72. Consider leaving a radio running inside your home when you are away. A radio which is on implies that someone is home; and, thus, the burglar might decide not to try to break in.

73. When you are gone from your home at night, use timers to turn lights on and off at various times and at different locations throughout your home. Another, less expensive option is to use light-sensitive devices to automatically turn lights on at the appropriate degree of outside darkness and off at the appropriate degree of outside lightness. The lights could help deter burglars.

74. If you plan to be away from home for more than a few days, consider asking the police or sheriff's department to check your house regularly while you are gone. Such checks, if observed by a would-be burglar, could discourage the planned break in. The checks could also stop a break in while in progress.

75. Make your home look as though you are there. For example, if you leave draperies open while you are home, do so while you are away from home. If burglars think people are home, they might decide not to try to break into your residence.

76. Have someone to keep your lawn mowed if you will be away from your home for an extended length of time. An overgrown lawn implies that no one is at home. Therefore, a burglar assumes that your home is easy prey.

77. Ask someone to stay in your home when you are away from it at a family member's funeral (if the deceased resided at your residence). Burglars read the obituary column and often burglarize homes while the residents are at funerals.

78. Consider utilizing a house-sitter while you are away from home. The presence of a person within your home could prevent a possible burglary.

79. Install sufficient outside lighting to light up all entrances to your home at night. A well-lighted home should help to discourage a break in.

80. Use only solid-core or metal-clad doors on the outside entrances to your home. Such doors are more difficult to break through than ordinary hollow-core doors.

81. Make sure outside door frames are solid, substantial, and firmly attached to your home. Door frames with these qualities should make it harder for someone to break down your doors.

82. Make sure door hinges are on the inside of doors and not on the outside. If hinges are on the outside, they can more easily be removed to allow entrance by a dishonest person.

83. Install wide-angle peepholes in all outside doors of your home. These door viewers enable you to see who is at your door, to decide whether or not to acknowledge their presence, and to determine if you should open your door to them. If they are strangers, there is always a possibility they could be burglars.

84. Use deadbolt locks with at least a one-inch throw on all outside doors of your home, including the door leading from the garage to your house. If glass is near enough to a lock to allow someone to break the glass and reach through to the lock, make sure the lock requires a key to unlock it from the inside. These precautions could help to prevent an unauthorized entry.

85. Have heavy-duty night chains on all appropriate outside doors of your home, and make sure they are mounted so as to withstand an attempted forced intrusion. Heavy-duty night chains provide added protection. (Ordinary night chain systems are relatively easy to break through.)

86. Make sure windows and sliding glass doors are securely constructed and have strong, dependable, and tight-fitting locks. Consider additional locks and latches. These precautions could help to prevent break ins.

87. With the sliding glass door closed and locked, wedge a wooden dowel into its bottom track. The dowel should prevent the door from being opened if unlocked by a potential intruder.

88. Consider installing reinforced glass in vulnerable places in your home. This glass will be more difficult than ordinary glass to penetrate.

89. Consider installing burglar bars over windows which are excessively susceptible to being entered by a burglar. Bars will provide a high degree of resistance to entry.

90. Consider installing a burglar alarm system in your home. An alarm system could scare off a burglar if accidentally activated by him or her.

WAYS TO PROTECT YOUR HOME FROM FIRE

Take steps beforehand to help prevent fires in your home. Replacing or making repairs to your home, furniture, appliances, and other personal possessions could cost you money even if you do have homeowners insurance. A few examples of what you can do to help avoid fires in your home are listed below. Most of the suggestions will cost you nothing or only a relatively small amount of money.

91. Don't smoke in bed. There is always a risk of your falling asleep with a lighted cigarette in your hand and igniting bed coverings or other items.

92. Don't let children play with matches. They could accidentally start fires.

93. Be careful with natural Christmas trees. They can dry out quickly and become fire hazards.

94. If you store a container of gasoline for use in your lawn mower, for example, make sure the container is safe for storing gasoline and that you store it away from heat. Store the container in an outbuilding, if possible, and not in your home or attached garage. Following these suggestions could help you to prevent a fire in your home.

95. If you have a chimney and use it, have it inspected regularly. Inspections can detect problems which could, if not corrected, cause fires in your home.

96. If you have built a fire in your fireplace, close the front of the fireplace when leaving your home or going to bed. Otherwise, sparks from the fireplace could start a fire without your being immediately aware of it.

97. If you have a furnace, have it inspected regularly. Routine inspections could reveal problems which might, if not corrected, start fires in your home.

98. Don't overload your electrical wiring system. If you have reasons to suspect that the wiring is faulty or is not adequate, pay an electrician to check it for you. This inspection might possibly prevent a fire in your home.

99. Install smoke alarms throughout your home according to the instructions which come with them. Smoke alarms could alert you to fires in their early stages; and, thus, considerable loss of property might be prevented.

100. Keep several fire extinguishers at different locations throughout your home, as they can be used to put out fires while the fires are still relatively small.

MISCELLANEOUS WAYS TO SAVE ON HOUSING COSTS

101. If you are planning to build a house, consider if you have the knowledge and expertise to be your own contractor and also to do some of the actual, physical work yourself. Cutting out the cost of hiring a contractor could save you thousands of dollars. Friends of mine took this route and saved over $25,000 on the cost of building their new home.

102. If you own your home, consider selling it if it is much larger than you need; and buy a smaller, less expensive one.

Generally, the smaller and less expensive the home, the lower the property taxes, utility bills, homeowners insurance, and expenses for upkeep.

103. If you are a senior citizen or low-income person, check with your local housing authority or office on aging to see if you qualify for subsidized house payments or rental payments. Getting help with your payments can save you money out of your own pocket.

104. Rent out one or more bedrooms in your home. You could rent the bedroom(s) on a long-term lease of one year, on a short-term lease of anywhere from several months up to a year, or on a weekly or monthly basis. Be sure to check local ordinances to make sure renting out a room to someone is permissible in your area. The rent you receive could offset part or all of your housing costs.

105. Rent out one or more rooms in your home on the bed-and-breakfast format to tourists for one or more days at a time. Check with the local Tourist Bureau, Chamber of Commerce, and Zoning Commission concerning the laws, required permits, and publicizing of your bed-and-breakfast arrangement. The money you receive could partially or totally compensate you for your rent or house payments, utilities, and upkeep.

106. Check with the local Internal Revenue Service (IRS) office concerning the possible tax advantages of using an area or room in your home as an office for business purposes. Such use could help lower your federal income taxes.

CHAPTER 15

HOW TO SAVE ON YOUR INSURANCE COSTS

Who will not lay up a penny
shall never have many
Thomas Fuller

INTRODUCTION

Many people, perhaps you, can scarcely afford all the various kinds of insurance available to them. However, you cannot afford to be without some types of insurance, such as automobile insurance, if you own a vehicle; homeowners insurance, if you own living accommodations; insurance on your personal property; life insurance, if you want to make sure your survivors are adequately cared for; and disability income insurance, if you and others depend on your monthly paycheck for survival.

This chapter suggests some ways to keep necessary insurance expenditures as low as possible.

WAYS TO SAVE ON AUTOMOBILE INSURANCE

1. Shop around for the best prices on automobile insurance. Call a half-dozen or so different, reputable, independent insurance agencies representing different auto insurance companies. Also, check with insurance companies which sell directly to customers. See if your employer offers group auto insurance. In addition, check with professional organizations and other groups to which you (or your spouse) belong or could belong for possible group auto insurance. Joining and paying membership dues just to be eligible for the group policy may be worthwhile.

Always compare prices for similar coverage. The premiums usually vary quite a lot among different companies. Even a small difference in premiums can add up to a substantial amount over many years, not to mention the interest you could earn on the savings. Ask the various agents to fully explain the coverage in their policies in simple terms so you can understand what their policies cover and do not cover. Choose the policy which you think is the best for your particular situation. After you receive your copy of the policy in the mail, read it carefully and thoroughly. If there is anything in it you don't understand, call your agent and ask for clarification.

2. When you are checking around to compare premiums and coverage of automobile insurance, ask about discounts. Some companies give discounts on premiums for the following:

    a.   For not smoking.

    b.   For insuring two or more autos in the same family with the company.

    c.   For having a good driving record (for not having had an auto accident in so many years).

    d.   For having successfully completed a driver training course. For example, the American Association of

Retired Persons (AARP) offers the 55 Alive/Mature Driving Program. This is a driver-improvement, six-session, eight-hour course which helps older people update their driving knowledge and sharpen their driving skills.

Check your telephone directory to see if a local AARP Chapter is listed. If so, an officer in the chapter should be able to give you information on the driving course. If you can't locate a local chapter, contact AARP at 1909 K Street, N. W., Washington, D. C. 20049 to get additional information and to find out when the course might possibly be offered in your area. Also, ask around to see if other organizations or local schools offer driver training courses.

e.   For driving limited miles (low-mileage drivers).

f.   For being, for example, over 60 years of age (mature drivers, senior citizens). Age requirements may vary among companies.

g.   For having outstanding student scholastic records.

Simply put, discounts decrease the amount of money you must pay for automobile insurance.

3.   Consider raising the deductibles on your "collision" and "other than collision" automobile insurance coverage. Generally, the higher the deductibles, the lower your premiums. Discuss the issue of deductibles with your present insurance agent and also with other agents when you are comparing premiums for similar coverage.

4.   If your car is an older one, paid for, and not worth much dollar-wise, discuss with your present insurance agent (and other agents with whom you check on prices) the advisability of dropping the coverage for damage to your automobile

("collision" and "other than collision"). Dropping this coverage could cut your premiums by a large amount.

5. If you retire, move closer to your job, or stop using your automobile to drive to and from work, ask your automobile insurance agent if you are entitled to lower rates. Lower rates will cut your outlay for premiums.

6. If you are buying an automobile, don't automatically accept the auto insurance offered by the auto dealer. Rather, check around with several insurance companies and agencies to see if you can get better rates for similar coverage. Even a small difference in premiums could be worth your effort, especially over a period of time.

7. If you are thinking of buying an expensive, high-powered automobile, before you buy it, check with several insurance agents for premiums to see if you will be able to afford the relatively expensive auto insurance on the vehicle. If you can't keep up the insurance payments, you might have to sell the car; and you could lose money on the sale.

8. Read your automobile insurance policy carefully to know exactly what it covers and doesn't cover and to what extent. Update your coverage when there are pertinent changes in your life. Having the coverage you really need could save you money in the long run.

WAYS TO SAVE ON DISABILITY INCOME INSURANCE

9. Seriously consider taking out disability income insurance if you and/or others depend on your paycheck for survival. Compare premiums and coverage among several reputable insurance companies and agencies. Perhaps your employer or organizations to which you (or your spouse) belong offer group policies. If the membership dues are low, it may pay you to join a particular organization just to be eligible for its group policy. A group policy usually can be obtained at a lower cost than an individual policy.

If you become disabled and do not have disability income insurance, your savings might not last until you are able to return to work. Therefore, you could end up having to borrow money to live on. Even worse, you could end up losing your house, car, and other possessions because you can't continue to make payments on them. Or, if you own these items, you might have to sell them to get money to live on.

WAYS TO SAVE ON HEALTH/MEDICAL INSURANCE

10.   Make sure you have adequate health insurance coverage. An extended illness in your family could possibly "wipe you out" financially. In general, buy as good a policy as you can possibly afford. Do without some nonessentials if you have to in order to pay for adequate coverage.

11.   Usually the higher the deductibles and copayments in your health insurance policy, the lower the premiums. Ask your present agent about the possibility and advisability of increasing your deductibles and copayments. Also, ask other agents about deductibles and copayments when you are talking with them about their premiums and coverage.

12.   Check on group health insurance offered by your employer. Group rates usually are cheaper than rates on individual policies. Some employers even pay all or part of the premiums for their employees for the group coverage.

13.   When you retire, inquire about the possibility of continuing in your employer's group health insurance plan. Group policies usually cost less than individual policies. Some employers will even continue to pay part of the premiums for their retirees. If you are not permitted to continue in the group plan, ask if it would be possible and cheaper to convert your group coverage to individual coverage with the same insurance company rather than take out a new policy with another insurance company.

14.   If group health insurance coverage is not available where you work, or if you are not employed, then shop around for the best prices. Compare prices for similar coverage. Check with six or eight different, reputable insurance companies and independent agencies. Confer with nonprofit organizations, special-interest groups, your professional organizations, and other organizations and associations to which you (or your spouse) belong or could belong; these may offer low-cost group policies. Joining and paying membership dues just to qualify for a group policy may be worth the expense.

Ask the insurance agents to explain their coverage in simple terms, and make sure you understand what the coverage is and is not. Ask about discounts on premiums for certain things, for example, for not smoking. The premiums can vary by a large amount from company to company. Even if the difference in premiums is small, it could become a substantial amount over 10, 15, or 20 years, not to mention the interest the savings could draw.   Make sure you understand the policy before buying the insurance.

15.   If you are a university or college student, see if low-cost student health insurance is offered at the institution where you are enrolled.

16.   Check into the cost of medical care through a Health Maintenance Organization (HMO). You pay a specified, fixed monthly premium or fee to the HMO; and you receive health care services as outlined in your enrollment contract. There are usually little or no out-of-pocket expenses such as deductibles or copayments. However, under some HMOs, you may be asked to pay small fees for certain things. HMOs usually cover most office visits and hospital expenses, though you often must choose a physician from the list of doctors participating in the program.   Look in your telephone directory under

Health Maintenance Organization, call several insurance companies and agencies to ask if they know of any HMOs in your area, or ask at the hospital business office for information.

You may be able to obtain adequate medical care through a HMO for less than the cost of traditional health insurance. Before you make a final decision to go the HMO route, however, find out the reputation of any HMO you are considering by talking with friends; your physician; appropriate persons at the local Better Business Bureau, Chamber of Commerce, and hospital; and others. Also, compare the monthly premium charged by a HMO for its services and that charged by insurance companies for comparable, traditional health insurance.

17.   Several months before you reach age 65, visit your nearest Social Security office concerning your eligibility for medical benefits under Medicare. You might be able to save money on your overall health insurance premiums if you have Medicare, so ask your private insurance agent what private insurance options are available to you if you have Medicare.

18.   Always read your health insurance policy very carefully, and make sure you know what it covers and does not cover. Thinking it covers something when it doesn't could cost you additional money out of your pocket when you have a claim.

19.   Update your coverage when the need arises. For example, if you get married, do you need to add your spouse to your policy? Not covering those who need to be covered on your policy could cost you money out of your pocket for health care expenses.

20.   When planning a trip outside the United States, see if your health insurance covers you while you are outside the U.S. Some do not. For example, Medicare does not pay for medical care outside the U.S.

WAYS TO SAVE ON HOMEOWNERS INSURANCE

21. When purchasing homeowners insurance, you need to understand the following three terms:

> **Replacement cost** is the cost of repairing or replacing property with materials of like kind and quality, without any deduction for depreciation. It is the full cost of replacing property at today's prices.

> **Actual cash value** means the replacement cost of property minus a charge for depreciation.

> **Market value...**is what you could sell the property for today.[1]

Knowing what these three terms mean can help you choose the coverage you really want. Otherwise, you may not actually have the coverage you think you have. You may not realize what coverage you really have until you file a claim, and then it's too late. You could be paid much less than you thought you would be paid on your claim. It probably would not be your agent's fault at all, but your fault because you simply did not buy the coverage you thought you were buying--since you had not informed yourself of the various types of coverage.

Understand exactly what coverage you would have with a particular homeowners policy before you decide to take it. For example, do you want actual-cash-value coverage on your contents, or do you want to pay higher premiums to get replacement-cost coverage? Getting the type of coverage you want could save you money in the long run.

22. Shop around for the best price for similar coverage under homeowners insurance. (Other names used for specific coverage might be renter's insurance, condominium owner's insurance, or mobile home insurance.) Compare prices at a half-dozen or so reputable insurance agencies. The premiums could vary a great deal from company to company. Even if the difference in premiums is small, it could add up to a relatively large amount over a number of years. Also, you could be drawing interest on the money you saved on premiums. Ask the agents to explain their coverage in simple language so that you can fully understand what the coverage is and is not.

Don't forget to check out group policies offered by your professional associations and various other organizations or groups to which you (or your spouse) belong or could belong. If you can come out ahead financially by joining a specific organization and paying the membership dues in order to qualify for its group policy, then consider joining. Also, find out if your employer has group homeowners insurance available to employees. Group policies should cost less than individual policies of comparable coverage.

23. Talk to your agent and get his or her advice about how much and what type of homeowners insurance coverage you should have on your home and your personal property and how much personal liability coverage you should have. For example, significantly increasing your personal liability insurance coverage increases your homeowners insurance premium very little. Being adequately covered should decrease your burden of loss when you file a claim.

24. When you are calling around for prices, ask about discounts. Some companies give discounts on homeowners insurance premiums for the following:

a. Installing smoke alarms.

b. Installing fire extinguishers.

c. Installing deadbolt locks, burglar alarms, and other security devices.

d. Being retired.

e. Living in a home 15 years old or less.

f. Being a nonsmoker.

Also, ask if discounts are available for senior citizens. Discounts lower your premiums.

25. The higher the deductibles, the lower the premium. Talk to your agent about the advisability of increasing the deductibles in your homeowners insurance policy.

26. Remember that most standard homeowners policies have limits on losses on such things as jewelry, silverware, furs, collectibles, china, paintings, stamps, and coins. The coverage could be as low as several hundred dollars. If you want coverage in addition to what is offered by the standard homeowners policy for such personal property items, then you will need to purchase the extra coverage. You may need to attach "riders" or "endorsements" to your present homeowners policy; or you might have to take out special policies to cover these items. Adding riders or endorsements may be cheaper than buying additional, separate policies. Discuss this whole matter with your insurance agent.

27. Damage by floods normally is not covered under a standard homeowners policy. Usually, you will need to buy a separate flood insurance policy. If you live in a flood-prone area, not having flood insurance could set you back financially if your home is flooded. Confer with your insurance agent on the issue of flood insurance.

28. Before you move, check your homeowners insurance policy to see if it covers your possessions during your move. Some policies may cover moves; others don't. If your policy isn't clear as to whether or not it covers moves, call your insurance agent to be sure. If your present policy doesn't, consider taking out a separate policy to cover the move. Not being covered could cost you money should you suffer losses during your move.

29. If bags of groceries are stolen from your car while you are downtown shopping, your clothes are stolen from your hotel room while you are on vacation, or your coat is stolen from the coat rack in the restaurant where you are eating, confer with your insurance agent to see if these stolen items are covered ˙ nder your homeowners insurance policy. If such losses are covered, the money you get from your claim could help to replace the items.

30. Photograph your personal property for insurance purposes. Photographs will provide additional proof of your ownership, description, and valuation of particular items should you ever need this information. Having or not having photographs could mean a difference in how much money you actually get from your claim.

31. Make a list of your personal property. Update your list each time you make purchases. In case of damage, destruction, or theft, you won't forget to report a particular item to your homeowners insurance company if the item is on your list. If you must rely on your memory, you may forget to report some items, which will result in a financial loss to you.

32. Review your homeowners insurance policy each year, and increase coverage as necessary. If you don't, then after several years your coverage might no longer be adequate; and you could be out a substantial amount of money should you suffer a loss.

WAYS TO SAVE ON LIFE INSURANCE

33. Shop around for the best prices for life insurance. Talk with a number of agents representing several different companies. The rates can vary significantly from company to company on a given type of insurance. Ask about discounts on premiums for nonsmokers. Also, ask if any other discounts are available. Even a small difference in premiums over many years can be substantial. You could, also, be drawing interest on the money you save.

34. Check to see if your employer offers group life insurance to employees. Group coverage usually will be cheaper than an individual policy you buy on your own.

35. When you retire, see if you can continue your group life insurance. Some employers will even continue to pay all or part of the premium for the retiree. Continuing the group coverage should cost less than individual coverage.

36. Check with professional and fraternal organizations, clubs, various associations, and other groups to which you (or your spouse) belong to see if any of them offer group life insurance plans. It could be to your financial benefit to join one of the above just to qualify for its group insurance if the membership fee is not too high. Group rates will be less than individual rates.

37. Don't buy more life insurance than you really need. Determine how much coverage you actually need and take this amount into consideration when buying life insurance.

One rule of thumb is that you need coverage equal to seven times your annual salary. So, if you make $30,000 a year, you would need $210,000 worth of life insurance under this rule. However, the amount of your savings should be taken into account. Let's say you have $150,000 in CDs--then you might need only $60,000 worth of coverage.

On the other hand, consider if you need any life insurance at all if no one depends on you for his or her livelihood and if you have enough money to settle your debts and pay for your funeral and burial expenses. However, if the direct opposite of this is true, you probably need life insurance.

38. Consider which type of life insurance is affordable and adequate for you. Ask the agents with whom you talk to explain to you all of the various types of life insurance. (Term life insurance is the least expensive type of life insurance and, thus, can provide the most protection for the least amount of money.) If you have all of the necessary information on the types of life insurance, you will then be equipped to make a wise decision about what type you should buy for your particular situation.

39. If you want additional life insurance coverage, ask your insurance agent about increasing the coverage in your present policy to see if that would be cheaper than buying a second, new policy either from your present company or from another company. It usually will be cheaper to buy one large life insurance policy rather than several small ones totaling the same amount as the one large policy. Depending on the breaking point, the more life insurance you buy, the less the cost per $1,000 worth of coverage.

40. If you had particular medical problems when you took out your life insurance policy which caused your rates to be higher than the standard rates, and if these medical problems have improved or completely disappeared, ask your insurance agent if you might now qualify for lower rates. The lower premiums could leave you with extra money to save, pay other bills, or buy necessary items.

41. If you were working in a dangerous occupation when you took out your life insurance policy but are no longer in that occupation, talk with your insurance agent to see if you are now eligible for reduced premiums, that is if you were paying higher than standard rates because of your dangerous occupation. Even if you are still working in the dangerous job, discuss the matter with your agent. Your occupation may no longer be considered as hazardous as in the past because of safety improvements. Reduced premiums means you are left with extra money you can use for other things.

42. Increase your coverage when necessary. For example, you may need more life insurance when you get married, when you have children, and when you buy a house. The premiums will be higher for additional coverage, but the increased coverage could be financially advantageous for your survivors.

43.　When you buy an airline ticket, charge it to one of your credit cards if, by doing so, the credit card company provides accident life insurance which will be payable to your beneficiary(s) should you be killed while you are a passenger on the airplane. Some credit card companies automatically provide $100,000 (or more) worth of such coverage. The coverage is free.

44.　When you purchase an airline ticket, do so through a travel agency which automatically provides accident life insurance on you which will be payable to your beneficiary(s) should you be killed while you are a passenger on the airplane. Some travel agencies provide $100,000 (or more) worth of coverage. This coverage is free.

MISCELLANEOUS WAYS TO SAVE ON INSURANCE

45.　Ask people you know what insurance companies or agencies they use and if they would recommend them to others. Getting favorable recommendations could help you find reliable and stable insurance companies or agencies which can give you the most coverage at the lowest cost.

46.　By paying premiums annually, rather than monthly, quarterly, or semiannually, you usually can save some money on your premiums. Ask about this when taking out insurance. On one particular policy I have, when I pay the premium yearly, I am given a discount of one month's premium. Some companies will add several dollars onto the regular premium if a policyholder pays other than yearly to help cover the cost of the extra paperwork. Saving a few dollars each year can add up to an important amount over many years.

47. If you switch from one policy to another, make sure there will not be a lapse between the time your coverage will be effective on your new policy and the time you are no longer covered on your old policy. If you don't plan this switch very carefully, there is a chance you could be out an enormous amount of money should you experience a need for the coverage between policies--for instance, if you have an automobile accident, you become disabled, you have to go into the hospital, or you have a fire in your home.

48. If you switch from one insurance company to another, make sure you collect any refunds of premiums due you from the previous insurance company. Even a small refund is worth your effort.

49. Make sure painters, construction workers, and others doing work for you while they are located on your property have adequate liability insurance, so that if they are injured on your property they will be covered by their own policies. You could be held liable if they are injured on your property, and such liability could have the potential of stripping you of many of your worldly possessions.

50. Make sure you have adequate liability or other appropriate insurance to cover household employees, farm workers, and others who work for you. Otherwise, you are leaving yourself open to possible lawsuits if these persons are hurt while in your employ.

51. It is extremely important that you read all of your insurance policies carefully and understand what they do and do not cover before you take out the insurance. If, however, you discover later that a policy you have really doesn't cover what you thought it covered, then contact your insurance agent immediately and have the situation corrected, if possible. Having the coverage you need could save you money in the long run.

SOURCES FOR ADDITIONAL INFORMATION

52. Consult *Best's Insurance Guide* or *Best's Insurance Reports* for the ratings of various insurance companies. These ratings will help you to choose insurance companies which are financially strong. Check for the publications at your local public library.

ENDNOTES

1. Douglas F. Beech, *Home Insurance* (Manhattan, Kansas: Cooperative Extension Service, Kansas State University, March, 1982), p. 3.

CHAPTER 16

HOW TO SAVE ON YOUR PERSONAL GROOMING EXPENSES

How many things I can do without
Socrates

INTRODUCTION

Simply put, most people have to have at least a minimum amount of grooming. Some may require more than others because of their particular jobs or contact with the public.

If not carefully controlled, the buying of grooming aids and services can take a large bite out of your budget. The suggestions in this chapter will help you keep you and your family properly groomed while keeping the expenses to a minimum.

WAYS TO SAVE ON MAKEUP COSTS

1. Use a lip brush to get the remaining lipstick from down inside the tube. The lip brush will quickly pay for itself by

enabling you to get additional lipstick. Since about one-fourth to one-third of the lipstick is down inside the tube, the use of the brush should cut your lipstick expenditures by approximately 25 to 33 percent. Over the years, you could save several hundred dollars.

2. Add a few drops of water to your mascara tube when the mascara becomes too thick for satisfactory use. By doing this, you can delay spending your money for a new tube. You probably will be able to continue adding drops of water for several months before the mascara becomes too diluted for the desired results.

3. Use petroleum jelly for cleaning makeup from your eyes and face. Petroleum jelly usually is much lower in price than facial cleansers.

4. Some stores which sell cosmetics will do a complete makeup job free of charge. If you are going to have to replace a makeup item which you have exhausted or if you would like to try a new inexpensive item, such as a lipstick or blush, why not take advantage of the expertise of the makeup demonstrator. Don't be pressured into buying every item that the demonstrator uses on your face, but don't go through the makeup session if you have no intention whatsoever of buying anything. The prices of the items normally are higher than comparable items at a discount store, for example, so watch yourself; or you could end up "paying" for the makeup session.

WAYS TO SAVE ON HAIR CARE COSTS

5. Shampoo and style your own hair and that of family members at home. Doing this at home is far cheaper than having it done at the beauty or barber shop.

6. Dye or color rinse your and family members' hair at home. Coloring hair will be much more expensive at the beauty salon or barber shop.

7. Unless your hair is in "bad" condition, don't let your beautician or barber put special conditioners on it or give it special oil treatments. You could save several dollars. Even if your hair does need special conditioners or treatments, give your hair this special care at home yourself and save the several dollars.

8. If you have the ability, cut your hair and family members' hair at home rather than go to the beauty shop or barber shop. You could save $10 to $25 or more per haircut.

9. If you can't cut your or family members' hair, perhaps you can at least trim your own and family members' hair between cuts by a professional. This will result in fewer visits to the beauty shop or barber shop and less expense for you.

10. Give yourself and family members home permanents instead of getting them done at the beauty shop. Home perms will be much cheaper. Follow carefully the directions which come with the home permanents. If you can't give yourself perms, maybe a friend or family member could help.

11. Wash (roll, if necessary) and dry your own hair and that of your family at home, and just get a "comb-out" at the beauty salon. A "comb-out" will cost only a fraction of the price of the complete works.

12. Call the local cosmetology schools (beauty schools/colleges) or barber schools and volunteer to have your name placed on the list of people to serve as models on which the instructors can demonstrate haircutting, perming, shampooing, conditioning, hair rolling, coloring, styling, and blow drying to students. Getting occasional free hair care decreases your outlay.

13. Get permanents, shampoos and sets, cuts, and other hair care at cosmetology schools (beauty schools/colleges) or barber schools. Their regular prices could easily save you from 50 to 85 percent of the prices at beauty salons and barber shops.

Call for information and an appointment. Even though students will be doing the work, instructors will oversee their work. I have always been pleased with the quality of the work students have done on my hair.

14. Watch the newspaper for specials at cosmetology schools (beauty schools/colleges) and barber schools. For example, at a cosmetology school I once got a permanent on sale for $7.50 (one-half off the regular price) which also included a cut, shampoo, and set. There is a wide gap between $7.50 and what most beauty salons charge for a permanent.

15. Watch the newspaper for specials at beauty salons and barber shops. For example, one advertisement read, "Hair specials--permanents, shampoo and styling, cuts--2 for 1 on Thursdays in March. Bring a friend and split the cost." Another stated, "Permanents half-price for the month of January." Such specials could ease your financial burden for hair care.

16. If you have to resort to paying full price at a beauty salon or barber shop, then call eight to ten different ones. Ask what their prices are for particular items, such as permanents, cuts, shampoos and styling, conditioning, coloring, and "comb-outs." The prices normally vary a great deal among the different salons and barber shops.

17. Let your hair dry naturally and save yourself the expense of buying a hair dryer.

MISCELLANEOUS WAYS TO SAVE ON GROOMING EXPENSES

18. Buy grooming aids (such as hair color, hair spray, makeup, nail polish, facial tissue, razor blades, soap, toothpaste, shampoo, deodorant, shaving cream, hand and body lotion, and cleansing cream) on sale whenever possible instead of paying full price for them. Sometimes you can even find them at half-price or on special at "buy one, get one free." Buying your grooming aids on sale could amount to sizable savings. If the sale prices warrant it, then stock up. You may even want to buy as much as a one-year (or more) supply if you have adequate storage space.

19. Buy the generic grooming aids. The quality should be relatively comparable to store brands and name brands, and the prices should be much lower than the name brands and somewhat lower than the store brands. At least give the generics a try; if you like them, you could save yourself a substantial amount of money.

20. If you absolutely refuse to try the generic grooming aids, then at least give the store brands a try. Store brands usually are considerably cheaper than name brands. Many store brands will be of comparable quality to that of name brands.

21. In general, select grooming aids that are reasonably priced. Don't just assume that a particular lipstick selling for $7.50 a tube, for example, is better than a $1.50 tube or that a certain men's hair spray at twice the price of another hair spray (not labeled "men's" hair spray) is really superior. At least, give the less expensive ones a try. When you consider all of the many different grooming aids you use, say, over a year's time, you could save yourself a big chunk of money.

22. If you simply don't intend to change from your long-time national name brands of particular grooming aids, then at least shop around for the best prices. The prices of identical items can vary from store to store. The same item may be cheaper, for example, at discount stores, but more expensive at some drugstores and at cosmetic counters at "ritzy" stores. Saving even small amounts on several items can make a noticeable difference over time.

23. Regardless of whether you buy generics, store brands, off brands, or national name brands of grooming aids, shop around for the best prices. Compare prices at various places such as discount stores, general department stores, dollar stores, drugstores, grocery stores, cosmetic stores, clothing stores, cosmetic companies selling door-to-door, cosmetic companies selling through home party plans, various specialty shops, and mail-order companies. Also, prices on identical items can vary among the same types of stores, for example, from one drugstore to another drugstore or from one grocery store to another grocery store. Buy your grooming aids where they are the cheapest.

24. If you must buy a particular name-brand grooming item, then shop around to see if some stores may be offering a free item or several free items with the purchase of the particular item you need. For example, one well-known cosmetic company has periodically given a free gift package of several of its full-size cosmetic items with a $7.50 purchase of a company product or products. If you are going to buy a grooming item anyway, why not get some free items with your purchase. Getting free items decreases your overall cost for grooming aids.

25. Buy in quantity if you can save money over buying the same items individually. For example, if soap selling at 49 cents a bar can be bought for three for $1.00, that would be a saving of 47 cents on the three bars. If shampoo selling for $1.89 a bottle is available at two for $3.00, you could save 78 cents on two bottles.

26. Pick up free samples and trial sizes of cosmetics, cologne, body lotion, and other grooming aids at various stores. These free items often will be in small baskets on a counter in the cosmetic area or possibly other areas where various grooming aids are displayed. These items could reduce (even by a small amount) your expenditures for grooming aids.

27. Check out the garage sales for various grooming equipment. The best performing electric razor I've ever owned, I purchased for $1.50 at a garage sale. I've used it for years, and it still works well. This particular model of razor sold for approximately $50 new. My savings, therefore, amounted to $48.50, which went a long way in buying groceries and paying bills.

28. When you need to buy grooming equipment, consider putting an advertisement in the newspaper. The ad might be worded, "Want to buy a good, used hair dryer on floor stand. Call --------." You should be able to save a great deal over the price of similar, new equipment. However, do be very careful in buying used equipment. You could be buying the problems of the owner. It is probably doubtful that the seller will be willing to give you a guarantee on the used equipment. Even if you are given a guarantee, you might have difficulty in getting the seller to stand behind it if you experience trouble with the equipment. On the other hand, buying used grooming equipment might prove to be an extremely wise investment.

29. If you use cologne, buy a bottle without an atomizer if it is cheaper than one with an atomizer. Also, one large bottle without an atomizer may be less expensive than the same amount in two small bottles. If you want spray application, then pour the contents of the bottle into a clean pump bottle (hair spray or other suitable container). I, personally, prefer using an old, clean, pump hair spray bottle rather than one of the empty atomizer bottles with screw-off lids which are for sale at various stores. Anyway, buying an atomizer bottle costs money. Using an old hair spray bottle is free.

30. Get the last, possible bit of body lotion, liquid makeup, mouthwash, roll-on deodorant, and cologne (without an atomizer) from containers by storing them upside-down when you have used nearly all of the contents to allow the remaining contents to drain down for use. You may be pleasantly surprised at how many more days' use you can get from the containers.

31. After draining bottles of shampoo, bath "bubbles," liquid soap, and hair conditioner upside-down, rinse them out with a small amount of water to get the last possible drop for use.

32.　Soak several small pieces of soap in a small amount of water for 15 to 30 minutes or more, if necessary, to soften the outsides.　Then squeeze them together in your hand to form one larger piece.　There is never a need to throw away even tiny pieces of soap.　Throwing away soap is throwing away money.

33.　If pop-up, wet, disposable "towels" dry out, run a little water over the top of the towels in the container to rewet them. Rewetting them allows you to continue to use them.

34.　Squeeze the toothpaste tube from the bottom and flatten and roll the tube up from the bottom as you use the contents. I find that a piece of tape or a clamp is needed on a plastic tube to hold it in place after I have rolled it up.　With the above method, I find that I can get the maximum amount of toothpaste from a tube.

35.　Give yourself your own facials, manicures, and pedicures rather than go to the beauty shop for them.　You can do them yourself for much less money.

CHAPTER 17

HOW TO SAVE ON YOUR VACATION EXPENSES

Frugality enhances all other virtues
Cicero

INTRODUCTION

Vacations can be fun, but expenses can quickly and easily get out of control if you aren't extremely careful. This chapter gives you some suggestions for keeping your vacation expenses to a minimum but at the same time enabling you to have an enjoyable time.

WAYS TO SAVE ON VACATION TRAVEL EXPENSES

1. Vacation close to home this year. Many people are located relatively near interesting and exciting things to see and do. Check with your local and/or state (and nearby states) tourist offices or local and nearby Chambers of Commerce for literature on tourist attractions. Also, a nearby motel or campground might provide you with just as happy and enjoyable a change from your routine, everyday activities as accommodations that are hundreds or thousands of miles from home.

Don't just assume that a vacation must be a long distance away to be pleasurable. Vacationing close to home should save you a great deal on your travel expenses.

2. If you are planning to travel by air, ask about Super Saver fares (or whatever the particular airlines are calling their absolutely cheapest airfares at the time you call). Check with your local travel agent or directly with the airlines several months prior to the time you will need to fly. You could save 50 percent or more off the regular price of the ticket. Ask about any special restrictions (such as what time or day you must travel, how far in advance you must make your reservations and pay for your ticket, and the minimum required length of stay) associated with the lower-priced ticket. Also, ask if night travel, off-peak days, off-peak hours, off-season rates, midweek rates, or group rates are cheaper? If you plan sufficiently ahead, you should rarely ever have to pay full price for an airline ticket.

3. Ask your travel agent about "stand-by" airfares--they should provide tremendous savings.

4. Take advantage of special programs which some airlines are offering for senior citizens of a specified age (and up) entitling them to reduced prices for air travel. The terms and conditions of the programs vary from airline to airline. Some of the airlines which have advertised special programs include: Northwest Orient, Eastern, Delta, American, United, and TWA. Check with your travel agent or directly with these and other airlines for additional information.

5. If you have bought an airline ticket; but your plans have changed, and you no longer need the ticket and cannot get a refund, put an advertisement in the newspaper to sell it (if the ticket is transferable). Your ad might read, "For sale. One round-trip airline ticket from New York to San Francisco. Transferable. Cheap. Call------- before July 28." Being able to sell the ticket, even at a loss, helps you to recover some of your cost.

6.   Watch the newspapers for airline tickets for sale by individuals. Perhaps their plans have changed since they bought the tickets, and they no longer need them. Be sure that the tickets are transferable and the prices are really cheaper than tickets you can buy yourself from your travel agent or directly from the airlines. Negotiate with the sellers for drastically reduced prices. If they are unable to use the tickets and cannot obtain refunds, they will probably be glad to get whatever they can for the tickets. Their loss is your gain.

7.   When you are calling airlines for prices of tickets, ask each airline if it has a program in which you can enroll to receive free travel after you have traveled a designated number of "paid" miles on that particular airline. If you call travel agents, ask them about such special airline programs. For example, TWA calls its program "Frequent Flight Bonus Program." Getting free flights saves you the expense of having to buy tickets for those flights. For example, after you have traveled 20,000 miles on a particular airline, you might be allowed one free round-trip coach ticket to any U.S. destination to which its planes fly.

8.   When flying, don't take more weight than the maximum free allowance. Baggage weighing in excess of the free allowance is subject to an extra charge. The airlines and your travel agent will be able to tell you the weight limits. Having to pay for excess weight adds to the overall cost of your travel.

9.   Travel by your personal automobile if this would be cheaper than traveling by airplane, bus, or train. (See the "Introduction" to Chapter 1 for information on the cost per mile of owning and operating your automobile.) Of course, if your time is too short, you may have to take a plane. Other factors, also, must be taken into consideration when thinking about driving.

10.   Consider traveling by bus on special, low-cost deals. Check with your travel agent and directly with the bus lines. Ask about 30- and 60-day passes, round-trip fares, "off-season"

rates, and any other specials presently being offered. One special I saw in the newspaper comes to mind: "Student Special. Ride our bus to any destination we travel in the U.S. for $86 round trip during spring break. Present valid college ID." By taking advantage of special offers, you will not be out as much money for your bus fare.

11. Check to see if travel by train would be a less expensive method of transportation. Check on special rates for "limited duration, unlimited mileage" tickets. Check on prices for special one-way and round-trip tickets. Ask about "off-season" rates. Riding the train, for example, might be much cheaper than flying.

12. When flying or riding the train or bus, always ask about any discounts for senior citizens, disabled persons, children, and students. Discounts decrease the cost of your travel.

13. If you are into bicycling, then use this method of transportation when applicable. Bicycling will save tremendously on your travel costs, especially if you already own your bicycle. However, take safety into particular account when deciding whether to use this method of travel.

WAYS TO SAVE ON VACATION LODGING EXPENSES

14. Stay in appropriate low-cost hotels and motels. The low-cost chains and other hotels and motels can save you a sizable amount of money when compared with the cost of staying in higher-priced ones. The low-cost and the higher-priced establishments sometimes are even located side-by-side or across the street from each other. My husband and I have found no relationship between the price of the room and its cleanliness. Ask your travel agent for additional information on low-cost hotels and motels.

15. When checking into hotels or motels without reservations or when calling to make reservations in advance, ask about their least expensive type of room. The following words are sometimes used to refer to such accommodations: Economy rooms, special-priced rooms, minimum rates, or some other similar term. Regardless of what the least expensive rooms are called, they should provide big savings over the prices of other rooms.

16. When asking about room rates at hotels and motels, ask about weekend specials. Friday, Saturday, and/or Sunday rates are often much cheaper at some hotels and motels than their weekday rates. Some have periodical specials of one-half price for Sunday night if you also stay Saturday or Monday night. Others give special rates if you stay two consecutive nights during the weekend. Even though the nature of weekend specials varies from establishment to establishment, they usually do provide sizable savings.

17. When checking on hotel and motel room rates, ask about "off-season" rates and what dates they are in effect. Delaying or moving back the dates of your vacation could save you an important amount on the cost of your lodging.

18. When inquiring about room rates at hotels and motels, ask about family plans, if you are traveling with your children. Family plans may vary somewhat from place to place. Some places permit children under 18 years of age to stay in their parents' room free-of-charge. In addition, some offer special, reduced meal prices for children.

19. When asking about room rates at various hotels and motels, see if they provide special discounts to senior citizens. (However, don't always assume that the senior citizens' discounts will provide you with the least expensive room rates. Some other specials--such as group, family, business, or weekend--may provide you greater savings.)

20. Ask about group rates. They are usually cheaper than the regular room rates for individuals.

21. If you plan to be on a combined business trip and vacation, always ask what the business room rates are when you inquire in advance about prices at various hotels and motels. If you do not make advance inquiries, be sure to ask about business rates upon arrival. These rates usually are considerably lower than the regular rates.

22. If you are a government employee, ask hotels and motels about their government rates. Government rates could save you money.

23. If it seems appropriate to do so, negotiate lower hotel and motel prices. Once when my husband and I were in Africa, we stayed in an independently-owned hotel recommended by friends. When we arrived, we asked about the room rates. The price given was twice what our friends had paid one year earlier. We told the manager about this difference, and immediately we were given a rate even lower than our friends had paid the year before. In this particular case, we felt that it was quite appropriate to voice our concern; and by doing so, we saved a large amount of money.

24. Some low-priced hotels and motels charge extra for a television. If you don't really plan to watch television, then don't pay the extra price for it. Also, color may be more expensive than black-and-white.

25. When inquiring about room rates, also ask about the cost of parking. Some hotels and motels provide free parking, while others may charge a "hefty" fee for parking. At others, you may have to pay to park in an adjacent parking garage not owned by the hotel or motel. Figure any parking fees into the overall cost of your room.

26. Vacate your room by check-out time unless you have asked and received permission to stay in your room longer without an additional charge. Otherwise, staying overtime could cost you an extra day's charge.

27. Check on bed-and-breakfast arrangements. People in some cities rent out one or more rooms in their homes and include breakfast in the room rate. Call or write the Tourist Office or Chamber of Commerce where you plan to go and ask for information. In addition, you might check the newspapers in the area where you are going for bed-and-breakfast advertisements. Also, check at your public library for a directory of bed-and-breakfast offerings. The bed-and-breakfast rates could be less than the rates at some hotels and motels.

28. If you are going to be in an area for several days, a week, or longer, check on renting a furnished apartment. Renting an apartment for this period of time should be much cheaper than renting a hotel or motel room. You could also save on the cost of meals by preparing them in the apartment. There are such apartments in many cities. Check with the Chamber of Commerce, Tourist Office, and local newspapers in the area where you plan to vacation.

29. Check out the possibility of staying in college or university dormitories. Some colleges and universities rent rooms, permit meals to be eaten in the student cafeterias, and allow use of recreational facilities by vacationers. Check with your library for a list of colleges and universities making such offers, or write directly to the ones in the area where you plan to vacation. The daily rates should be much less than those at most hotels and motels.

30. When you go on vacation, plan the route of your trip in such a way that you can spend some nights with friends and relatives. This will save on lodging and also give you a chance to visit. However, be careful not to wear out your welcome or stay with people who might have wished that you had taken a different route.

31. If you are the nature-loving type, you might want to camp out. This could range from sleeping on the ground in a sleeping bag all the way up to camping out in a motor home. However, the more sophisticated the camping out, the greater the expense. By keeping the type of accommodation relatively simple, you should save a substantial amount on your lodging expenses by camping out.

WAYS TO SAVE ON VACATION FOOD COSTS

32. If you travel by automobile, take along a box and/or cooler of assorted foods and beverages for meals and snacks. My husband and I call this our "chop box," a term my husband picked up during his two-year stay in Nigeria in the mid 1960s where it was absolutely essential to take along food and beverages, including water, when traveling. By eating many of your meals and snacks from your "chop box," you should be able to cut your food expenditures by a very large amount.

33. If it isn't practical for you to carry a supply of food with you from home (for example, if you take a plane, bus, or train), then when you arrive at your destination, purchase food items from a grocery store for some of your meals and snacks. You could eat in your room, in the park, or some other suitable place. (Even when using the above methods of travel, however, you could possibly put a small amount of certain types of prepared, nonperishable, securely-sealed food items in your luggage.) Not having to eat all of your meals "out" should reduce your food expenses greatly.

34. Eat at fast-food, serve-yourself, and limited-service places. Such places ordinarily are less expensive than most full-service restaurants. However, even at these lower-priced places, you must choose carefully; or you could find yourself spending too much.

35. When you are staying in hotels and motels, don't use room service for snacks or meals. There is usually a room-service or tray charge. Also, the prices of the items in the room-service menu usually are higher than the prices of the same items in the hotel or motel restaurant or coffee shop.

WAYS TO SAVE ON TOURIST ATTRACTIONS

36.   Consider vacationing during the "off" season if fees for tourist attractions are much lower. (Lodging and commercial travel rates may also be considerably cheaper during the "off" season.)

37.   Ask if discounts on admission prices to tourist attractions are available for senior citizens, students, children, and disabled persons.

38.   Ask about group rates. They are usually less per person than regular, individual rates.

39.   Ask if entrance fees are less on certain days of the week. If so, go on those days.

40.   Visit free and low-cost attractions. Order free literature from states or specific places where you plan to visit. When you receive the literature, flip through it looking especially for such attractions. Also, check at your public library for information on free and low-cost things to see and do where you are planning to go. Including free and low-cost attractions in your plans will help lower your vacation costs.

41.   Visit National and State parks. Ask at your local library for publications or write directly to specific parks for information. Ask your librarian for mailing addresses. These parks should provide interesting and enjoyable activities and attractions at relatively reasonable prices. There may even be such parks near where you live.

42.   Take do-it-yourself tours rather than pay for guided tours. Guided tours can be quite expensive. For example, take your own tour through the botanical gardens, the art gallery, or historical museum rather than pay several dollars more to join the guided tour. Also, touring on your own enables you to move at your own pace, and you see what you want to see along the way.

WAYS TO SAVE ON VACATIONS ABROAD

In addition to the following, many of the suggestions listed in the other sections in this chapter are also applicable to foreign travel.

43. Buy a good book on money-saving foreign travel--one containing information, of course, on the countries and cities you plan to visit. For example, my husband and I used Frommer's *Europe on $25 a Day* for information on some of the cities we have visited in Europe. This book provides information on inexpensive hotels, pensions, and other suitable lodging; free and low-cost activities and attractions; low-cost meals; do-it-yourself tours; the least expensive ways to get around locally; and hundreds of other valuable bits of information.

Be sure to take whatever travel book you buy with you on your trip. A book like the one mentioned above will pay for itself in savings in less than a day. (I have mentioned the Frommer book only as an example. There are other good books and, of course, a later edition of the Frommer book on the market.)

44. Ask your travel agent for free brochures on inexpensive lodging and places to eat, free and low-cost things to see and do, the cheapest methods of local transportation, and other information to help you keep your vacation expenses abroad as low as possible. Having such information should help you make decisions which will save you a relatively large amount of money.

45. Obtain the cheapest airfare available. For example, travel during the "off" season (low tourist traffic) should be cheaper. Initially, check with your travel agent far in advance of your planned trip abroad. There is usually an enormously wide gap between the highest and lowest airfares for a particular destination.

46. Ask your travel agent about "stand-by" airfares. They should offer worthwhile savings.

47. Check with your travel agent on group charter flights. They could provide very favorable savings.

48. Try to choose methods of transportation other than the taxi to get around locally. For example, the bus, train, subway, and trolley are usually much less expensive than the taxi.

49. Buy food items from a grocery store or other similar place and eat in your room, at a park, or at other suitable places. Buying such food should be much cheaper than eating in restaurants all of the time.

50. Rather than pay substantially more for commercially planned and guided tours, do your own do-it-yourself tours. As merely one example of many, my husband and I planned our own trip from downtown Paris to Versailles for a small fraction of the cost of the commercial tour. We took the metro to the correct exit, where we caught the correct bus; and we were soon at the gates of the Palace.

51. In some cities abroad, having a hotel room with a bathroom in it could nearly double the price of a fairly comparable room without its own bathroom. In the lower-priced hotels, there usually will be one "toilet" and one bath and/or shower room on each floor or a "toilet" on each floor and a bath and/or shower room on every other floor. The specific arrangements may vary from place to place. Most of these lower-priced rooms, however, will have a lavatory in them. If you can convince yourself that you do not have to have a private bathroom, you can save yourself a big chunk of money on your lodging.

MISCELLANEOUS WAYS TO SAVE ON
VACATION EXPENSES

52. In general, don't borrow money to go on vacations. Also, don't charge items related to your vacations unless charging them is merely for convenience and unless you intend to pay the bills by the due date to avoid interest charges.

Vacations can be fun, and many of us need a vacation occasionally. However, the word vacation does not have to be necessarily synonymous with spending a lot of money. Take the type of vacation your pocketbook will allow you to take. If you borrow money and charge things on a long-term basis, the interest could add up to a substantial amount. Also, while you are making payments on the vacation loan and the charge accounts, you may get behind with other bills.

In addition, it seems very unwise to finance a vacation if, for example, you are already behind on your rent, you have very little food in the house, and the hospital is threatening to sue you for unpaid medical bills. You could end up with a bad credit rating; and, worse yet, some of your purchases could be repossessed. Unless your bills are paid up-to-date and you have the extra cash to spend on a traditional vacation, see number 65 at the end of this chapter for suggestions on how to vacation on a shoestring.

53. If they are available, always use toll-free numbers for contacting hotels, motels, airlines, bus companies, tourist attractions, and other places rather than pay for the telephone calls yourself. If you don't know the toll-free numbers, don't know whether or not the places you want to call have toll-free numbers, or can't locate the toll-free numbers in your local telephone directory, then dial 1-800-555-1212 (free) and ask the operator for the toll-free numbers. If particular hotels, etc. you want to call don't have toll-free numbers, then the operator will tell you so. Having to pay for long distance calls adds to the cost of your vacation.

54. Pick up free literature at travel agencies by browsing through the racks and selecting publications of interest to you. Also, order free information in advance from the Department of Tourism in the states which you plan to visit. In addition, many cities have their own tourist offices. The Chambers of Commerce in the cities you plan to visit may have information, too. Ask at your local library for mailing addresses. Your library may even have publications on tourist attractions and lodging in the places you plan to visit. Getting free information saves you the expense of having to buy similar information. Also, hopefully, the information you get will enable you to save money on the various aspects of your vacation.

55. Obtain assistance from travel agencies. Most travel agencies charge you nothing for their help. They normally are paid commissions by the airlines, hotels, etc. Travel agencies have a wealth of information at their fingertips. They should be able to get you the lowest hotel and motel rates, airfares, etc. Using their assistance can save you the work and expense of handling all of the arrangements for your vacation. However, ask them if there will be any charges for the particular assistance you need. Some travel agencies may charge a fee for certain specialized services.

56. Ask if the professional associations and other organizations to which you belong have discount agreements with various hotels, motels, and car rental agencies. If so, obtain a special card entitling you to these discounts if your membership card is not sufficient. Discounts, of course, will help to lower the cost of your vacation. Even a 10 percent discount is well worth the effort.

57. Take advantage of trips offered by senior citizens centers. These group trips usually will be less expensive than similar, individual ones you arrange on your own.

58. Take advantage of trips offered by various organizations and colleges, for example. Contact these and other groups directly for additional information. The trips may be open to the general public; or they may be restricted to certain people, such as the alumni of a particular college. Because these are usually group trips, the prices should be less than you could get on your own.

59. Participate in the Elderhostel program. The costs are minimal. The program is for people 60 years old and over. "Students" spend a one-week learning vacation on a college or university campus, eat in the campus cafeteria, live in a dormitory, and take particular courses in which they are interested. (Similar arrangements, not connected with Elderhostel, are available at some colleges and universities.) Contact colleges and universities for details or ask at your local library for a publication listing colleges and universities participating in the Elderhostel program.

60. Consider backpacking. If you are into backpacking, walking, hiking, climbing, camping out, and "roughing it," backpacking should provide you enormous savings on your vacationing expenses in terms of travel, lodging, and food costs.

61. Consider bargain vacation "packages." Such a "package" was advertised by a local travel agency in a local U.S. newspaper for $324 and included round-trip airfare to a designated city in Europe, six nights lodging in a hotel (double occupancy), and a free round-trip ticket on a participating bus from your home city to the U.S. city of departure. Such "packages" could save you a lot of money on your vacation expenditures.

62. Plan your vacations in conjunction with your business trips and conventions. If planned very carefully, the vacations could cost you relatively little additional money.

63. Vacation with friends or another family and share expenses. For example, if you travel by automobile, stay in hotels, and share these expenses with three other adults, you could save 75 percent on your travel expenses and roughly 60 to 75 percent on lodging.

64. In general, always try to travel as lightly as possible, especially if you use public transportation. Traveling lightly should save you a considerable amount of money in several ways. For example, if you are flying commercially, and you take several bags with you, have several places on your flight itinerary, and don't want to take all of your bags with you from the airport to your hotel every time you fly to a different place, then you must pay to store the bags at the airport until you return a few days later to pick them up and catch a plane to your next stop. Storage fees are quite high at airports in some countries. You could easily spend up to $50 or more in several days just on storage charges.

Traveling lightly also provides you greater freedom in choice of local transportation, for example, from the airport, train station, or bus station to your hotel. If you have one small, lightweight bag, you can more easily catch a local bus, subway, etc. instead of having to take a taxi just to transport your bags. Normally, a taxi will be much more expensive.

In addition, where appropriate, (for instance, in some cities in Europe), you can walk around shopping for an inexpensive hotel if you are not weighted down with luggage. Furthermore, you don't have to pay (tip) porters and others to carry your luggage to your hotel room and in various other situations. At $1.00 or more per bag, you could be out many dollars just moving your luggage around. It is important also to remember, when flying, that baggage in excess of the free allowance is subject to an extra charge--a very high charge with some airlines in some countries.

65. Consider vacationing at "home" this year. You could do such things as: puttering around the house; window-shopping; going to a matinee movie; doing some enjoyable volunteer work; visiting nearby friends; going on a picnic; sleeping late; relaxing in your home or backyard; watching a late, late movie on TV; reading at the library; working at an interesting and exciting paid job; going to free and low-cost local attractions; having a late breakfast out at one of the fast food places;

having a few friends over; working in your yard or vegetable garden; playing your musical instrument; fishing at a local lake; enjoying your hobby; visiting free exhibits in the mall; going to open houses and grand openings; walking; riding your bicycle; getting started in couponing and refunding; writing letters; having a garage sale; going to garage sales; or doing dozens of other things which would be free or very inexpensive yet provide an enjoyable change from your regular, routine work-week.

CHAPTER 18

HOW TO SAVE ON YOUR WATER BILLS

Waste not, want not
Franklin

INTRODUCTION

The table on the following page shows the average number of gallons of water used each day by the typical American family of four for specific activities such as dishwashing, cooking and drinking, utility sink (washing hands, etc.), laundry, bathing, bathroom sink, and toilet.

Using less water means saving money whether you are on a city water line or own your own well. If you are on the city water line, your bills come regularly. If you own your own well, you must take into account the investment you have in your water system, repair and maintenance costs, and the cost of electricity used in operating the pump.

This chapter suggests many ways you can use less water and, thus, save money.

DAILY WATER USE BY AMERICAN FAMILY OF FOUR[1]

Activity	Gallons
Dishwashing	15
Cooking and Drinking	12
Utility sink (washing hands, etc.)	05
Laundry	35
Bathing	80
Bathroom sink	08
Toilet	100
Total	255

WAYS TO SAVE IN THE BATHROOM

1. Cut down on the number of showers and tub baths you take. Replace some of them with "sponge" baths using the bathroom lavatory. The ordinary shower, equipped with a conventional shower head, uses from 5 to 10 gallons of water per minute.[2] Showering accounts for approximately 30 percent of the total water used in the home.[3] The amount of water used for a tub bath can vary greatly from person to person.

2. When taking a shower, turn on the water only long enough to wet your body. Then, turn off the water. Soap your body. Turn the water back on only long enough to rinse off the soap. Follow the same steps when washing your hair in the shower.

3. Use low-flow shower heads. They can reduce water flow by as much as 40 percent.[4]

4. Run a small amount of water for a tub bath. Do you really need a full tub or a half tub of water? Will a one-fourth tubful or less be sufficient? Be sure to place the stopper in the drain before turning on the water. Run only as much water as absolutely necessary for your bath.

5.   Don't allow the water to run continuously in the lavatory while you shave or brush your teeth. Running the tap for two minutes while you are brushing your teeth uses roughly 2 1/2 to 4 gallons of water.[5]

6.   If possible, install aerators in the faucets in your bathroom lavatories. Aerators will reduce the flow of water.

7.   Make sure that the water is not running continuously in the commode. Listen very quietly for the faint sound of running water. An alternative and probably a better way to determine whether water is escaping is to place several drops of food coloring in the commode tank. Wait 15 to 30 minutes and don't flush the commode. If the color appears in the water in the commode bowl, you have a "leak." Locate the leak and make the necessary repairs or have them made as soon as possible. Depending on the severity of the leak, it is possible that up to 100 gallons of water could be wasted each day.

8.   Put one to three tightly closed, quart plastic bottles (with rocks inside them to weight them down) inside the commode tank. Be sure to place the bottles in such a position as to not interfere with the flushing mechanism. When you flush the commode, one to three fewer quarts of water will be used. Don't use bricks for displacement of water in the commode tank. They may flake off and cause damage to the system. The flush volume of five gallons (for most conventional commodes) can be reduced by 15 percent without hindering performance.[6]

9.   Place plastic "dams" in your commode tanks. These flexible partitions are used to displace water in the tank and reduce the amount of water used with each flush of the commode. The plastic "dams" are inexpensive and should pay for themselves in a short time.

10. Don't flush the commode unnecessarily. For instance, if the commode has been flushed after its last use, there is really no reason to flush it again before cleaning the bowl with a brush and cleaner. Also, if you happen to toss a piece of facial tissue into the commode, wait until the commode is used again before flushing the tissue away.

11. Don't use the commode to dispose of such items as facial tissues, cotton swabs, and cotton balls. Put them in a waste-paper basket. Using the commode for trash disposal probably will lead to unnecessary flushings.

12. If you must install a new commode, consider a water-saving model. Some use as little as 3 1/2 to 4 gallons of water, or less, per flush.[7] In the Summer, 1987 issue of a popular magazine, I saw an ad for a commode which requires only 2 and 1/2 gallons.

13. If you purchase a new commode, consider a dual-flush model. The advantages of this type of commode are: A relatively small amount of water can be released for flushing only liquid waste, and a larger amount can be released when solid waste is present.

WAYS TO SAVE IN THE LAUNDRY

Washing clothes in a conventional automatic washer uses approximately 40 to 60 gallons of water per load.[8]

14. Check clothes to make sure they really need washing. Some pieces of clothing can be worn several times between washings. Get as many wearings as possible from a garment before washing it.

15. Save your laundry until you have enough to load your washing machine to its recommended capacity. Don't wash small or medium loads unless your washer has water level settings for such loads. If it does have such settings, don't forget to set them before you wash a small or medium load.

16. The permanent press cycle on automatic clothes washers uses approximately one-third more water than the regular cycle.[9] Therefore, limiting your use of the permanent press cycle will save water.

17. If you have only a few, small pieces of laundry, wash and rinse them by hand in the lavatory or laundry sink rather than in the clothes washer. Place the stopper in the lavatory or sink drain and run only the needed amount of water. Don't let the water run continuously while washing and rinsing.

18. Buy clothing and household items which don't have to be washed separately. Washing them separately will require additional use of the clothes washer (unless you wash them by hand) which means additional money for water.

19. When purchasing a clothes washer, consider a model with choices of water levels (small, medium, and large load settings). By merely pressing a button, you can save many gallons of water per load.

WAYS TO SAVE IN THE KITCHEN

20. If possible, install aerators in the kitchen water faucets. They will reduce the flow of water through the faucets.

21. Avoid unnecessary rinsing of dishes that go directly from the table into the automatic dishwasher for immediate washing. Scrape off leftover food, place them in your dishwasher, and let it do the rinsing for you.

22. Run your dishwasher only when it is full. The same amount of water will be used regardless of the size of the load. Get as much as you can for your water dollar.

23. Compare the water requirements of different dishwashers before buying one. If all other things are almost equal, consider purchasing the model which has a "water miser" cycle, which uses less water than the normal wash cycle.

24. After washing, rinsing, and drying dishes which you use only occasionally, wrap them in plastic wrap, put them in plastic bags, or cover them in some other manner to keep them clean. This will save you the time and the water required for washing them again before the next use.

25. Heat a kettle of water for various uses rather than draw hot water from the tap. Depending on the distance of the water heater from the tap, many gallons of water may have to be run off before the hot water reaches the tap.

26. Use a pan when washing vegetables and fruits. When you have finished, use the water to water plants. Reusing water is like getting double value for your water dollar.

27. Limit the number of utensils you use in preparing food as well as plates, flatware, glasses, and other dishes used with meals. Generally, the more items you have to wash, the more water will be required.

28. Use the smallest amount of water necessary in pans to cook foods. Saving a cup here and a pint there will add up to a considerable number of gallons over a month's time.

29. Use tight-fitting lids on pans when cooking to minimize the loss of steam. Steam that escapes is water wasted. There are, of course, certain foods and recipes which necessitate the pan to be uncovered while cooking. Follow the instructions given in the recipe and also use your own good judgement. Saving even a small amount of water when you cook can add up to significant savings on your water bill over time.

30. Place drinking water on the table only if people really drink it. Pouring unused water down the drain is like throwing money out of the window. (Incidentally, some restaurants will bring water to your table only if you request it.)

31.   Keep a container of water for drinking in the refrigerator or in an insulated container on the counter. This will save your having to run extra water from the cold water tap to get water cool enough for drinking. During hot weather, you could waste one or more gallons of water each time you go to the tap for a drink.

32.   Take ice trays from the refrigerator a few minutes before the ice is needed so that the ice cubes can be removed without having to run water over the trays.

33.   If you want to save money on your water bill, don't use running water to thaw frozen foods. Take them from the freezer in time for them to thaw before eating or cooking them. (Thaw meat, poultry, and fish in the refrigerator to avoid possible spoilage. Other foods or dishes, also, may need to be thawed in the refrigerator, rather than on the kitchen counter. Use your good judgement.)

34.   Use your garbage disposer sparingly. Consider putting certain kinds of food scraps in the garbage bag. Put selected food scraps in a compost for use in fertilizing the plants in your yard or vegetable garden. There will be fewer remaining scraps to go in the garbage disposer. Garbage disposers require water for proper operation, and water costs money.

WAYS TO SAVE ON HOUSEHOLD CLEANING

35.   Wipe up small spills and spots immediately to avoid frequent and widespread mopping of floors. Cleaning small areas requires less water than mopping the entire floor.

36.   Save up routine household cleaning jobs and do them all at one time to conserve water. Using the same water, start with the lightest soiled surface and end with the heaviest soiled surface. For example, start with the mirrors and end, eventually, with the floors. A few gallons of water saved each time you clean can add up to noticeable savings, moneywise, over time.

WAYS TO SAVE IN THE YARD AND
VEGETABLE GARDEN

37.   Water your vegetable garden, lawn, and outdoor plants only when necessary. Unnecessary watering wastes water, time, and your money.

38.   Mulch plants in your yard and vegetable garden to help hold moisture in the soil. Spread leaves, cut grass, pieces of bark, plastic, and other appropriate materials around the plants. (Make sure that the mulch does not prevent water from soaking into the soil when you do water or when it rains.) The longer you can keep the soil moist through mulching, the more money you will save on watering.

39.   Whenever possible, water your lawn, yard plants, and the vegetable garden only in the early morning, late afternoon, or evening. It is best to refrain from watering in the heat of the day, when it is windy, or when the sun is shining brightly. Under these conditions, you waste a large amount of water through evaporation.

40.   Use a "soaker" hose rather than a sprinkler, where possible. Less water is required when a "soaker" hose is used because the water is concentrated on the soil nearer the roots; and there is, also, less evaporation.

41.   Use drought resistant grasses and plants which can survive on limited amounts of water. Ask your County Agricultural Extension Agent about drought resistant grasses and plants that are adapted to your area. The fewer times you must water your yard, the lower your water bill.

42. Remove weeds from your yard and vegetable garden. Weeds use water which could be used by your vegetables, flowers, shrubs, trees, and grass. A weed-free yard or garden will require less water than one infested with weeds.

WAYS TO SAVE ON CAR WASHING

43. Rinse off your car with the water hose first. Use low pressure so as not to cause the grit to scratch the finish. Then, turn off the water. Next, wash your car with a soft cloth or sponge and bucket of water. Finally, rinse the car again with the water hose. Don't let the water run continuously while you wash the car. Letting the water hose run gently for a 20-minute car wash uses approximately 79 gallons of water.[10] Turning the water on only for the initial and final rinsings could save you quite a tidy sum of money on water over the period of time you own your car.

44. When it is raining gently, leave your car out of the garage and let the rain "wash" the car for you. Rainwater is free.

MISCELLANEOUS WAYS TO SAVE WATER

45. Turn off water faucets completely and immediately after each use to avoid wasting water and money.

46. Repair dripping faucets. A slow, steady drip (100 drops per minute) wastes 330 gallons of water in a month.[11] That's nearly 4,000 gallons per year.

47. Locate and repair, as soon as possible, all leaking water pipes detected by visual inspection. For example, you normally can suspect a leak if you find unexplained dark green patches of grass or a permanently damp area of ground on your property. An unexplained jump in your water bill may also indicate a leak in your water mains.

48. Check to see if there are leaks in your plumbing system which are not evident from visual inspection. To do this, first turn off completely all water faucets inside and outside of the house, turn off the automatic icemaker, and don't flush the commode. Watch your water meter for one-half hour. If the dial on the water meter moves, you have a leak somewhere. Locate the leak and repair it as soon as possible. The longer you delay repairs, the more water and money you will waste.

49. Don't let children play with the water hose. Thirty minutes of fun could waste up to several hundred gallons of water. Even water used for play costs money.

50. Install your water heater as near as possible to the area in which the most hot water is used. The farther the water heater is away from the point of use, the greater the amount of cool water which must be run off before hot water reaches the tap.

51. Insulate hot water pipes. Insulation will help minimize the cooling down of hot water in the pipes; therefore, less cool water should have to be drawn off before the hot water is available for use at the tap.

52. Cover wading and swimming pools when they are not in use to reduce evaporation. Evaporation necessitates the use of more water to keep the pools filled.

53. Use a broom to sweep the garage, sidewalks, and driveway. Don't remove debris by hosing it off with water. You could use over 100 gallons of water in hosing off the above.

54. When you are away from home for more than a day, consider turning off the water supply to your outside faucets. This will prevent loss of water should someone turn on the outside faucets while you are away. Or, you might consider placing locks on the outside faucets to prevent someone from turning them on. These precautions could save you from an unexpected rise in your water bill.

ENDNOTES

1. William M. Eberle and James G. Thomas, *Some Water Saving Ways* (Manhattan, Kansas: Cooperative Extension Service, Kansas State University, May, 1981).

2. Cooperative Extension Service, *Water Watch* (Little Rock, Arkansas: University of Arkansas), No date.

3. Jay Knorr, "Professors Develop Water Conservation Computer Program," *Kansas State Collegian* (Manhattan, Kansas: Kansas State University), April 23, 1986, p. 10.

4. *Ibid.*

5. N. J. Wilkinson, *Water Conservation in Urban Botswana* (Gaborone, Botswana: Botswana Technology Center, July, 1986).

6. Jay Knorr, "Professors Develop Water Conservation Computer Program," *Kansas State Collegian* (Manhattan, Kansas: Kansas State University), April 23, 1986, p. 10.

7. Cooperative Extension Service, *Water Watch* (Little Rock, Arkansas: University of Arkansas), No date.

8. *Ibid.*

9. *Ibid.*

10. N. J. Wilkinson, *Water Conservation in Urban Botswana* (Gaborone, Botswana: Botswana Technology Center, July, 1986).

11. *Ibid.*

BIBLIOGRAPHY

Baker, Sydney. "Lady Tarzan." *Fair Lady*. Cape Town, South Africa, August 22, 1984, p. 68.

Beech, Douglas F. *Home Insurance*. Manhattan, Kansas: Cooperative Extension Service, Kansas State University, March, 1982.

"College Tuition Costs Outpace Inflation." *Kansas State Collegian* (Manhattan, Kansas: Kansas State University), February 25, 1987, p. 8.

Cooperative Extension Service. *Water Watch*. Little Rock, Arkansas: University of Arkansas, No date.

Eberle, William M. and James G. Thomas. *Some Water Saving Ways*. Manhattan, Kansas: Cooperative Extension Service, Kansas State University, May, 1981.

Federal Trade Commission, Bureau of Consumer Protection. *Consumer Guide to the FTC Funeral Rule*. Washington, D.C., April, 1984.

Knorr, Jay. "Professors Develop Water Conservation Computer Program." *Kansas State Collegian* (Manhattan, Kansas: Kansas State University), April 23, 1986, p. 10.

Loucks, William L. *Windbreaks and Home Energy Conservation*. Manhattan, Kansas: Cooperative Extension Service, Kansas State University, May, 1984.

Snead, Bruce. *Choosing a Solar Water Heater*. Manhattan, Kansas: Cooperative Extension Service, Kansas State University, August, 1983.

Stephenson, Mary J. *Risk Management: Health Insurance and Disability Income Insurance, Fact Sheet 407*. College Park, Maryland: Cooperative Extension Service, University of Maryland, 1984-85.

Stephenson, Mary J. *Writing Wills in Maryland, Fact Sheet 283*. College Park, Maryland: Cooperative Extension Service, University of Maryland, 1983-84.

U.S. Department of Agriculture and U.S. Department of Health and Human Services. "Dietary Guidelines for Americans." in *Home and Garden Bulletin No. 232*, Second Edition. Washington, D.C.: Government Printing Office, 1985.

U.S. Department of Energy. *1987 Gas Mileage Guide*. Washington, D.C., October, 1986.

U.S. Department of Energy. *Heating With Wood*. Washington, D.C., May, 1980.

U.S. Department of Energy. *Tips for Energy Savers*. Washington, D.C., 1986.

U.S. Department of Health and Human Services. *Generic Drugs: Cutting Costs, Not Corners*, by Bill Rados. HHS Publication No. (FDA) 86-3156. Washington, D.C.: Government Printing Office, 1987.

U.S. Office of Consumer Affairs. *Hypothermia - A Winter Hazard for Older Americans*, by Virginia H. Knauer. Washington, D.C., Revised November, 1985.

U.S. Office of Consumer Affairs and U.S. Department of Energy. *Your Keys to Energy Efficiency*. Washington, D.C., July, 1985.

van der Hoeven, Gustaaf A. *Energy Efficient Landscaping*. Manhattan, Kansas: Cooperative Extension Service, Kansas State University, November, 1982.

Wilkinson, N. J. *Water Conservation in Urban Botswana*. Gaborone, Botswana: Botswana Technology Center, July, 1986.

INDEX

AUTOMOBILE, 1-28
  alternatives to owning, 23-26
  cost of owning and operating,
    1, 2
  financing, 8
  gasoline, 13
    saving, 17-22
  insurance, 8, 9
  maintenance, 9-17
    do-it-yourself, 12, 13
    oil, 9, 11
    parts, 11
    repairs, 2, 3, 9, 12, 13, 14, 15, 22
    tires, 9, 10, 11, 20
    tune-ups, 9
    undercoating, 13
  parking, 15, 22, 23
  protection, 14-17
    denting, 14
    finish, 15, 22
    interior, 15
    theft, 16, 17
  purchasing, 2-9
    demonstrator, 3
    new car, 4
    optional equipment, 4, 5
    used car, 6-8
  rental, 24, 25, 26
  selling, 7, 8
  sources of additional
    information, 26, 27

CLOTHING, 29-59
  accessories, 29, 48, 57-59
    purchasing, 57, 58
    repairing, 57, 58
    warranties, 58
  altering, 40
  care, 38, 39, 42-48
    dry cleaning, 38, 39, 46
    laundering, 39, 46
    protecting, 43, 44, 47
  construction, 40-42

  do-it-yourself, 40, 41
  hiring-it-done, 40
  designer, 31, 37
  discarded, 51-53
    salvaging, 51, 52
    selling, 41, 45, 52, 53, 58
    swapping, 52
  purchasing, 29-39
    children's, 31, 35, 37, 38,
    exchanging, 36, 59
    sources, 30-33
  recycling, 48-51
  repairing, 42, 43, 47, 48
  shoes, 53-56
    care, 53, 56
    protection, 56
    purchasing, 53-55
    repairing, 55, 56

COMMUNICATIONS, 60-69
  home office supplies, 65-67
    calendars, 66-67
    copying, 66
    correction tapes, 67
    envelopes, 66
    free supplies, 66
    paper, 65-67
    paperweights, 67
    pencils, 66, 67
    scratch pads, 66
  postage, 67-68
    aerogrammes, 68
    packages, 68
    postage-paid envelopes, 68
    postage scales, 68
    post cards, 67
  telephone, 61-65
    extensions, 62
    extra services, 62
    long distance calls, 63-65
    measured service, 61-62
    party lines, 61
    purchasing instruments, 62-63

renting instruments, 62-63
toll-free numbers, 65

COUPONING AND REFUNDING,
70-84
couponing, 70-74
coupon, 70-74, 82, 83
books, 72
clubs, 78, 81-82
collecting, 74
conventions, 82
file boxes, 72, 78
information on, 81
locating, 73-74
magazines, 81
organizing, 71-72
saving, 71
trading, 73, 74, 82
refunding, 74-80
clubs, 78, 81-82,
conventions, 82
forms, 74-79
collecting, 74, 79
locating, 77-79
organizing, 74, 75
purchasing, 79
trading, 78-79, 81, 82
magazines, 81
qualifiers, 74, 79-81
examples, 80
organizing, 79-80
sources, 80-81, 82

EDUCATION, 85-99
college and university, 86
correspondence study, 88
costs, 85, 86, 89
external degrees, 88
financial aid, 88, 89, 90-91
housing, 87
independent study, 88
night courses, 87
off-campus courses, 87
remote courses, 87
summer sessions, 86, 87
testing out, 88

tuition, 86, 89
weekend courses, 87
work-study, 88
community colleges, 86
informal education, 92-94
Elderhostel, 93
free or low-cost, 92-94
nature walks, 94
noncredit courses, 92
tours, 93, 94
trips, 94
information, educational, 94-96
sources, 94-96
Extension Service, 94
free literature, 94-95
library, 95-96
mass media, 95, 96
private schools, 86
public schools, 86

ENERGY, 100-135
alternative sources, 131-132
solar energy, 132
wind power, 132
wood, 131-132
fireplaces, 131-132
heater, 131
purchasing, 131, 132
species of wood, 131
awnings, 110
bathroom, 128
aerators, 128
showerhead, 128
showers, 128
tub baths, 128
cooling, 104-108
attic fans, 107
ceiling fans, 106
cooling systems, 104-105
exhaust fans, 107
insulation, 108
roof, 108
spot cooling, 104-105, 106
thermostat settings, 105, 106
draperies, 108, 110-111
entertainment equipment, 129

hair drying, 133
heating, 100-104
  body heat, 103
  central heating, 101-102
  insulation, 104
  obstructions, 103-104
  oven heat, 103
  spot heating, 101-103
  thermostat settings, 101
  ventilating fans, 103
kitchen, 113-120
  aerators, 120
  coffee makers, 120
  cooking, 117-119
  dishwashing, 115-116
  freezers, 113-115
  garbage disposers, 116
  microwave ovens, 116-117
  oven, 117
  pots and pans, 118-119
  pressure cookers, 118
  range, 116, 118-120
  refrigerator, 113-115
laundry, 124-127
  dryer, 125-126
    electric, 126
    gas, 126
  drying, 125-126
    line-drying, 125
    machine drying, 125-126
  ironing, 126, 127
  washing, 124-125
    load size, 124
    pre-soaking, 125
    water temperature,125
lighting, 120-124
  area lighting, 122-123
  daylight, 121, 123
  desk lamps, 123
  dimmer switches, 123
  fluorescent lights, 121, 122
  gas lights, 124
  incandescent lights, 121, 122,
    123
  night lights, 122
  outdoor lighting, 123, 124

special utility rates, 130-131
  energy switches, 130
  financial assistance, 130-131
  off-peak rates, 130
  time-of-day rates, 130
water heater, 111-113
  draining, 112
  insulation, 112
  location, 112
  solar power, 113
  temperature setting, 111-112
weatherizing, 108-110
  electrical outlets, 110
  insulating, 109
  reflective film, 111
  storm doors, 109
  storm windows, 109
  weatherstripping, 110
yard care, 129-130
  landscaping, 129
  power equipment, 129-130
  windbreaks, 129

ENTERTAINMENT, 136-147
at-home activities, 137-139
  card games, 137, 139
  conversations, 137
  cookouts, 137
  crafts, 139
  gardening, 137
  playing musical
    instruments, 139
  plays, 137
  puzzles, 138
  radio listening, 137
  reading, 138
  singing, 139
  table games, 137
  TV watching, 138
hobbies, 144-145
public activities, 140-144
  art galleries, 141
  beach, 143
  church activities, 142-143
  concerts, 142
  free exhibits, 140, 141, 142

hikes, 144
museums, 141
national parks, 143-144
nature walks, 144
open houses, 141
picnics, 144
reading at library, 140-141
theater, 142
tours, 141, 142
travel, 144
trips, 144
window-shopping, 140
zoos, 144
sports events, 145

FOOD, 148-175
couponing, 149, 151, 152, 162-163, 168
eating out, 166-169
children's menus, 168
discounts, 168
drinks, 169
happy hours, 169
open houses, 169
restaurants, 167-168
specials, 168
entertaining others, 169-171
cocktails, 170
hors d'oeuvres, 170
menus, 169-170
potlucks, 170
scheduling, 170-171
snacks, 170
government and other programs, 173-174
churches, 174
food banks, 174
food stamps, 173
nonprofit organizations, 174
school lunches, 173
senior citizens, 173
WIC, 174
growing your own, 171
costs, 171
gardens, 171
preparation, 163-164

baby food, 164
casseroles, 164
from scratch, 164
leftovers, 164
meats, 163
soups, 164
stews, 164
substitutes, 163
preserving, 172-173
canning, 172
costs, 172, 173
freezing, 172, 173
purchasing, 148-161
bargains, 149, 151
bread, 159
canned foods, 155
cash register tapes, 150-151
cereals, 159
condiments, 154-155
container dating, 152
containers, 156
convenience stores, 150
co-ops, 150
costs, 148-161
couponing, 149, 152
department stores, 150
diet foods, 154
driving distance, 150
farmers' markets, 161
fish, 157
fresh foods, 156, 158
frozen foods, 156
generic labels, 152
ingredients, 155
"junk" foods, 154
marked prices, 151-152
meat, 157
milk, 159
national brands, 152
pick-your-own, 161
poultry, 157
shopping trips, 160-161
snack items, 154
soft drinks, 159-160
specials, 149, 151, 152, 153, 158
stocking up, 153, 156

store brands, 152
store circulars, 148, 151
substituting, 149, 158
unit prices, 155
storing, 165-166
dating containers, 166
freezing, 165-166
heat, 165
moisture, 165
refrigerating, 165-166
rotating, 166

FUNERALS AND BURIALS,
176-188
before a death occurs,
177-183
cemetery plot, 178, 182
cremation, 182
emergency information, 178
grave markers, 180, 183
insurance, 177, 178, 179
memorial societies, 179
organ donation, 182
papers, 177-179
prearranged funerals, 180-181
Social Security benefits, 180
veteran's benefits, 179-180
will, 177
following a death,183-187
check on
credit card death benefits, 185
credit union benefits, 185
debts of the deceased, 186
employee benefits, 184
financial assistance, 183
income tax obligations, 187
insurance, 184, 185, 186
labor union benefits, 184
pension benefits, 184
prearrangements, 183
retirement benefits, 184
Social Security benefits, 184
veteran's benefits, 183
house-sitting, 183
source of information, 188

**GIFTS, GIFT WRAPPING,
GREETING CARDS, AND
DECORATIONS,** 189-195
gifts, 190-192
buying on sale, 190
exchanging, 192
free gifts, 192
gift vouchers, 190
making gifts, 191
shopping garage sales, 192
greeting cards, 193-194
holiday decorations, 194-195
making decorations, 194
purchasing, 194, 195
saving, 194
wrapping paper, 193

HEALTH CARE, 196-212
blood banks, 211
dental care, 204
"discount" dentists, 204
eye care, 204-205
eyeglasses, 204-205
prescriptions, 204
tests, 205
free or low-cost, 206-208
hearing aids, 205-206
batteries, 205-206
purchasing, 205
hospital care, 201-203
checking in and out, 202-203
costs, 201-203
insurance, 209-210, 211
medicines and drugs, 196-199
purchasing, 196-199
brand names, 196-197
by mail, 198-199
discounts, 199, 211
free samples, 198, 199
generics, 196-197
over-the-counter drugs,
199, 211
out-patient, 201-202, 203
physicians, 199-201
selecting, 200

preventive medicine
and dentistry, 208-209

HOME FURNISHINGS, 213-226
cooking and eating utensils
and items, 223-224
dishes, 223, 224
paper plates, 223
paper towels, 223
plastic dinnerware, 224
pots and pans, 223, 224
floor coverings, 219-220
cleaning, 220
purchasing, 219-220
furniture, 213-218
purchasing, 213-215
refinishing, 216-217
repairing, 216-217
reupholstering, 216, 217
interior decorating, 221-223
accessories, 222
do-it-yourself, 222, 223
free advice, 221
purchasing items, 222
sheets, towels and tablecloths,
220-221
making your own, 221
purchasing, 220-221
window coverings, 218
making your own, 218
purchasing, 218

HOUSEHOLD APPLIANCES,
227-238
installing, 233
operating costs, 228
purchasing, 227-233, 235-236,
237-238
delivery costs, 233, 236
features, 229, 230, 237-238
financing, 233, 236, 238
floor models, 231
models, 229-230, 235
new appliances, 229-230
prices, 228, 230
used appliances, 231-232, 235,
238
repairing, 228, 233-234, 236-237
service, 233, 236
service contracts, 237
warranties, 231, 232, 233, 234,
235, 236, 238

HOUSING, 239-259
home maintenance, 248-250
painting, 249
repairing, 248, 249, 250
weatherizing, 249
home protection, 252-258
burglaries, 252-257
fires, 257-258
moving, 250-252
do-it-yourself, 250
hiring it done, 251
packing, 251
purchasing, 239-246
condition, 240, 241, 242, 243
financing, 240, 244-246
location, 240, 241
real estate agent, 240
size, 241
taxes, 241, 244, 245, 246
type, 241, 242
warranties, 240-241
renting, 247-248
apartment, 247
free rent, 247
house, 247
rental agreements, 248
room, 247, 259
roommate, 247
selling, 246
do-it-yourself, 246
real estate agent, 246

INSURANCE, 260-275
additional information, 275
automobile, 260, 261-263
disability income, 260, 263-264
health/medical, 264-266
homeowners, 260, 267-270
liability, 274

life, 260, 270-273
  selecting a company, 273

PERSONAL GROOMING,
  276-283
  grooming aids, 279-283
  hair care, 277-279
  makeup, 276-277

VACATIONS, 284-299
  at home, 284-285, 298-299
  financing, 295
  lodging, 287-291, 296
    discounts, 288, 296
  meals, 291
  planning, 296
  selecting a spot, 284-285, 296
  tourist attractions, 292
    discounts, 292
  travel, 284-287
    airlines, 285-286
    automobile, 286
    bicycle, 287
    bus, 286-287
    train, 287

vacations abroad, 293-294

WATER, 300-310
  bathroom, 300, 301-303
    bathtub, 301-302
    commode, 302-303
    lavatory, 302
    shower, 301
  car washing, 308
  cleaning, 306-307
  kitchen, 304-306
    cooking, 300, 305
    dishwasher, 304-305
    drinking water, 305-306
    garbage disposer, 306
    ice trays, 306
    thawing frozen foods, 306
  laundry, 300, 303-304
    washer, 303-304
  leaks, 308-309
  yard and garden, 307-308
    drought resistant plants, 307
    mulching, 307
    watering, 307
    weeding, 308

NOTE TO READERS

If you have money saving tips which have worked for you that you would like to share with others, send them to the Author:

> Dr. Charlotte Gorman
> c/o *Nottingham Books*
> Department TRB
> P.O. Box 2454
> Denton, Texas 76202

Please <u>print</u> your name, complete mailing address, and zip code.

Those tips submitted will become the property of the Author to be used as she chooses. The tips might be used in future editions of this book and in other ways to help people better manage their resources.

THE AUTHOR

NOTE: If you would like to have Dr. Gorman speak to your group, write to her at the above address.

ORDERING INFORMATION

Copies of *The Frugal Mind* can be ordered from:

Nottingham Books
Department IBOB
P.O. Box 2454
Denton, TX 76202

-Enclose $16.95 for each book ordered.

-Add $2.95 for shipping and handling for **each** book.

-Texas residents add $1.39 for sales tax for **each** book.

**Enclose your check or money order (payable
to Nottingham Books) with your order.
Please do not send cash.**

Print or type your name and complete mailing address,
including zip code.

Allow 3 to 6 weeks for delivery.

The above prices are subject to change without notice.

The Frugal Mind is available at special, discount prices for bulk
orders (for fund-raising activities, for retail or wholesale resale,
etc.). Write for prices and details.

THE AUTHOR

Dr. Charlotte Gorman was born on April 12, 1945, in Alabama and grew up on a farm in the Mississippi Delta. She worked her way through under-graduate and graduate school, an experience which gave birth to many of the tips included in her book. Other tips have come from her experiences as a wife, homemaker, and Resource Management Consultant.

She earned a Bachelor's degree in Home Economics at Delta State University and a Master's degree in Home Economics at Ball State University. She has a Master's in Sociology from the University of Tennessee. Her doctorate in Educational Administration with minors in Home Economics and Sociology is also from Ball State.

Her varied work experiences have included teaching in the public schools in a low resource area; serving as a County Extension Home Economist in Mississippi working with low-income homemakers in the area of resource management; teaching "Social Problems" at Ball State University; serving as a State Extension Specialist in Public and Consumer Affairs at the University of Arkansas; and doing research on Rural Social Organization and on Needs, Wants, and Characteristics of Homemakers.

Her other experiences have included writing educational literature and newspaper articles, appearing on radio and television, serving as an officer of various state-wide organizations, conducting seminars and workshops, and speaking before groups.

Currently, the author is President of GT Associates, a Management and Communications Consulting Group, with headquarters in Denton, Texas.